INTERNATIONAL STUDIES

Détente and the Nixon Doctrine

INTERNATIONAL STUDIES

DÉTENTE AND THE NIXON DOCTRINE

American Foreign Policy and the
Pursuit of Stability, 1969–1976

ROBERT S. LITWAK

The right of the
University of Cambridge
to print and sell
all manner of books
was granted by
Henry VIII in 1534.
The University has printed
and published continuously
since 1584.

CAMBRIDGE UNIVERSITY PRESS
Cambridge
London New York New Rochelle
Melbourne Sydney

Published by the Press Syndicate of the University of Cambridge
The Pitt Building, Trumpington Street, Cambridge CB2 1RP
32 East 57th Street, New York, NY 10022, USA
296 Beaconsfield Parade, Middle Park, Melbourne 3206, Australia

© Cambridge University Press 1984

First published 1984

Printed in Great Britain at the
University Press, Cambridge

Library of Congress catalogue card number: 83-15053

British Library Cataloguing in Publication Data

Litwak, Robert S.
Détente and the Nixon doctrine.—(International
studies)
1. United States—Foreign relations—1969–1974
2. United States—Foreign relations—1974–1977
I. Title   II. Series
327.73   E744

ISBN 0-521-25094-3

BO

CONTENTS

TO MY PARENTS

ACKNOWLEDGMENTS

This book could not have been completed without the help of many teachers, colleagues, and friends in England and America. Special thanks go to those who commented on the manuscript, especially Desmond Ball, Christoph Bertram, Fergus Carr, Shahram Chubin, Lynn Davis, Aaron Friedberg, Stanley Hoffmann, Robert Jaster, James Mayall, John Mojdehi, George Moffett, Peter Nailor, Avi Plascov, Daniel Poneman, Jack Snyder, Gregory Treverton, Larry Trachtenberg, and Michael Yahuda. The book grew out of a doctoral dissertation prepared for the London School of Economics and Political Science, University of London. The manuscript benefited from the trenchant insights of my LSE supervisor, Philip Windsor, whose own work provided inspiration.

I am deeply grateful to Samuel Huntington, Director of the Center for International Affairs, Harvard University, for ideal working conditions to convert the original dissertation into its present published form. I wish to thank the Olin Foundation for their generous support of this project while I was at Harvard. Thanks are also due to Ian Nish and Michael Leifer of the Centre for International Studies, LSE, and Elizabeth Wetton of Cambridge University Press for their kind assistance and counsel in the production of this book. The librarians and staff of the British Library of Political and Economic Science (LSE), the International Institute for Strategic Studies, and the Center for International Affairs, Harvard University, offered unstinting support. Marianna Tappas and Hilary Parker typed the manuscript expertly and cheerfully. Janet Haouchine meticulously edited the copy for typesetting. Finally, I would like to express my deepest gratitude to family and friends. I am, of course, responsible for all of the book's shortcomings.

Cambridge, Massachusetts
March 1983

WRITTEN UNDER THE AUSPICES OF THE
CENTER FOR INTERNATIONAL AFFAIRS,
HARVARD UNIVERSITY

INTRODUCTION

No work of history ever begins soon enough or ends late enough to be wholly rounded.

George F. Kennan, 1959[1]

A quarter of a century ago, Henry Kissinger, concluding his study of the Congress of Vienna, wrote: 'Those statesmen who have achieved final greatness did not do so through resignation, however well founded. It was given to them not only to maintain the perfection of order, but to have *the strength to contemplate chaos*, there to find material for fresh creation' (emphasis added).[2] Richard Nixon assumed the Presidency, with Kissinger as his Assistant for National Security Affairs, at a juncture in history when chaos appeared to threaten. The multiple pressures of Vietnam underscored the extent to which the coherence of American foreign policy, and the domestic consensus sustaining it, had broken down. Out of the chaos they sought to forge a new 'structure of peace' – a stable international equilibrium in which the philosophy and practice of American policy would be altered to meet the complexities and exigencies of the new epoch.

While acknowledging the inefficacy of previous American policies, the Administration steadfastly contended that the primary impetus behind this radical departure was to be found in the evolving nature of the international system itself. Major qualitative changes, many of which were depicted as achievements of American policies, demanded a 'fresh approach' – a new philosophical framework which heralded the end of the bipolar postwar era and underscored 'the potential and the imperative of a pluralistic world.'[3] Henry Kissinger, in a 1968 essay addressed to the question of restoring coherence to a troubled American diplomacy, observed that the principal challenge which confronted a new Administration and the American people was that of 'relating our commitments to our interests and our obligations to our purposes.'[4]

The postwar American image of the inter-state system, and its perceived unique role within that system, had been severely shaken by the Vietnam debacle. Moreover, the global diffusion of power, the

1

changing nature and utility of power, and the pervasive force of nationalism, *inter alia*, had served to reshape the global political landscape. With the major elements of the international environment in a simultaneous state of flux, the new Administration was presented with a compelling new agenda of international politics. Clearly, what one observer has described as 'the end of the postwar era'[5] positioned the United States at a political and, perhaps more significantly, a psychological crossroad. If the previous American vision of the world had indeed been flawed, the casting of a new image – one which would both clearly reflect the implications of pluralism and enjoy domestic support – would not be an easy task. Yet it was toward this end, and from this perspective, that the Nixon Administration ostensibly set itself to work in 1969.

Seven years later, as his stewardship of American foreign policy was drawing to a close, Henry Kissinger remarked: 'What will probably give me satisfaction in the longer term are structural achievements: the attempt to create a foreign policy based on permanent values and interests.'[6] The use of the word 'permanent' is highly significant and, though not intended, calls into question the essential aims and methods of the Nixon–Kissinger diplomacy. Did the policies of the new Administration truly reflect a fundamental re-evaluation of American interests, values, commitments and alliances within the context of politico-economic multipolarity? Or rather, was this 'new period of creativity' merely confined to the realm of devising new modalities to achieve the familiar ends of American postwar policy: containment, orderly change and stability?

The central issue here is one of contending perspectives. In essence, what image of world politics was to color the perception of events and thereby guide American policy in the post-Vietnam era? To be sure, the choice was not one of a simple either/or nature. Indeed, one might question the extent to which a conscious choice was involved.

The thesis to be advanced within this study is that the question of rival perspectives and choice of image might best be viewed as reflecting perhaps the principal foreign policy dilemma to confront American decision-makers in the post-1969 period: the ongoing dilemma of reconciling continued (indeed revitalized) military bipolarity with the new conditions of global pluralism. Within such a conception, it might be argued that the historical force which both mediated and propelled American policy-makers to the limits of choice was that which Raymond Aron has described as 'the inscrutable dialectic of the men and their circumstances.'[7]

Arthur Miller, writing in the wake of critical acclaim for his play *Death of a Salesman*, chose to characterize the essence of tragedy as being the dislocation of one's chosen image.[8] Such a definition serves to highlight the underlying ironic tragedy of American foreign policy during the Nixon–Kissinger era. At the very moment when the United States was psychologically prepared to cast off an admittedly defective bipolar image in favor of one which reflected the implications of multipolarity, the former image was ostensibly being reconfirmed by events within the new context. That is, the emergence of the Soviet Union as a fully-fledged global military power (i.e. the attainment of strategic nuclear parity with the United States and the dramatic expansion of its conventional capabilities), in conjunction with the unfolding nature of the détente process, had the net effect of conferring an ostensibly new legitimacy to the image of bipolarity during a period in which its relevance across a spectrum of issues was clearly waning.

The ironic-tragic element in these developments is that they occurred at the precise moment in history when the logic of bipolarity within the Cold War context had seemingly been worked out.[9] It was hoped that the promulgation of a new philosophical framework – a resultant of the 'new period of creativity' – would allow the United States to transcend the image of bipolarity and the disastrous policy of undifferentiated globalism which it had sustained. And yet, *pari passu*, the former image was finding fresh bases of support within the new context. In time, the *obiter dicta* of Henry Kissinger signalled a marked retreat from his earlier espousals of 'the potential and the imperative of a pluralistic world.' Indeed, by the winter of 1975, the Secretary of State went so far as to declare that '*the problem of our age* is how to manage the emergence of the Soviet Union as a superpower' (emphasis added).[10]

It is this confluence of contending images – what might almost be regarded as a kind of historical dissonance – which will emerge as the leitmotif of this study. But in attempting to understand the complex cause and effect inter-relationships of international politics, one is challenged to seek a level of explanation that goes beyond the essential dilemma of foreign policy decision-making – Aron's inscrutable dialectic of the men and their circumstances.

The purpose of this study is to analyze the nature and implications of the evolving international system characterized above and to examine the policy dilemmas that American decision-makers encountered in attempting to reconcile the contending demands which it reflected. In concrete terms, this was to require the design of policies to harmonize (1) the necessity of containing the new realities of Soviet power with (2) the imperative of post-Vietnam retrenchment (with its logical implication of a devolution of responsibility in favor of emerging regional centers of power).[11] Thus, in endeavoring to erect a new 'structure of peace' – that is, the pursuit of stability based upon 'permanent values and interests' – the Nixon–Kissinger strategy came to embody the twin policies of superpower détente and the Nixon Doctrine. While such an approach possessed the elegance of the architectonic, the question remained as to whether it could prove successful in reconciling seemingly contradictory foreign policy demands. The argument advanced within this study is that the presumed efficacy of the Nixon–Kissinger strategy was predicated upon the almost symbiotic relationship which the United States sought to effect between the dual policies of superpower détente and the Nixon Doctrine.

Such, at least, was the design. What is of central concern is the precise nature of this relationship and those forces (both domestic and international) which militated for or against it. In attempting to address these questions, this study will meld an historical analysis of the Nixon–Kissinger years with an analysis of the ideas that shaped the policies of that period.

Within the context of this analysis two unifying themes will emerge: first, the question of 'image' in international politics; and second, the special difficulties of integrating force and policy in the nuclear age (e.g. the impact of nuclear weapons on the means–ends relationship). A brief exposition of each would be useful at this initial point.

What is meant by an 'image' of the international system? The concept of image, in conjunction with the study of the function of perceptions and misperceptions in decision-making, is a relatively recent area of enquiry in the field of international relations. In addition to its clear relationship to the more traditional historical concept of world view (*Weltanschauung*), it figures prominently in studies on belief systems and operational codes in those allied fields of social psychology and political science, respectively. The burgeoning literature devoted to the concept of image has tended to place greatest emphasis on its importance in governing behavior.[12] However, the assertion that it is a decision-maker's *image* which colors his perceptions and serves as a guide to policy – that is, its role as a unifying view of the world which renders external reality intelligible – has sparked considerable controversy. Alexander George, in his analysis of the function of operational codes, has sought to clarify the issues in question:

The term 'operational code' is a misnomer. It really refers to a general belief system about the nature of history and politics; it is *not* a set of recipes or repertoires for political action that an elite applies mechanically in its decision-making . . . These general beliefs serve, as it were, as a prism that influences the actor's perception of the flow of political events and his definition or estimate of particular situations. The beliefs also provide norms and standards that influence the actor's choice of strategy and tactics, and his structuring and weighing of alternative courses of action.[13]

As can be readily observed, all three terms – operational code, world view and image – share a more or less common meaning.

The importance of comprehending the nature of these 'images' of the world has been underscored by Weber: 'Not ideas, but material and ideal interests, directly govern men's conduct. Yet very frequently the "world images" that have been created by "ideas" have, like switchmen, determined the tracks along which action has been pushed by the dynamic of interest.'[14]

In considering the interplay of ideas and interests, one interpretation of Weber immediately comes to the fore: though man (or the state) is initially motivated into action through the dynamism of interests (both material and ideal), it is his mental construct or 'image' of the external world which determines the nature or direction of this movement. Thus, for example, Robert Jervis has observed that neither neo-Marxist nor traditional liberal theorists have been able convincingly to explain American postwar foreign policy in terms of interests alone. Such an endeavor requires an initial reference to and exploration of the images, ideas and beliefs held by the policy-makers. Once the nature of these images or ideas has been explicated, an analysis of interests can go far in explaining policy, but that should not divert attention from the crucial importance of images – the 'switchmen' – in the decision-making process.[15]

However, by reversing the terms of this argument, an alternative interpretation of Weber's comment *vis-à-vis* the role of ideas in social action might be obtained. That is, it may be possible to derive a converse proposition of equal validity to the fairly orthodox one offered above – and perhaps in the process shed considerable light on the underlying dynamics of American Cold War policy. The alternative view would embody the assertion that it is often a nation–state's *image* of the world, and its role or position therein, which is crucial in the delineation and articulation of its interests and values. Indeed, the latter may come to be viewed as its supreme interest. Such a conception suggests quite a different relationship between images and interests. Within it, interests do not serve as the pre-articulate basis for social action to be channelled by the switchmen of ideas; rather, they come to evolve in themselves as a *consequence* of the prevailing idea or image.

In light of this analysis one can, for example, find substance in Dean Rusk's declaration that 'other nations have interests; the United States has responsibilities.'[16] It reflects a policy-making process in which the American image of the international system contributed both to the proliferation of interests (i.e. commitments) and the sustenance of the psychological milieu in which these newly-articulated 'interests' would be safeguarded. Indeed, in an important study of American postwar policy, Bernard Brodie argues that within the context of its perceived role in the international system, the American notion of security became a highly flexible and inherently expansible concept:

In some situations viewed as distantly menacing or disturbing, a superpower, in considering its appropriate response, allows itself the luxury (or burden) of thinking in terms of national responsibility rather than simply of national peril. In so doing it will not usually acknowledge that it is departing from the criterion of self-interest fixed as security; it merely finds it convenient to broaden the terminology as it broadens its conception. The whole idea of 'containment' is one convenient way of expressing and at the same time of justifying a preoccupation with affairs far from home, and doing so ultimately in the name of national security.[17]

Recapitulating, it has been argued that images or ideas serve not only in defining the manner and situations in which interests are pursued but, indeed, may often come to define the interests themselves. As suggested above, it is this latter interpretation of the interplay of images and interests which may prove to be of particular use in the analysis of American postwar foreign policy.

The second unifying theme of this study centers on the special difficulties of integrating force and policy in the nuclear age: that is, the unique impact of nuclear weapons on the means–ends relationship in the decision-making process. Here, one must return to Clausewitz and the continuing relevance of his work. In examining the fundamental nature of war, Clausewitz, in a manner unrivalled in the history of strategic thought, articulated the necessity of rationally conducting war within the context of and in constant reference to explicitly stated political objectives. While able to contemplate the specter of total war, he wrote at a moment in history when both the objectives and the instrumentalities of warfare could be limited. To be sure, the Congress of Vienna system provided a political and philosophical framework within which limited objectives could be derived and rationally related to the means requisite to realize them. This restraint was as much a function of technology as it was of politics.

The postwar era differs from preceding historical periods in at least two major respects: first, the extension of diplomacy to a global concept; and second, the existence of total means. Together they present unique problems for the soldier and statesman alike – particularly for those of a 'superpower' who believes it possible to affect political and military outcomes far from its borders. While the former concern has supported the extension of commitments on a global scale, the latter has sparked and sustained a serious debate *vis-à-vis* the defense of those commitments. In short, with perhaps the sole exception of the preservation of the state or regime itself, how is it rationally possible to relate *total* means – means which for the first time threaten the survival of man as a species – to the defense of any commitment? It is this dilemma of the nuclear age which has resulted in an 'inversion' of the traditional Clausewitzian means–ends relationship. Whereas the age of Clausewitz was one in which statesmen could rationally proceed from a consideration of the objectives of war to the modalities of war, the contemporary period has been marked by an overriding concentration on the question of means – total means whose employment rational statesmen seek to avoid at all costs. With the attention of policy-makers and strategic analysts sharply fixed on the dilemma of total means, the process underscored by Clausewitz of delineating appropriate ends within the political context has been both distorted and ignored. Thus, while admittedly the challenge of integrating force and policy has never been more profound, so too has that process never been subject to more distortion as a consequence of the specter of total means.

The nature and interplay of the two central themes of this study – that is, the concept of image and the integration of force and policy in the nuclear age – will be developed in the following discussion. It will be seen that during the Cold War – a period in which America pursued what has been characterized as a foreign policy of 'undifferentiated globalism'[18] there was extreme resistance to any reappraisal of the prevailing image of the international system: policy-makers essentially perceived a bipolar world in which the United States was engaged in a relentless Manichean struggle against pro-Communist forces. Results not fully consonant with the implications of that image (such as the inability of the United States to relate credibly the policy of massive retaliation to the defense of its far-flung commitments, or the Sino-Soviet rift) prompted not a reevaluation of the validity and utility of the underlying image as a guide to policy; rather, these circumstances precipitated a search for more efficacious means to achieve objectives upon which there was a continuity of Cold War consensus. In short, when confronted with contradictory or otherwise dissonant information, it was the strategic doctrine of the Cold War period which was subject to alteration in order to ensure the maintenance of the prevalent American image of the international system. In time, for a multitude of reasons, it proved impossible for the United States to relate credibly the magnitude of its multiple security commitments on an equal basis.

Consequently, rather than accept a more complex and differentiated image of the inter-state system, successive administrations chose instead to assert that the image of anti-Communist global engagement remained fundamentally valid, but that it was the insidious nature of the *threat* which had become diversified. Thus, they contended that it was necessary for the United States to differentiate critically amongst the means at its disposal so as to enable it, in any given crisis situation, to differentiate adroitly the type of reciprocal threat (i.e. from all-out nuclear to guerrilla warfare) which could be credibly brought to bear. In retrospect, it is apparent that this process of deftly discriminating between the categories and levels of threat – that is, the differentiation of means within the Cold War context – belied a tacit differentiation of ends or commitments.

'What's past is prologue' would appear to be particularly pertinent

in the realm of foreign policy analysis. It is hoped that the importance of comprehending the dynamics of Cold War decision-making
shall become clear when attention is squarely focused on the nature
of the Nixon–Kissinger strategy. It is at this point, and within this
historical context, that the twin considerations of image and the
means–ends relationship shall converge. In essence the question
arises as to whether the Nixon–Kissinger strategy truly reflected the
shift in image which the accompanying rhetoric would have had one
believe. Or rather, did the dilemma of contending with the consequences of revitalized bipolarity (i.e. the emergence of the Soviet
Union as a true global power) result in the transformation of the
Nixon Doctrine into yet another instrument of containment – that is,
just one more link in a chain of policies whose unifying process
accentuated the differentiation of means. Otherwise stated, was the
Nixon Doctrine more a legacy of the Truman Doctrine than a new
initiative consonant with the image of a pluralistic world?

In concluding this brief exposition of the major themes and questions to which this study is addressed, a short outline of its structure
would prove useful. The following chapter is devoted to an analysis
of American Cold War policy – from the Truman Doctrine to the Tet
offensive. The importance of this section, as suggested above, goes
beyond the bounds of that usually attributed to historical background in a work such as this. Thereafter, the discussion considers
the nature of the international environment as it existed in 1969 and
the rudiments of the Nixon–Kissinger strategy as a response to the
challenge which it posed. Also included are analyses of pertinent
writings by Henry Kissinger prior to his entry into government service, and the organizational changes which the new President and
his National Security Adviser brought to the foreign policy decision-
making process.

Chapter 3 deals with the nature of US–Soviet détente during its
initial 'euphoric' phase, which culminated in the accords of May
1972 and June 1973. The following section considers the Nixon
Doctrine both as a specific strategy for American disengagement
from Indochina and a general philosophy governing American
security policy in the Third World. It also seeks to explore the ways
in which the United States hoped to establish a symbiotic
relationship between this devolutionary strategy and the policy of
superpower détente.

Chapter 5 focuses on the nature of US–Soviet détente in the wake of the October 1973 Middle East War and the shattering impact of that episode on the underlying assumptions of the Nixon–Kissinger strategy. This discussion leads to an analysis of the Angolan Civil War. Rooted in that nation-state's unstable domestic structure but having rapidly assumed a new and alarming international dimension, this conflict proved one in which the principal elements of the Nixon–Kissinger strategy were severely tested. Finally, the book attempts to assess the efficacy of the Nixon–Kissinger strategy as a response to the challenge of the international environment and, in this context, to delineate those dilemmas of an ongoing nature which continue to have a critical bearing on the formulation and conduct of American foreign policy.

1 . AMERICA AS THE NIGHT-WATCHMAN STATE, 1947–1968[1]

We must consider first and last the American national interest. If we do not, if we construct our foreign policy on some kind of abstract theory of rights and duties, we shall build castles in the air . . . If, in our search for the true American interest, we fail to find it correctly and explore its implications exhaustively, our policies will be unworkable in practice because in fact they do not recognize the realities of our position. In short we shall succeed in so far as we become fully enlightened American nationalists.

Walter Lippmann, 1943[2]

The advent of the Cold War: 'two versions of the new spirit'

During the Cold War, American foreign policy was conceived of and expressed in universal terms: the containment of the Soviet Union as a political and military force became the centerpiece of American strategy. In this period of recognized American military superiority, terms such as security, commitment and vital interests were used almost interchangeably and without precision. The tendency of American postwar foreign policy towards undifferentiated globalism was manifested as early as March 1947 when the Truman Doctrine affirmed that the United States would 'support free peoples who are resisting attempted subjugation by armed minorities or by outside pressures.' Such phrases, and the ambiguous concept of aggression which they reflected, led to the proliferation of American commitments. In time, the extension of the American global mission was completed as the United States sought to preserve the integrity of specific national regimes from whatever threat. The pursuit of stability became the driving force behind an American policy of global containment which viewed Communist ideology and Soviet power as a monolithic force. This served to foster a psychological environment in which the American conception of national interest, traditionally a minimalist notion governed largely by economic criteria, came to be transmuted into the more expansive and ambiguous *national security interest*.

11

The origins of the Cold War – from initial differences on the Polish question to a final rupturing of relations over the German question – have been skillfully analyzed in depth elsewhere.³ The central concern of this chapter is twofold: first, to examine the process whereby a predominant and well-articulated image of the inter-state system came to be institutionalized within American governmental structures; and second, to assess the impact and influence of this image on the means–ends relationship in the foreign policy decision-making process.

In the period just prior to the enunciation of the Truman Doctrine, two highly influential reports concerning the overall state of US–Soviet relations and the more speculative question of Soviet intentions circulated amongst officials in the top echelon of the American government. Together, these studies provided an important part of the ideological and intellectual context within which the specific request for aid to Greece and Turkey was discussed. The first comprehensive American report on the evolving state of postwar relations between the United States and the Soviet Union was written by George Kennan, then the relatively obscure chargé d'affaires in the Moscow embassy. Kennan's response to a State Department request in February 1946 for an 'interpretative analysis' of Soviet intentions was an 8,000-word 'long telegram.' As he later recorded in his autobiography: 'Now, suddenly my opinion was being asked . . . It would not do to give them just a fragment of the truth. They had asked for it. Now, by God, they would have it.'⁴

Kennan's assessment of Soviet intentions arrived in Washington at a moment when Soviet pressures on Iran and Turkey were being viewed as an immediate threat to the global balance of power. It was followed seven months later by a similar report written by the Special Counsel to the President, Clark Clifford. According to journalist Arthur Krock, Clifford's study, running to nearly 100,000 words, not only supplied the new President 'with every detail of the wartime relationship with the USSR, it charted the postwar prospect with startling prescience in which the shape and thrust of Truman's subsequent great programs – the Greek–Turk aid legislation, the Marshall Plan, the North Atlantic Alliance . . . and what later became known as the 'Truman Doctrine' – were outlined.'⁵

In recognition of his informative and incisive cables from Moscow, Kennan was brought to Washington in early 1947 and asked, shortly thereafter, to assume the directorship of the State Department's newly founded Policy Planning Staff. This body, functioning within the office of the Under Secretary of State, was established in the hope of ensuring the competent development of long-range policy. Upon the initiative of the then Secretary of the Navy, James V. Forrestal, Kennan was invited to elaborate his views on the nature of Soviet behavior. With this charge, he submitted a working paper in January 1947 to Secretary of State Marshall entitled 'Psychological Background of Soviet Policy.' Subsequently, when Kennan was asked by the editor of *Foreign Affairs* for a contribution to the journal, it was this article which was given security clearance by the State Department and published anonymously in the July 1947 issue. Given these circumstances, many analysts of the development of American Cold War policy have tended to view the 'X' article as *the* authoritative public pronouncement of the premises governing official US policy. While the article did reflect an 'operating consensus' amongst members of the decision-making elite, it is important nonetheless to emphasize that many of the underlying assumptions of containment – and in particular their application – continued to be vigorously debated within the Truman Administration.

It is significant to note that of the X article's seventeen pages, only three were in any sense prescriptive with respect to the postwar direction of American foreign policy towards the Soviet Union – and even those were quite general. This feature prompted one observer to quip that, like the subject to which it was devoted, the X article also turned out to be something of a riddle wrapped in a mystery inside an enigma. Indeed, this central ambiguity contributed to the ultimate transformation of the containment doctrine into an abstraction within the American political context. It truly became a policy of all things to all men – one which could be used to initiate or rationalize such diverse undertakings as the Marshall Plan and the Vietnam intervention.

Having been asked by Forrestal to assess the role of ideology in Soviet foreign policy, Kennan subsequently acknowledged that this was to account for the thrust of his own piece for *Foreign Affairs*. Basically, the question which the Truman Administration sought to clarify was whether the United States should regard the Soviet Union as a great power with imperial (though limited) ambitions or as a messianic revolutionary power with unlimited aims. Kennan asserted that 'the political personality' of Soviet power under Stalin was 'the product of ideology and circumstances.' Whereas the former postulated an ongoing Manichean struggle with the capitalist world, the latter provided an historical backdrop of civil war, foreign intervention, and internal dictatorship. Given the axiomatic nature of the US–Soviet antagonism that Kennan posited, a number of conclusions followed. Thus, with regard to negotiations: 'If the Soviet government occasionally sets its signature to documents which would indicate the contrary, this is to be regarded as a tactical maneuver permissible in dealing with the enemy . . .' Indeed, believing 'the logic of history' to be on their side, the Soviets were prepared for 'a duel of infinite duration.'

In most respects, Kennan's basic line of argument in the X article represented an extrapolation upon those themes that he had introduced in the celebrated long telegram. The image of the Soviet Union that he depicted was indeed that of the revolutionary power – albeit one with severe internal vulnerabilities which the West might one day hope to exploit. Soviet 'political action,' Kennan observed,

is a fluid stream which moves constantly, wherever it is permitted to move, toward a given goal. The main concern is to make sure that it has filled every nook and cranny available to it in the basin of world power. But if it finds unassailable barriers in its path, it accepts these philosophically and accommodates itself to them. The main thing is that there should always be pressure, unceasing constant pressure, toward the desired goal.

Given the mercurial nature of this threat, Kennan warned that 'sporadic acts' of Western resistance would prove inadequate. Rather, he advocated the adoption of 'a long-term, patient but firm and vigilant' policy of 'containment' to thwart Soviet expansive tendencies. It thus followed that Kennan came to define loosely his new doctrine of 'containment' as 'the adroit and vigilant application of counter-force at a series of constantly shifting geographical and political points corresponding to the shifts and maneuvres of Soviet policy . . .' The X article concluded on a note of universalism consistent with the language and tenor of the Truman Doctrine, as Kennan expressed 'a certain gratitude to a Providence which, by providing the American people with this implacable challenge, has made their security as a nation dependent on their pulling themselves together and accepting the responsibilities of moral and political leadership that history plainly intended them to bear'.[6]

Domestic critics of Kennan's relatively ambiguous counterforce strategy crossed the American spectrum and included such diverse voices as those of John Foster Dulles, Robert Taft, J. W. Fulbright, and Henry A. Wallace. Without question, however, the most detailed and sustained critique of the containment doctrine came from journalist Walter Lippmann. Lippmann sought to demonstrate the fallacious reasoning and the dangers of the politico-military route suggested by the X article in a series of columns written in the late summer of 1947.[7] An analysis of the critique developed in the 12 columns reveals four pervading themes. First, Lippmann asserted that Kennan's 'Sources of Soviet Conduct' rested upon questionable assumptions and presented an inadequate explanation of Soviet behavior. Challenging Kennan's emphasis upon the primacy of ideology in Soviet foreign policy, he demonstrated from Russian history that the drive for a sphere of influence in Eastern Europe and along the Soviet periphery was a long-standing Czarist ambition. Moreover, Lippmann attacked Mr X's 'disbelief in the possibility of a settlement of the issue raised by [the] war.' This again was a conclusion which could be sustained only by an ideological interpretation of Soviet behavior and was, in Lippmann's assessment, unfortunately the basic premise underlying the orientation of the Truman Doctrine.

Second, on the politico-military plane, Lippmann argued that the prescriptive elements of the X article for American policy were potentially disastrous and embodied a 'strategic monstrosity.' Here, in many respects, he anticipated the Republican critics of the 1950s who regarded containment as a wholly negative policy that would deprive the United States of any foreign policy initiatives. Kennan's recommendation of a counterforce strategy to meet Soviet probes along the periphery would, in Lippmann's view, invariably lead to a postwar world of perpetual crises, whose timing and location would be determined by the Kremlin. Thus, he observed that the United States military was 'not designed for, or adopted to, a strategy of containing, waiting, countering, blocking, with no more specific objective than the eventual "frustration" of the opponent ...' The Americans would probably be frustrated by Mr X's policy long before the Russians.'

Third, Lippmann challenged the hierarchy of priorities ostensibly suggested by the X article. He warned that the acceptance of an interventionist policy of universal application – the global extension of the containment doctrine – would result in the foolhardy proliferation of American commitments. Indeed, such commitments could only be sustained within the context of a misleading Manichean image of the international system rather than through intimate reference to traditional American core values and interests.

Lippmann accurately predicted that the containment strategy of the Truman Doctrine would create many strange bedfellows for the United States. Hence, his observation that 'the policy can be implemented only by recruiting, subsidizing and supporting a heterogeneous array of satellites, clients, dependents and puppets.' Merely maintaining the *status quo* along the periphery would require 'continual and complicated intervention by the United States' – that is, a foreign policy of perpetual *tour de force* – while the Soviets could easily frustrate such a strategy through the undermining of those states' already unstable domestic structures.[8]

While Lippmann's detailed critique of the X article failed to include an alternative vision of the international system (and America's proper role within that system), his recommendation of an Atlanticist policy reflected a conviction that American engagement abroad must take the form of 'natural alliance' with those countries where the United States perceived a consonance of interests and values. Arnold Wolfers has observed that within Lippmann's conception of national security 'a nation is secure to the extent to which it is not in danger of having to sacrifice core values, if it wishes to avoid war, and is able, if challenged, to maintain them by victory in such a way.'[9] Thus, while rejecting the *universalist* orientation of the Truman Doctrine, Lippmann unabashedly advocated what he considered to be an 'enlightened' internationalist line for American foreign policy (as manifested, for example, in his enthusiastic support of the Marshall Plan). This important dichotomy between contending universalist and internationalist conceptions of the postwar inter-state system shall be further considered in the final section of this chapter.

Fourth, and finally, Lippmann's critique of Kennan's containment doctrine highlighted the serious domestic problems that it would present given the nature of the American polity. He argued that the implementation of this interventionist policy would require the organization of a highly centralized and secretive foreign policy apparatus more Soviet than American in style. Observing that the United States constitution itself might pose a barrier to the implementation of containment, he concluded: 'A policy of shifts and maneuvers may be suited to the Soviet system of government, which as Mr X tells us, is animated by patient persistence. It is not suited to the American system of government.'[10]

A century earlier, Alexis de Tocqueville had expressed similar reservations concerning the conduct of American foreign policy in his seminal study, *Democracy in America*:

Foreign politics demand scarcely any of those qualities which are peculiar to a democracy; they require on the contrary, the perfect use of almost all those in which it is deficient . . . A democracy can only with great difficulty regulate the details of an important undertaking, persevere in a fixed design, and work out its execution in spite of serious obstacles. It cannot combine its measures with secrecy or await their consequences with patience. These are qualities which more especially belong to an individual or an aristocracy; and they are qualities by which a nation, like an individual, attains a dominant position.[11]

The ultimate challenge to confront the statesman in the realm of policy-making, particularly within a democracy, is the articulation and pursuit of a foreign policy line that can be sustained within the limits and possibilities of the domestic consensus. This policy dilemma was underscored by Henry Kissinger in his Harvard doctoral dissertation, when he characterized the ability to obtain domestic support as 'the acid test of a policy.'[12] That said, it is not then without irony that during his own eight-year stewardship of American foreign policy, this scholar turned statesman encountered (and, to a degree, fostered) such intense domestic opposition to his policies. Indeed, Kissinger's distinctive brand of *Realpolitik* was often compared, in form if not content, to Kennan's containment strategy with its emphasis on the 'adroit and vigilant application of counter-force at a series of constantly shifting geographical and political points.' Moreover, it was this feature of the Kissinger diplomacy which prompted observers to speculate whether the balance that he sought abroad could balance at home.[13]

In the public mind, there was a clear link between the X article and the Truman Doctrine. Kennan's piece was widely quoted and cited in the American press. Hailed as a grand new formula for American foreign policy, it was perceived, whatever its original intent, as the intellectual justification for the Truman Doctrine. This was hotly denied by Kennan, whose own particular brand of anti-Communism was of a much more subtle variety. Rejecting the undifferentiated globalism suggested by the rhetoric of the Truman Doctrine, he sought in his *Memoirs* to explain the precise nature of the strategy that he had advocated in the X article: '. . . what I was talking about when I mentioned the containment of Soviet power was not the containment by military means of a military threat, but the political containment of a political threat.'[14]

The course of events in 1948–9 (e.g. the Berlin blockade, the Soviet detonation of an atomic bomb three years ahead of US intelligence estimates, the collapse of the Nationalist Government in China, and developments in Czechoslovakia and Yugoslavia, *inter alia*) reinforced the image of global confrontation and provided added impetus to the militarization of containment. The convergence of these events, in conjunction with the necessity of arriving at a decision whether to proceed with the development of a fusion bomb or not, prompted the Truman Administration to order a systematic reappraisal of American foreign and defense policies (just as the British withdrawal from Greece in 1947 had precipitated the review leading to the enunciation of the Truman Doctrine). Overall responsibility for the drafting of this study (NSC-68) fell to Paul Nitze who, upon the succession of George Marshall by Dean Acheson as Secretary of State in January 1949, had assumed the directorship of the department's Policy Planning Staff. Acheson and Nitze shared a common strategic outlook. In rejecting the false alternatives of isolation, appeasement and preventive war, they advocated the creation of 'situations of strength' so as to lead to an eventual political settlement with the Soviet Union without recourse to war.

The merging of the containment doctrine with the idea of 'negotiation from strength' had two powerful consequences *vis-à-vis* the conduct of American Cold War policy. First, it established a policy pattern (e.g. the emphasis upon 'war-winning' strategies) through which the United States sought to *impose* its notion of strategic stability upon the Soviet Union. As shall be discussed in a later section of this chapter, the logical culmination of this process was manifested in the strategic doctrine of the Kennedy Administration. At that time, however, the very attempt by the American government to dictate the terms of strategic stability to the Soviet Union paradoxically resulted in the most destabilizing episode of the Cold War – the Cuban missile crisis. Second, the slogan 'negotiation from strength' (taking, in effect, the prevailing American image of the international system as a given) implied that the problems and dilemmas of global containment could be solved through adroit adjustments of the instrumentalities of American power. As Bernard Brodie observed in a 1953 study assessing attitudes towards the use of force:

This slogan suggests that there is some marvelously effective mode of negotiation which we thoroughly understand and which we are quite ready to use but which is presently denied us because of marginal imperfections in our strength. This is patently false ... The obverse of this principle of postponing for a future of presumably greater strength the obligation to practice a shrewd and determined diplomacy is the doctrine that our military policy and our foreign policy must be intimately coordinated at every stage, and that neither can proceed without constant reference to the other.[15]

The expression of containment as the creation of 'situations of strength' spurred the process whereby the American mode of strategic analysis assumed an increasingly instrumental nature. In time, this quality came largely to shape the character of the internal dialogue on foreign and defense policies. With the *ends* of American power taken as given, the focus of debate centered upon the delineation of the requisite *instrumentalities* of American power. When confronted with contradictory or otherwise dissonant evidence, it was the strategic doctrine of the Cold War period which was subject to alteration in order to ensure the maintenance of the prevailing bipolar image. In this way, the differentiation of American commitments was accomplished via the *differentiation of means*, rather than through the elaboration of a more diversified image or world view.

NSC-68, like its predecessor NSC-20/4, represented an extrapolation of the analysis of Soviet intentions that had originated with the long telegram and found public expression in the Truman Doctrine. As for Soviet capabilities, the Nitze study group concluded that the United States would face a 'crisis year' in 1954 when the Soviets would have sufficient atomic (and perhaps thermonuclear) capability to neutralize the deterrent value of the American nuclear arsenal for the preservation of local stability. With the end of the American atomic monopoly, the implications with respect to the development of conventional capabilities were clear. Thus, with the uncritical acceptance of a bipolar, zero-sum image of the international system, the focus of NSC-68 centered upon the expansion of American capabilities to meet the Soviet threat within the context of (what *Pravda* would call) new objective circumstances.

In recommending increased defense expenditure, the Nitze *ad hoc* study group was directly challenging the major economic premise underlying American security policy in the immediate postwar period. Until 1950, the White House and the Bureau of the Budget had imposed strict budgetary limits on defense spending, fearing that such expenditures might trigger unacceptable inflation. Nitze and his staff economists, with the avid support of members of the President's Council of Economic Advisers, cited the American experience during World War II, when vastly increased defense expenditures had not caused damaging inflation. In light both of this experience and the projected exigencies of the 1950s, they argued that defense spending could conservatively be increased by a factor of three while still satisfying the 'welfare' demands of American society.[16] Ironically, this call for increased defense expenditures came from Acheson and Nitze at the State Department, while Secretary of Defense Louis Johnson, a confirmed fiscal conservative, was perhaps the plan's most vociferous opponent within the Truman Administration.

Critics of NSC-68 also included Soviet experts George Kennan and Charles Bohlen who, in challenging the document's Manichean world view, questioned whether the Soviet Union had, in fact, a 'fundamental design' of world conquest. Whereas Kennan and Bohlen 'emphasized the need to define interests in terms of limited capabilities, NSC-68 took the approach that, because capabilities were not limited as had been thought, interests need not be either.'[17]

With its recommendation for increased defense expenditures and its anticipation of the need for an American doctrine of limited war, NSC-68 was formally submitted to the White House in April 1950. Two months later, the outbreak of hostilities on the Korean peninsula appeared to validate both the study's policy prescriptions and the prevailing image of the international system upon which it was predicated. At that juncture, NSC-68 provided a coherent conceptual framework upon which the expansion of American forces in the early months of the Korean War was based. Indeed, as Paul Hammond observes in his study of this seminal document, NSC-68 had at least the initial effect of consolidating contending bureaucratic perspectives *vis-à-vis* the nature and economic feasibility of the expansion of American capabilities:

The existence of NSC-68 at the outset of the war contributed a particular quality to [the Korean War] build-up. From the beginning, and through its most frantic phases, the Korean War remained only a part of the larger picture of national strategy. For the small number of people in the executive branch who had read it, and for a large number who knew it by reputation, NSC-68 represented that larger picture . . . It is easy for a crisis, particularly war, to break down the separate and conflicting views and interests of government and infuse them with a common purpose. The common purpose, however, may have to be oversimplified . . . NSC-68 provided a partial substitute within the executive branch for the oversimplification of objectives in war. Before the Korean War had started, and, of course, without reference to it, a question had been asked and an answer provided which transcended organization perspectives and, when the time for implementation came, consolidated them. NSC-68 became a milestone in the consolidation of perspectives . . .[18]

Beyond the 'consolidation of perspectives' – that is, the institutionalization of a set of operational premises concerning the nature of Soviet behavior and the international system – NSC-68 had a more tangible impact on the structuring of American forces. Indeed, the Korean War left a material legacy of forces-in-being fully consonant with the general policy prescriptions made by the Nitze *ad hoc* study group in 1950.

Containment and the differentiation of means: (1) The search for the 'Great Equation'

Although the Truman Doctrine signified the globalization of containment on the rhetorical plane, it was the Korean War that marked the actual extension of American operational commitments. Those American policy-makers who had previously focused almost exclusively on the problems and dilemmas of European security now asserted that even a marginal shift in a secondary theater could be decisive, given the Manichean nature of the struggle with the Soviet Union. In this way, American universalism (as discussed in the final section of this chapter) engendered a foreign policy orientation which, having activated the American sense of moral mission, precluded a balanced differentiation of issues and commitments. The institutionalization of this approach, with its highly flexible and inherently expansible concept of national security, had powerful consequences. It fostered a decision-making environment in which considerations of the center – those few areas where American 'core' commitments are founded upon the consonance of material interests and values – and the periphery became blurred.

The Korean experience had demonstrated the credibility of the American will to counter the Soviet threat by proxy along the Eurasian periphery. The further proliferation of American commitments (within the context of this universalist foreign policy approach and its concomitant image of the international system) was reflected in the decisions to interpose the Seventh Fleet in the Taiwan Straits and to place anti-colonial qualms aside in support of the deteriorating French position in Indochina. Along with this globalization of containment came the transformation of the periphery into the center. Universalism thus proved inimical to foreign policy selectivity. With the *ends* of American policy undisputed, attention invariably focused on the requisite *means* of containment. This mode of analysis largely accounts for the instrumental nature of the foreign policy debate during the Cold War period.

The conclusion of the Korean War, coupled with the advent of the thermonuclear age, prompted a renewed high-level policy debate as to the most efficacious means for implementing the American strategy of global containment. The incoming Eisenhower Administration faced the problem of harmonizing foreign and defense policies within the bounds of the constraints imposed by this confluence of political and technological circumstance. In addition, this 'New Look' in the American approach to its external environment was expected to be wholly consonant with the 'New Look' that the Administration sought to bring in the realm of domestic and fiscal policy. This conclusion, as it came to be operationalized, ran contrary to the final assessment offered by the outgoing Truman Administration in the form of NSC document 141. This study, representing an extrapolation of the NSC-68 position *vis-à-vis* rearmament, was commissioned specifically to facilitate the transition between administrations. It concluded that the termination of hostilities on the Korean peninsula held no realistic prospects for reduced defense expenditure. Rather, in the face of projected developments in the Soviet strategic nuclear capability, NSC-141 argued for the creation of a more balanced and flexible military establishment (including substantial limited war forces) in order to rectify local imbalances between Communist and non-Communist nations. It was estimated that this essential requisite for the maintenance of American global commitments would entail budgetary increases of $7–8 billion.[19]

The planners of NSC-141 envisioned that much of this increased expenditure would be devoted to upgrading North American air defense systems in order to counter the anticipated Soviet strategic threat via manned bomber. Paradoxically, this and other early American responses to the development of Soviet retaliatory power, while at once providing added impetus to the Cold War arms race, simultaneously signalled the initiation of the process through which the prerequisites for a strategic dialogue were established. Though attention has generally focused here upon the material requirements, it is clear that to a very large extent this Cold War process entailed (to paraphrase Bernard Brodie) the adjustment of society's politics to its physics.[20] Yet the attempt to elaborate a common philosophy of deterrence, as later institutionalized within SALT, was sidetracked in at least two ways.

First, the American drive on the strategic plane, in effect, to operationalize a slogan – whether 'negotiation from strength,' 'massive retaliation' or even, in its initial presentation, 'flexible response' – necessitated that general nuclear war be presented as constituting a rational option for the United States. This orientation engendered an atmosphere in which many statesmen and analysts came to regard strategy as the pursuit of the master-key: the securing of those specific instruments of power which would perpetuate American 'superiority' and thereby allow it to continue to *impose* its notion of strategic stability upon the Soviet Union. This chimerical, non-Clausewitzian approach with its emphasis upon 'rational,' war-fighting postures invariably became more difficult to sustain as the Soviet Union moved to develop its own capability for 'assured destruction.' Hence there would remain an inherent tension – if not at times outright contradiction – between the ostensible demands of American strategic doctrine and the realities of a changing external environment. In part, the American approach to the means–ends relationship, characterized above as the *differentiation of means*, provided a way of coping with this dilemma while thus avoiding a fundamental re-evaluation of the universalistic assumptions governing the execution and formulation of American Cold War policy.

The US drive to perpetuate American military superiority over the Soviet Union had its counterpart on the political plane. The Eisenhower Administration was ushered into office upon the vague promise of 'a new, positive foreign policy' to upgrade somehow the 'negative,' status quo oriented doctrine of containment. This stance reflected the domestic disquiet of a people who fundamentally believed in the efficacy of a MacArthur-type approach ('no substitute for victory') and who therefore found it difficult to adjust to the demands and indecision of the Cold War. This domestic orientation undoubtedly contributed to the Cold War's virulent nature and resulted at times in the denigration both of the utility of dialogue with the Soviet bloc and, by implication, those individuals who advocated such a course. As Emmet J. Hughes observed in his chronicle of the Eisenhower years, 'words like "negotiation" were spat out like obscenities.'[21]

The second impediment to the establishment of a meaningful US–Soviet dialogue arose from the political consequences of the material disparity between the two sides. For much of the Cold War period this material imbalance was reflected in the asymmetry of reciprocal threats that each superpower could invoke against the other (*viz.* the American nuclear capability to devastate the Soviet homeland as countered by the Soviet threat to overrun Western Europe). While this Soviet emphasis upon the European theater is in one sense an understandable consequence of the centrality of the German question in Cold War politics, it might also be regarded as a reflection of Soviet weakness in strategic terms. Indeed, during the very period which political scientists characterize as 'rigid bipolarity,' the Soviet Union, for lack of a true global reach and advanced strategic systems, was perhaps least able to undertake discussions with the United States as a full negotiating partner. Hence, the initiation of a strategic dialogue and the subsequent elaboration of a common philosophy of deterrence was required to await both the advent of rough material parity (as embodied in that fitting acronym MAD – Mutual Assured Destruction) and the political perception of that reality.

For the Eisenhower Administration, however, the essential task was one of providing maximum security – albeit as defined *vis-à-vis* the inherently expansible 'national security interest' of global containment – at a sustainable cost. As the precise nature of the New Look continued to be debated, the prior assumption of an impending 'crisis year' gave way to the 'new' perspective of meeting the pervasive Soviet challenge over the 'long-haul.' John Foster Dulles captured the spirit of this shift when he asserted that the Soviets were planning for 'an entire historical period and we should do the same.'[22] During the spring and summer of 1953 three presidential task forces labored to balance what they termed the 'Great Equation' or, in other words, to provide substance to the New Look within the context of the new political, economic, and technological realities.

Three alternative grand strategies and their implications were explored by each task force: (1) the continuation of 'containment' as practiced by the Truman Administration; (2) global deterrence by threat of nuclear punishment (i.e. 'draw a line' around the globe); and (3) the 'liberation' of Communist-controlled territories through an amalgam of politico-economic and paramilitary methods.

The Planning Board of the NSC issued a preliminary report, designated NSC-162, which sought to integrate the best ideas of the task force studies and thereby reconcile the competing demands of economy and security. The authors of this document favored the adoption of a strategy characterized by one observer as 'containment plus' – a basic continuation of option (1) with some slight modification in the direction of option (2). While providing a coherent statement of American strategic policy, it failed to offer the Administration any real hope of reduced defense expenditures. Similar conclusions were reached in a separate report prepared by the Joint Chiefs of Staff (JCS) which included contingency planning across the categories and levels of potential conflict. Eisenhower and his fiscal planners, who had expected some savings as a result of the cessation of hostilities in Korea, rejected the strategic posture advanced within these studies. In response, Admiral Radford, the newly elected Chairman of the JCS, argued that considerable savings could be achieved only if American doctrine stipulated the early use of nuclear weapons upon the recommendation of battlefield commanders to the President. The prevailing view was that such a dependency upon nuclear weapons would permit reductions in conventional capabilities, particularly manpower.[23]

On 30 October 1953, the Radford line won presidential approval in the form of NSC-162/2. This document, providing much of the substance to the New Look, represented a landmark in the development of postwar strategic doctrine as it signified the final movement away from the idea that future wars would conform to the pattern of World War II. The JCS were directed to develop a narrower range of contingency plans upon the assumption that nuclear weapons would be employed whenever it was *technologically* advantageous to do so. Such an approach, while ostensibly adopted out of domestic considerations of economy, clearly reflected the American political and psychological preference at that juncture. In many respects, it represented a military counterpart to the political manifestation of containment as undifferentiated globalism.

The New Look doctrine was most strikingly presented in the 'massive retaliation' speech of Secretary John Foster Dulles in January 1954. Dulles, who had led the Republican assault upon the Truman–Acheson containment line during the 1952 presidential campaign, sought to underscore the Eisenhower Administration's shift away from a Korean-type mobilization posture in favor of a comprehensive strategy of deterrence. It was his belief that the initial Communist miscalculations in Korea had been the direct result of the failure of American declaratory policy – specifically, the Acheson 'defense perimeter' statement of January 1950. Dulles hoped that the global extension of collective defense arrangements would affirm American resolve and lessen the likelihood of such political miscalculation.

For reasons of economy, efficacy, and political preference, Dulles asserted that local defense must be reinforced by 'the further deterrent of massive retaliatory power.' This 'positive' approach to the strategy of containment would, he further argued, allow the United States to seize the initiative, as it would 'depend primarily upon a great capacity to retaliate, instantly, by means and at places of our own choosing.'

With the enunciation of the massive retaliation doctrine, Dulles had dramatically, if somewhat misleadingly, extrapolated upon the planning premises of the New Look. The emphasis which he placed in the address upon the role of nuclear weapons, coupled with his understatement of the continued utility and importance of conventional and indigenous forces, clearly went beyond the bounds which the planners of NSC-162/2 had envisioned. The press immediately seized upon the slogan of massive retaliation and portrayed it as a formula for turning every border skirmish into a nuclear showdown. Subsequent attempts to clarify the meaning of the massive retaliation address could not overcome the ambiguity and inherent contradictions of the New Look. Like the Nixon Doctrine a quarter century later, critics asked how the United States intended to support a global network of security commitments within the context of reduced, or at least static, capabilities.

The New Look offered the chimerical vision of a postwar world in which the United States could impose its notion of strategic stability upon the Soviet Union, and thereby ensure international order, on the basis of American technological superiority. Ironically, the Administration sought to give substance to the New Look at the precise moment when the nascent development of Soviet strategic nuclear capabilities was already beginning to undermine its assumptions and goals. To be sure, the advent of the 'balance of terror' raised the awkward questions of 'credibility' that came to so dominate the Western strategic debate in the ensuing years. In terms of American decision-making, this reflected the ongoing dilemma of integrating force and diplomacy – the traditional Clausewitzian question – in a revolutionary period of total means. The often sterile debate over credibility belied the fact that, despite a zero-sum image of global engagement, the United States proved unable to equate indefinitely the value of importance accorded its far-flung security commitments. Hence, the growth of Soviet strategic nuclear power demanded a degree of foreign policy selectivity which the rhetoric of the kind of the Truman Doctrine ostensibly precluded.

How were American decision-makers of the Cold War period able to reconcile these competing demands? One argument advanced within this study is that the process characterized above as the 'differentiation of means' became the mechanism for differentiating amongst American commitments while thus avoiding a fundamental re-examination of the prevailing image of the international system. In this way, the American image of global containment could remain intact and unchallenged as the instrumentalities of that policy were adroitly adjusted to meet (so it was argued) an insidious and multi-variegated Communist threat.

Critics of the Dulles–Radford line argued that a strategy based upon an over-reliance on nuclear weapons provided no answer to the pressing challenge of local aggression. To these analysts of American national security policy, the dawn of the era of truly total means demanded the development of a strategic doctrine and the capabilities requisite for the conduct of limited wars along the periphery. The Korean experience had demonstrated the possibility of placing such technological and political limitations upon warfare. The Dulles 'massive retaliation' speech served as the catalyst which both focused attention upon the manifold problems of limited war and initiated a lively debate in the public domain. The 'classic' critique of the Dulles massive retaliation position came from William W. Kaufmann, who laid out the requirements for a credible deterrent and emphasized the necessity of limited war forces for local defense. In advocating 'a broadly based policy of deterrence,' Kaufmann delineated a strategic posture subsequently characterized as 'flexible response': 'Our problem . . . is to find deterrents that forecast costs sufficient to discourage the enemy, but not provocative enough to make him turn, out of fear and desperation, to contingencies of the last resort. We must, in a word, try to fit the punishment to the crime.'[24] Kaufmann's critique of massive retaliation appeared all the more well taken coming as it did in the wake of the 1954 Indochina crisis when the paucity of non-nuclear options had been a major factor militating against intervention.

Henry Kissinger, then serving as rapporteur for a Council on Foreign Relations study group, followed the seminal works on limited war by Kaufmann and Brodie with an exploratory piece focusing upon the problems of defending the so-called 'gray areas.'[25] In this article, whose policy prescriptions bear a striking resemblance to the Nixon Doctrine proposals of a quarter century later, Kissinger argued that the prerequisites of effective local action by the United States lay in the establishment of stable indigenous governments. If these conditions were met he felt sure that American technological superiority could be translated into local superiority. Significantly, in this 'little war thesis,' Kissinger only hinted at the possible role of tactical nuclear weapons – a central concern of his 1957 best-seller, *Nuclear Weapons and Foreign Policy*. It is interesting to note that while Kissinger laid great stress in this volume upon the continuing relevance of Clausewitz, he rather uncritically accepted the underlying political assumptions then governing American strategy. Although he extensively explored the prerequisites of limited war in terms of American doctrine and capability, the political framework itself – the prevailing bipolar, zero-sum image of the international system – was not called into question. Kissinger's focus was, thus, on the modalities of containment. His elaboration of a strategy of *limited* nuclear war (written at that early point when American analysts generally believed that the employment of tactical nuclear weapons in local war would necessarily be to the advantage of the West) was but a further reflection of the instrumental nature of the American policy debate.[26]

While Kissinger advanced both a doctrine and strategic posture for limited war, Robert Osgood, in his important work of the same year, *Limited War: The Challenge to American Strategy*, examined how American attitudes towards war would affect the adoption of such a course. Osgood argued that the Dulles–Radford massive retaliation line was the logical outgrowth of an American tradition which knew no experience of war, save total war. In the final chapter he accurately articulated the challenge confronting American decision-makers:

> This study began with the recognition that an American strategy capable of meeting the threat of limited war must depend, ultimately, upon a transformation of the traditional American approach to war and to the re-lation between force and policy. We have come full circle. The fundamental question concerning the ability of this nation to sustain such a transform-ation remains unanswered.[27]

By the middle of 1957, the Eisenhower Administration ac-knowledged the need for both a doctrine and the forces for limited war as it sought a way to overcome the inherent strategic immobility of massive retaliation. In this instance, the differentiation of means was manifested in the wedding of new technology (*viz.* tactical nuclear weapons) with a Kissinger-type strategy of limited nuclear war. Previously, Administration spokesmen had failed to differen-tiate clearly between various types of nuclear weapons and the dif-ferent purposes to which they might be put. Hence, the distinguishing characteristic of what Samuel Huntington has described as 'the New New Look period' was the direct mating of tactical nuclear weapons with the idea of limited war: 'The wheel had come full circle from the early days of the New Look. In 1953 emphasis on tactical nuclear weapons had been part of the reaction against the concept of limited war. By 1957 it had become the means by which the United States proposed to implement that concept in any conflict of conse-quence.'[28]

In approaching the question of limited war, most of the analysts and decision-makers at the time, including Kissinger and Osgood, assumed the balance of terror to be inherently stable. That is, the balance of terror was regarded as a kind of stable strategic superstructure whose very nature, having made the limitation of war an imperative, had consequentially shifted the arena of challenge to the periphery. The dramatic impact of the Sputnik launch, coupled with the hard analysis of the Gaither Committee which followed it, cast serious doubt upon these assumptions and prompted the return of attention to the problems of maintaining the stability of the central strategic balance. In particular, concern was mounting *vis-à-vis* the potential vulnerability of American strategic forces. Seminal works by Bernard Brodie and Albert Wohlstetter challenged the assumption of stability upon which the Kissinger and Osgood analyses were predicated.[29] With this shift in emphasis, the necessity and problems of limited war appeared concomitantly to lose some of their urgency. The net result, however, was that the Eisenhower Administration again faced the acute task of reconciling the competitive demands of economy and security as it sought to finance the simultaneous development of a limited war capability and the improvement of American strategic capabilities. Although the Administration continued after 1957 to assert its recognition of the need for a limited war doctrine and capability, this acceptance was not reflected in its annual defense budgets. As a result, the pressing question as to the precise interrelationship between limited war and the central strategic balance was left unresolved.

Containment and the differentiation of means: (2) The Kennedy–Johnson years

The Kennedy foreign policy approach was premised upon the assumption that the arena of competition with the Soviet Union had dramatically shifted to the periphery. Khrushchev's historic foreign policy address of 6 January 1961, with its vision of a new epoch characterized by 'wars of national liberation,' had both confirmed this view and served as a catalyst to bring adjustments to the focus and modalities of containment. In his special defense budget message to Congress on 28 March 1961, Kennedy affirmed his Administration's commitment to the development of a panoply of forces in order to deter, and, if necessary, to counter, a spectrum of Communist threats. Unlike the Eisenhower Administration, the fiscal planners of the New Frontier felt that the adoption of a broadly based strategic posture ('flexible response') could be sustained through an overall expansion of the domestic economy.

The acceptance of flexible response marked a pronounced shift in attitude *vis-à-vis* the efficacy of tactical nuclear weapons in limited war. Previously there had been an attempt to blur somehow the difference between tactical nuclear and conventional weapons. At the time of the first Quemoy and Matsu crisis, for example, Vice President Nixon had proclaimed: 'tactical atomic explosives are now conventional and will be used against the targets of any aggressive force.'[30] Still later, Henry Kissinger, in a 1958 article examining the relationship between arms control negotiations and limited war, criticized the concept of test ban negotiations on the grounds that it implied that tactical nuclear weapons were in some way unsuitable for use in limited wars due to their unconventional nature.[31] By 1961, however, the threat to employ tactical nuclear weapons in a limited war situation, particularly along the periphery, had aroused concerns strikingly similar to those manifested in the massive retaliation controversy of 1954–5. Clearly, this proposed course of action neither commanded much credibility nor encouraged confidence in the American ability to effect any specific political outcome. In addition, analysts were increasingly concerned that the employment of tactical nuclear weapons would be a major escalatory factor, given the somewhat ambiguous interrelationship between limited and general war. The acceptance of these negative conclusions with respect to limited nuclear war scenarios amounted to yet another step away from a Dulles-type strategic posture with its reliance upon nuclear options. This position and its implications – acceptance of the need for conventional defense forces – would be articulated in the second of Kissinger's books devoted to strategy. In that volume (whose dialectical title conferred to it a Clausewitzian tone), Kissinger negotiated the first of many changes in a well-argued position.[32]

As an alternative to the strategic monism of the Eisenhower Administration, the so-called Kennedy–McNamara 'revolution' prompted two major shifts in the form that containment took. First, it prescribed the development of capabilities across the entire spectrum of warfare in order to counter, particularly along the periphery, the new and variegated Communist threat. Second, this acceptance of flexible response as a strategic posture was complemented by a new attitude towards the developing world in general and the modernization process in particular. This new approach (as expressed in the slogan 'nation-building') was informed by what Anthony Hartley has characterized as 'a spirit of positivistic optimism.'[33] In this view, Khrushchev's 'wars of national liberation' and the general politico-economic dislocation of modernization were regarded as components of a preliminary 'stage of development' which could be controlled through the appropriate mix of American policies. Military intervention, utilizing an array of counter-insurgency techniques, was viewed as a credible response to the problem of chronic political instability, should the other instrumentalities of American power be proved insufficient. It was hoped that the dual strategies of flexible response and nation-building – ostensibly reconciling the demands of security and modernity – would successfully transform and stabilize not only the international political landscape, but the domestic structures of the developing nation-states as well.

In terms of the hypotheses advanced within this study, one might regard the Kennedy–McNamara revolution as but one further step in the policy process characterized above as the differentiation of means. Upon their assumption of office, the policy-makers of the Kennedy Administration were obliged to confront an inherent contradiction within American strategic doctrine: the inability to relate credibly tactical nuclear weapons to a doctrine of limited war. That notwithstanding, the Administration continued to act uncritically upon the prevailing image of the international system as well as many of the planning premises bequeathed to it by the outgoing one. Instability along the periphery – often in the form of genuine nationalist movements – continued to be perceived as manifestations of a monolithic Communist threat. Elegant general theories of counter-insurgency and nation-building failed to take into account the political intricacies of local situations. As during the Eisenhower Administration, contradictions between doctrine and capabilities were regarded as evidence of the variegated and insidious nature of the Communist threat.

On the strategic nuclear plane, the acceleration of the *Polaris* and *Minutemen* missile programs provided the Administration with a relatively large and diversified second-strike force. With the expansion of the American strategic arsenal, policy-makers maintained the hope that it would be possible to impose a stable pattern of behavior upon the Soviet Union on the continuing basis of American superiority. This orientation found expression in Secretary of Defense Robert McNamara's Ann Arbor address of June 1962 – a coherent document which continues to be of seminal theoretical importance. In sharp contrast to the Dulles–Radford massive retaliation line which was repudiated as a consequence of its arbitrary, non-credible nature, the so-called 'McNamara Doctrine' sought to translate American numerical superiority – surprisingly not regarded at best as a transitory phenomenon – into a rational, credible, war-winning strategy. Here, one finds the quintessence of numbers within American strategic thinking. That is, in an attempt to extend deterrence to third parties (here, of course, the context was primarily European), American strategic planners felt that it would be necessary to demonstrate to the Soviet regime that the United States not only had the requisite capabilities to *fight* a nuclear war, but that it could, if necessary, *control* the course of a nuclear war.

Such a doctrinal shift, however, required some adjustments in the technical details of American strategy. Hence, just as the Kennedy Administration had quickly jettisoned the Eisenhower premise that any war larger than a 'brushfire' would be nuclear from the outset, so too did the demands of the McNamara Doctrine compel it quietly to drop the declaratory pledge that the United States would not be the first to employ nuclear weapons should there be an outbreak of hostilities. This appeared to be an internally logical prerequisite of the McNamara counterforce strategy – for in order to control the course of a nuclear war, the United States, in the words of Kennedy to journalist Stewart Alsop, 'might have to take the initiative.'

The problems with the McNamara Doctrine, however, were not to be encountered on the technical level. Rather, events exposed it to be a flawed strategy whose non-Clausewitzian nature was manifested in its failure to relate to the Soviet Union on the political plane. To be fair though, a large part of this failure may be attributed to the precarious nature of the strategic dialogue itself: that is, the attempt by each superpower to use its strategic posture as a means of imposing a political definition upon the relationship. In the eyes of American policy-makers, the McNamara Doctrine, framed as it was within the context of an unsatisfactory tactical situation in Europe (e.g. successive Berlin crises), was obviously addressed to the pressing problem of credibly extending deterrence to third parties. To a Soviet 'worst cast' planner, however, the emerging American strategic posture – *viz*. the dramatic expansion of the American strategic nuclear arsenal coupled with a more dynamic operational doctrine – roused the specter of a first-strike attack directed against the small and vulnerable Soviet ICBM force. Ironically, the American attempt to *impose* stability on the Soviet Union (based as it was upon maintaining a continuing degree of superiority) triggered a Soviet response, which, in turn, precipitated the most dangerous episode of the Cold War.

The background and chronology of the Cuban missile crisis – Khrushchev's Caribbean 'gamble' – have been skillfully analyzed in depth elsewhere.[34] In terms of this study, however, its significance lies in the fact that, despite the lofty rhetoric of the Kennedy–McNamara revolution, the truly fundamental shift in American strategic thinking occurred in its aftermath. It is interesting to note that in the Chinese written language, the character for 'crisis' has two meanings: danger and opportunity. The Cuban crisis underscored the dangers of a superpower dialogue in which contending strategic postures served as the mechanism for defining their political relationship. In the words of one observer, 'each was forced to consider the problems of deterence and defense in a context imposed by the other.' But the dangers of the brink also exposed the opportunities, or at least the potentialities, for altering the form (if not the content) of the strategic dialogue. Thus, paradoxically, the Cuban episode of October 1962 contained the seeds for a subsequent 'intellectual rapprochement.'[35]

During the crisis-ridden period from massive retaliation to the McNamara Doctrine, American policy-makers had felt it essential that the United States project a credible, rational, war-fighting strategic posture. This attempt was repeatedly frustrated, however, as the dramatic expansion of Soviet strategic nuclear capabilities steadily eroded the facade of credibility and rationality. Within this context, the internal policy-process characterized above as the *differentiation of means* served as the mechanism for ostensibly reconciling these contradictions between strategic doctrine and capability, while thus avoiding a fundamental re-examination of the political premises underlying the American doctrine of global containment.

In the wake of the Cuban crisis, the *real* revolution in American strategic thinking occurred when the United States abandoned any further attempts to demonstrate to the Soviet Union that general nuclear war could be a rational option. A shift of this kind, however, necessitated a transformation in the operational interrelationship between the American concepts of credibility, rationality, and commitment. As suggested above, with credibility regarded as the criterion of nuclear deterrence (and hence, of commitment), policy-makers had previously felt it necessary to demonstrate the rationality of the American war-fighting posture. In the face of the steady expansion of Soviet strategic nuclear capabilities, however, it required almost a perpetual *tour de force* to maintain such a form of credibility. Indeed, this was the function which the 'differentiation of means' had come to serve, namely, that of continuing to demonstrate the rationality of the war-fighting option. In time, there developed an almost inverse relationship between American attempts to demonstrate the rationality of their strategic posture and

European skepticism as to the credibility of the American commitment.

The Europeans, in particular the influential school of French strategists, quite naturally questioned the 'rationality' (and hence the credibility) of an American commitment to Europe in which the devastation of the American homeland was held in the balance. Hence, one of the consequences of the Cuban crisis was a fundamental shift in the criterion of credibility – that is, from the continued assertion of the rationality of war to a recognition that under certain circumstances the policy-maker would be willing to act irrationally. Here, of course, the circumstances were to comprise the all-important parameter. For, by necessity, it had to be a 'selective' irrationality operating on the principle of commitment – that is, 'irrationality carried to a consistent level of policy-making.' Within such a context of nuclear deterrence, a nation's core commitment might be regarded as 'ultimately a declaration that in given circumstances one would be prepared to act irrationally – or to put it in a different language, to incur terrible risks for the sake of values.' The mutual acceptance of the irrationality of commitment has proved a highly effective and credible form of deterrence. With the development of Soviet second-strike forces (and the consequential acceptance of MAD) it became possible to establish a meaningful strategic dialogue with the Soviet Union. This ensuing period of 'stabilized irrationality' was one characterized by 'a subtle and complex dialogue: one in which each superpower played two roles. In respect of its own commitments, it was prepared to demonstrate its irrationality; in respect of the other's it demonstrated its rationality. The dialogue was thus a four-way process, the irrational talking to the rational both ways round.'[36]

Though the prerequisite of such a superpower dialogue would ostensibly be a high degree of political differentiation – 'a selective irrationality' operating on the principle of commitment – there occurred no fundamental re-evaluation of the predominant American image of the international system in the aftermath of the Cuban crisis. Nonetheless, the acceptance of 'mutual assured destruction,' operating within the system of nuclear deterrence characterized above, necessitated at least a tacit acknowledgment of the center/periphery dichotomy – that is, a 'center' so defined as encompassing those few core commitments where the war-maker would be willing to incur terrible risks for the sake of values (i.e. would be prepared to act irrationally), and a 'periphery' in which the absence of shared values, and perhaps even of material interests, would militate against such a calculus of risk-taking. Unlike the arbitrary nature of the Dulles–Radford massive retaliation line, the regime of restraints embodied in that fitting acronym 'MAD' could only operate within the context of an acceptance, albeit tacit, of the center/periphery dichotomy. Yet, ironically, just as such a tacit understanding was being worked out on the strategic nuclear plane, the United States prepared to assume an active commitment in Indochina, which would ostensibly transform the periphery into the center. In this sense, the link between the Cuban missile and Gulf of Tonkin crises is a profound though paradoxical one. At least two sets of factors are to account for the paradox.

First, as stated above, despite the lessons of the Cuban episode (i.e. the *tacit* acceptance of the center/periphery dichotomy as the prerequisite for MAD), the well-institutionalized American image of the international system remained unchallenged and unchanged. However, this assessment of the external environment – one in which the United States was perceived to be engaged in a relentless Manichean struggle with the Communist bloc – appears to have been accepted more as an article of faith than as a result of reasoned analysis. This characteristic tended to reinforce the general rigidity of the American approach. Even political notions which clearly no longer corresponded to the external environment enjoyed rather long half-lives. In his chronicle of the Kennedy Administration, for example, Arthur Schlesinger recounted his unsuccessful effort to have the State Department drop its use of the phrase 'Sino-Soviet bloc.'[37] These themes of structural rigidity and continuity of the Cold War image are underscored by Doris Kearns in her study of Lyndon Johnson:

Johnson had inherited not only an office but a world view . . . Beside him were advisers who shared that view, and who represented that difficult to determine group of men – the so-called foreign policy establishment – who, from Acheson to Dulles to Rusk and Bundy, had developed, applied, and believed in the entire mode of reasoning that had dominated and given continuity to American foreign policy.[38]

The second set of factors which account for the paradoxical link between the Cuban missile and Gulf of Tonkin crises stems from the first. As argued above, despite the changes in rhetoric from the Truman Doctrine to massive retaliation to flexible response, the

American framework of analysis remained much the same: a bipolar, zero-sum image of the international system still prevailed and strategic thinking continued to focus almost exclusively on the instrumentalities of power. The quintessence of this approach was manifested in the psychological attitude of the New Frontier. The *hubris* reflected in such slogans as 'nation-building' and 'social engineering' led many observers to express concern over this reigning 'arrogance of power' and 'the illusion of American omnipotence.' With the ends of American power taken as a given, the focus of debate shifted to the question of requisite and efficacious means. In this light, Philip Geyelin's assessment of Lyndon Johnson is characteristic: 'His interest and expertise were not in policies and still less in ideas. His interest was in instrumentalities, and his supreme talent was in making them work to his timetable and to his ends.'[39] This instrumental approach to foreign policy problems extended down from the top echelon of the Administration into the heart of the bureaucracy. To Rusk, Vietnam had always been and would remain 'essentially a military problem.' To McNamara, the 'numbers' indicated the efficacy of the American course in Vietnam; as he would put it in May 1962, 'every quantitative measurement we have shows we're winning this war.'[40]

Yet, a theory of bureaucratic determinism fails to adequately explain the nature and weaknesses of the American decision-making process. Leslie Gelb and Richard Betts, in their important study, *The Irony of Vietnam: The System Worked*, argue that the critical decisions underlying American involvement in Vietnam were not imposed by the bureaucracy but were consonant both with elite and mass opinion. The American system is said to have 'worked' insofar as 'the core consensual goal of postwar foreign policy (containment of Communism) was pursued consistently.' Gelb and Betts conclude that '[like] the Frankenstein monster, the bureaucracy, once created, became uncontrollable. It played only a subsidiary role in setting the basic American commitment in Vietnam but a central role in shaping the war itself.'[41]

Within this context, the American instrumental approach to foreign policy (as operationalized within the bureaucratic structure) may be regarded as having enjoyed a consequential, rather than causal, status *vis-à-vis* the predominant image of the international system. Hence, the bureaucratic perspective, while useful in understanding decisions on the operational level, is of limited utility in analyzing the fundamental motivating dynamics of the decision-making process with respect to American involvement in Vietnam. In this case, the 'dialectics of intervention' can be explained only if one looks 'beyond the institutions into the American political style as it has been shaped by American history.'[42]

The publication of a major article on 2 September 1965 by the Chinese Defense Minister, Lin Piao, was regarded in Washington as confirmation of its conception *vis-à-vis* the nature and stakes of the war in Vietnam. Entitled 'Long Live the Victory of People's War!' the article was characterized by McNamara as China's *Mein Kampf*. Extrapolating upon this dubious analogy, it was possible for the Johnson Administration to identity Mao as the Asian Hitler, Vietnam as the new Czechoslovakia, and, importantly, domestic critics as would-be appeasers. Official pronouncements of 1965 and 1966 continued to emphasize the forward containment of Communist China as the principal objective of American involvement in Vietnam. In his important speech of 7 April 1965 at Johns Hopkins University – one which was designed to reiterate forcefully the case for 'why we are there' – the President made ominous references to the 'deepening shadow of Communist China.' From the vantage point of Washington, China was perceived as a revolutionary, non-rational power – one, unlike the Soviet Union, with which serious negotiations would not be possible. In the language of Henry Kissinger the scholar, this dichotomy between revolutionary and status quo orientated powers may be viewed as one whose basis centers around the question of legitimacy.

As reflected in the *Pentagon Papers*, the Johnson Administration regarded the Vietnam conflict as a decisive test case both of American will and the instrumentalities of American power (that is, nation-building and counterinsurgency versus 'people's war'). But in a broader sense Vietnam was more than a test case. It was the logical culmination (perhaps the inevitable consequence) of the American policy-making process characterized above – that is, the wedding of an undifferentiated, well-institutionalized image of the international system with an instrumental approach to foreign policy problems. Within this context, one can make sense of McGeorge Bundy's *obiter dictum* of February 1965 that 'pleikus are streetcars': given the style and orientation of the American foreign policy approach of that period, it was almost inevitable that one would come along.[43] With Peking perceived as the guiding hand of North Vietnamese aggression, the purpose of United States involvement was to frustrate people's war through the adroit application of American instrumentalities, and thereby accelerate the process to make China a rational, non-revolutionary power. The danger of failure was highlighted by Dean Rusk in testimony before the Senate Foreign Relations Committee on 18 February 1966: '. . . if we do not meet those responsibilities, we shall find a Red China more voracious and much more dangerous, if they should discover that this technique of aggression is successful.'[44]

Ironically, within months of Rusk's appearance before the Fulbright Committee, the United States and China achieved a tacit stand-off agreement about Vietnam which both triggered the real revolution in Sino-American relations and signified a fundamental transformation in the American rationale underlying its involvement in Indochina. The immediate context of this subtle and complex dialogue was the expanding air war over the skies of Vietnam in the Spring of 1966 when it appeared that the United States and China were on a clear collision course. On 27 April 1966, for example, *New York Times* columnist James Reston reported that the Administration had adopted a sweeping and potentially escalatory policy of 'hot pursuit': 'the official policy of the United States is that our bombers are now free to attack the base of any planes that intercept our fliers in North Vietnam, even if those bases are inside Communist China.'[45] In this atmosphere, the Chinese may have felt that the United States was considering a preemptive strike against their nuclear installations – a course which one American journalist colorfully referred to as 'nuclear castration.' An additional and perhaps more realistic concern of the Chinese was the possibility of an American move into North Vietnam. In his important study, *The Chinese Calculus of Deterrence*, Allen Whiting traces two repeated Chinese allusions in Autumn 1965–Spring 1966 to a 'Korean-type war' and unpublicized war preparations in south China were orchestrated so as to deter an expansion of the war: 'while there were other inhibitions against an invasion of North Vietnam, the available documents make explicit the prominent role of Chinese deterrence in foreclosing this choice of action.'[46]

The ominous escalation of the air war in Indochina during March 1966 coincided, paradoxically, with hearings before the Senate Foreign Relations Committee which reflected a strong desire in the American academic community for a shift in US policy towards

China. These sentiments were expressed in the testimony of Columbia University Professor A. Doak Barnett who, after characterizing American policy over the previous 17 years as 'containment and isolation,' advocated the adoption of a new posture based upon the formula of 'containment [without] isolation.' In the following month, lengthy statements by Premier Chou En-lai and Secretary of State Dean Rusk signalled respectively that China would refrain from intervention in a Vietnamese conflict confined below the 17th parallel and that the United States did not intend to attack China. That the United States and China had achieved a *modus vivendi* over Vietnam was reported by French journalist René Dabernat, the foreign editor of *Paris-Match* with close ties to the Quai d'Orsay in January 1967. Dabernat maintained that in April–May 1966 Peking had transmitted three conditions to Washington for abstaining from active participation in the Vietnam War: (1) that the United States not attack China; (2) that it not invade North Vietnam; and (3) that it not bomb the Red River dike system. Shortly after these conditions were communicated to Washington via the French foreign ministry, President Johnson and other top Administration officials were reported to have given necessary signals to Peking in various public speeches to indicate that they agreed to the Chinese terms.[47]

The importance of this tacit stand-off agreement between the United States and China over the Vietnam conflict cannot be overstated. For its achievement marked both a fundamental transformation in the American rationale underlying its involvement in Indochina and the start of the dialogue which culminated in the Sino-American *rapprochement* of 1971. The Chinese proposal of 26 November 1968 (N.B. three months after the Soviet invasion of Czechoslovakia) to resume ambassadorial talks at Warsaw symbolized the mutual desire for an improvement of relations in spite of the ongoing conflict in Vietnam. In announcing this proposal over Radio Peking, the Chinese government declared that highest priority should be given to the achievement of a bilateral agreement based upon its five principles of coexistence. During this period, the Soviet Union, naturally fearing the implications of *any* political understanding between the United States and China, claimed that the two powers had concluded a cynical deal at the expense of the Vietnamese people during their Warsaw 'get-together' – a charge which provoked an unprecedented denial by the Chinese ambassador to Poland.

By the time of the promulgation of the Nixon Doctrine in July

1969, the previous American perception of China as an irreconcilable adversary had already undergone a two to three year transformation. Indeed, the Nixon–Kissinger rationale for a continuing American involvement in Indochina (as shall be examined in chapters 2 and 3) was based not upon the forward containment of China, but rather upon a more convoluted argument which is best considered within the context of their approach to international order. However, this pronounced shift in American attitude cannot be solely attributed to the achievement of a Sino-American *modus vivendi* between 1966 and 1969. It also had much to do with the manner in which Americans conceived and conducted the war in Vietnam, and their resulting inability to achieve their desired (though ambiguous) political outcomes.

The Tet offensive of February 1968 all but shattered 'the illusion of American omnipotence.' The bravado and hopes of 1965 had turned into a nightmare which threatened to undermine the very social fabric of the country. Herbert Schandler, in his study of American decision-making in Vietnam, has assessed public reaction to the Tet offensive as follows:

The scope, intensity, and strength of the Viet Cong attacks caused extreme surprise and shock throughout the United States. Extensive television coverage of the offensive brought the blood, agony, and destruction of the battle directly into American homes and was a key factor in forming the popular conception of what had happened on the battlefield during the Communist offensive . . . Daily press reports filed from all parts of Vietnam also contributed to the sense of disaster, as they concentrated on reporting the destruction caused by the initial Communist attacks throughout Vietnam. One single quotation in a press report had a tremendous impact. 'It became necessary to destroy the town to save it,' an American major was reported to have said to newsmen in explaining how it had been necessary to rout the Viet Cong who had occupied the delta village of Ben Tre. This widely repeated sentence seemed to sum up the irony and the contradictions in the use of American power in Vietnam and caused many to question the purpose of our being there. If we had to destroy our friends in order to save them, was the effort really worthwhile, either for us or for our friends?[48]

Hence, the Tet offensive, in dramatically underscoring the inefficacy of the *instrumentalities* of American power (from 'controlled escalation' to 'strategic hamlets'), marked the end of the Cold War consensus upon which the *ends* of American power had so long been sustained. As Townsend Hoopes later recalled: 'the Tet offensive performed the curious service of fully revealing the doubters and dissenters to each other, as in a lightning flash.'[49]

Yet, a comprehensive re-evaluation of American objectives and purposes in the Vietnam War was precipitated not directly by the Tet debacle itself, but rather by the request of Generals Wheeler and Westmoreland for an additional 206,000 troops in its aftermath. Clark Clifford, who had succeeded Robert McNamara as Secretary of Defense in March 1968, was appointed by the President to chair an *ad hoc* task force on Vietnam, whose designated purpose was to examine the Wheeler–Westmoreland request for more forces and to determine its possible domestic implications. At Clifford's suggestion, a panel of senior presidential advisers – the so-called 'Wise Men' – was assembled at the State Department on 25 March to extensively question government officials on the post-Tet situation. On the following day, the Wise Men reported to President Johnson at the White House: with the exception of a small minority who supported the current course of action, the group reflected a growing consensus that direct American involvement should be reduced and that the South Vietnamese themselves should shoulder a greater share of the burden. In this sense, the sentiment and rationale later expressed in the slogan 'Vietnamization' predated the tenure of Messrs Nixon, Kissinger and Laird. Upon the completion of their oral presentation, the President expressed shock and dismay at the change in attitude of the Wise Men and demanded to know from which government officials they had received their briefing. 'Somebody,' Johnson intoned, 'had poisoned the well.'[50]

Johnson's initial reaction aside, the lengthy meeting with the Wise Men on 26 March served the purpose that Clifford had hoped it would. This *ad hoc* panel of senior presidential advisers (including such distinguished members as Dean Acheson, W. Averell Harriman, George Ball, Douglas Dillon, *et al.*) had made it clear that further escalation was unpalatable to Congress, the business community, and the public at large. It was this inexorable conclusion which prompted the President, however reluctantly, to adopt the conciliatory tone in his historic address to the nation on 31 March 1968. That speech, which announced both a partial bombing halt and Johnson's decision not to seek a second full term of office, represented something much more though than a change of policy *vis-à-vis* the Vietnam conflict. No longer would the United States consider itself the 'night-watchman state' – a nation once willing, in the language of John Kennedy's inaugural address, to 'pay any price, bear any burden . . . to assure the survival and success of liberty.' The Vietnam tragedy, like no other foreign or domestic crisis in its relatively brief history, had exposed the American soul to the dangers of *hubris*. From this nadir the incoming Nixon Administration faced the task of reshaping the shattered American foreign policy consensus in order to meet the demands and rigors of the coming period.

Containment and 'America's millennial role'

In terms of the evolution of the international system, the transition of the United States from a posture of relative isolation to that of superpower was negotiated in an extraordinarily short period of time. American isolationism during the period preceding its entry into World War II has generally been attributed to three sets of factors. First, the United States did not possess a truly global network of economic interests until after the war. Second, the presence of strong imperial powers (Britain and France) militated against a more active American role outside the Western hemisphere. And third, the American isolationist withdrawal was a logical consequence of its self-perception as an 'innocent nation [in a] wicked world.'[51]

This affirmation of American 'exceptionalism' – as reflected, for example, in Washington's 'Farewell Address' and such diverse political writings as those by de Tocqueville, Hegel, and Thomas Paine – became a powerful rationale both for American abstinence from the perceived dangers and intrigues of international (i.e. European) politics and its territorial expansion across the North American continent. 'Manifest Destiny,' as Daniel Bell has observed, 'was the civil religion of nineteenth-century America: not just the idea that a nation had the right to define its own fate, but the conviction of a special virtue of the American people different from anything known in Europe or even, hitherto, in the history of the world.'[52] Given this theme of Americans as a chosen people, building a new and better way of life in the New World, it is perhaps not surprising that the equation of America with Israel (and hence of Europe with Egypt) in the idea of the 'American Israel' is not infrequent.[53] This symbolic uniqueness, as manifested in American 'civil religion,' reinforced the isolationist impulse. Only with the lofty rhetoric of Woodrow Wilson (as Walter Lippmann took great pains to point out) did American isolationism find expression in different terms. For Wilsonian universalism not only proclaimed America's unique status within the international system, but its universal validity as well. This universalist approach, however, belied an active messianism – the sense of mission derived from the American character – which could 'like a recessive gene in the right situation . . . become dominant.'[54] Those circumstances would arise in the wake of World War II when the material prerequisites of continued American isolationism (factors 1 and 2 cited above) ceased to exist.

Fittingly enough, an initial attempt to define this new American mission was made by Henry Luce, the son of a missionary and publisher of *Time*, in a February 1941 *Life* magazine essay entitled 'The American Century.' The inability of Roosevelt and Stalin mutually to agree upon an internationalist approach to postwar planning led to the adoption by the United States of a different (i.e. universalist) foreign policy orientation. Though the core idea of this new approach (as expressed in the containment doctrine) was in part a reflection of reality, it was also a 'myth' in the sociological sense, as it was rooted in a universalistic conception of US 'national security' interests.[55] This characteristic of American postwar policy contributed to the general virulence of the Cold War. In a similar vein, Raymond Aron observed that although nuclear weapons made any major war insane, the possibility of 'ideological war,' to use Comte's expression, remained possible 'since instead of a clash between the *ancien regime* and a new spirit, we see a clash between two versions of the new spirit.'[56] This perception of the Cold War as 'a clash between two versions of the new spirit' (or 'between alternative ways of life' in the language of the Truman Doctrine) permitted questions of power to be translated into extrapolated questions of value.

However, the 'mobilization of moralism' (to use Aron's expression), which accompanied the postwar appeal to universalism, was not merely the logical consequence of the American civil religion. To policy-makers, it clearly had a political utility of its own. For given the legacy of America's post-World War I withdrawal, there was an underlying belief that only the portrayal of the postwar situation in the starkest of terms could prevent its recurrence. Thus, the Truman Administration arrived at the conscious decision to present publicly the specific matter of military assistance to Greece and Turkey as a statement of global policy with explicit reference to the ideological challenge of Communism. Following the crucial meeting with Congressional leaders on 27 February 1947, one of the participants reported that Acheson had 'discovered that he had to pull out all the stops and speak in the frankest, boldest, wildest terms to attract their support for a matter which in parliamentary democracies without a tradition of isolation would have been undertaken quietly and without fanfare.'[57] From the vantage of the Policy Planning Staff, George Kennan feared that the ideological tone of the Truman Doctrine, when coupled with the American foreign policy style, would lead to a posture of undifferentiated globalism: 'This universalistic approach has a strong appeal to US public opinion; for it appears to obviate the necessity of dealing with the national peculiarities and diverging political philosophies of foreign peoples; which many of our people find confusing and irritating. In this sense, it contains a strong vein of escapism.'[58] As discussed above, however, the very attempt to escape the traditional dilemmas of diplomacy (e.g. the impact of nuclear weapons on the means–ends relationship) invariably complicated the decision-making process and thereby heightened the dangers and uncertainties of the Cold War. But beyond this obstruction of foreign policy selectivity, the institutionalization of such a universalist approach had two powerful and far-reaching consequences – one in terms of the American perception of the world at large and another in terms of the American perception of itself.

With respect to the international environment, the American postwar appeal to universalism led it to be regarded as almost an extension of the US domestic environment. Thus, it was a garrulous isolationist, an undertaker turned statesman from Nebraska, Senator Kenneth Wherry, who could tell a cheering audience: 'With God's help, we will lift Shanghai up and up, ever up, until it is just like Kansas City,'[59] Twenty years later, Lyndon Johnson's proposal for an Asian 'Great Society' program similarly reflected this sense of national faith and mission. Moreover, this kind of approach to the international environment fostered a decision-making atmosphere in which it became possible to rationalize and thereby sustain a global network of security commitments through explicit reference to American core values. Writing in the wake of President Johnson's decision to escalate the war in Vietnam, Robert Bellah commented on this phenomenon:

With respect to America's role in the world, the dangers of distortion are greater and the built-in safeguards of the tradition weaker . . . Never has the danger been greater than today. The issue is not so much one of imperial expansion, of which we are accused, as a tendency to assimilate all governments or parties in the world which support our immediate policies or call upon our help by invoking the notion of free institutions and democratic values. Those nations that are for the moment 'on our side' become 'the free world.' A repressive and unstable military dictatorship in South Viet-Nam becomes 'the free people of South Viet-Nam and their government.' It is then part of the role of America as the New Jerusalem and 'the last hope of earth' to defend such governments with treasure and eventually with blood.[60]

On the domestic plane, the postwar expression of American civil religion (here again defined, in the words of Raymond Aron, as the American 'version of the new spirit') upon occasion gave rise to political intolerance and extremism. Within this context, the domestic drive for ideological conformity may be regarded as a powerful complement to the American postwar appeal to universalism. Contrary to popular notions, however, this zealous campaign did not merely rise and fall with the fortunes of that now notorious Senator from Wisconsin. Indeed, most of the institutional mechanisms associated with McCarthyism (e.g. the Federal Loyalty Program, the Internal Security Act, and the House Un-American Activities Committee) owed much of their existence to the psychological climate fostered by the promulgation of the Truman Doctrine.[61] The origins of American domestic anti-Communism aside, McCarthyism as a political phenomenon had a lasting impact on the nature and scope of the American foreign policy debate in that 20-year period between the Truman Doctrine and the Tet offensive. For, as a consequence of its influence, genuine liberalism, which might have provided an alternative (more differentiated) image of the international system, was discredited and thus of little sway in the development of the postwar foreign policy consensus. Ultimately, the foreign policy debate became a tight dialogue between the center-right and the right. With the ends of American power taken as a given (global containment), discussion invariably focused upon the conditions affecting the adroit application of the instrumentalities of American power.

In time, the institutionalization of a universalist foreign policy approach prompted American decision-makers to pursue policies based on the decisive and independent efficacy of power. Daniel Bell, writing of 'the end of American exceptionalism,' observes:

[One might] say that the centrality of the American world role was an inevitable consequence of the weakness of other states, or the inevitable rivalry with the Soviet Union, or that the idea of Manifest Destiny and mission inevitably would carry the United States into the moralistic role of world policeman. Whatever the truth of these cases, the fact is that these molds have now been broken. There is no longer a Manifest Destiny or mission. We have not been immune to the corruption of power. We have not been the exception. To a surprising extent there is now a greater range of choice available to the American polity. Our mortality now lies before us.[62]

With the Vietnam debacle bringing a premature conclusion to 'the American Century,' the ensuing period demanded that the United States navigate that difficult transition from preponderance to *primus inter pares*. Such a shift in foreign policy, however, required that a new balance be struck between what Raymond Aron has referred to as 'the antinomies of diplomatic–strategic conduct.' In charting the Nixon–Kissinger Strategy, the new Administration sought to forge such a new (hopefully favorable) balance and, in so doing, to restore coherence to a troubled American diplomacy.

2 . CHARTING THE NIXON–KISSINGER STRATEGY

The Statesman is . . . like one of the heroes in classical drama who has had a vision of the future but who cannot transmit it to his fellowmen and who cannot validate its 'truth.' Nations learn only by experience; they 'know' only when it is too late to act. But statesmen must act *as if* their intuition were already experience, as if their aspiration were truth.

Henry Kissinger, A World Restored, 1957

I feel my greatest strength was in intuition on where the main historical currents were.

Henry Kissinger, 12 November 1977[1]

Nixon and Kissinger: the development of a 'special relationship'[2]

The history of American diplomacy reveals several instances in which a close, even intense, working relationship was forged between a President and his chief adviser. In this century, the close collaboration between Woodrow Wilson and Colonel House as well as of that between Franklin D. Roosevelt and Harry Hopkins are examples which readily come to mind. Yet, beyond these precedents, the Nixon–Kissinger partnership stands apart as a wholly exceptional relationship – one, remarkably, in which the power and influence of the aide increased even as that of the patron diminished. On the operational level, their close rapport was firmly rooted in a shared conception *vis-à-vis* the style and substance which American foreign policy should assume as the nation entered the post-Vietnam period. The reality of this 'special relationship' accentuates the difficulty in differentiating the substantive role that each played in the negotiation of this arduous transition. Indeed, it is a problem which led one observer to quip that just as Churchill designated Hindenburg and Ludendorff in *The World Crisis* as HL, it might be more accurate to refer to the Nixon–Kissinger foreign policy by the symbol NK.[3]

At the outset of the new Administration, however, the Nixon–Kissinger relationship appeared to be a rather incongruous one. For Nixon – at least the 'old' Nixon – had built his constituency upon the kind of opportunistic appeal to insular politics which Kissinger deplored. During his 1968 service on behalf of the candidacy of Nelson Rockefeller, this quality prompted Kissinger to diagnose Nixon as 'paranoic' and to characterize him as 'the most dangerous, of all the men running, to have as President.'[4] Given this background, most observers were surprised when on 30 November 1968 the *New York Times* reported that Kissinger was to join the Nixon Administration as staff director of the National Security Council. (Kissinger himself believed that, if anything, he would be asked to head the State Department's ineffectual Policy Planning Staff.) The Kissinger appointment was hailed across the American political spectrum. From left to right (i.e. from *The New Republic* to the *New York Times* to William F. Buckley's *National Review*) it was regarded as a 'reassuring sign' that Nixon – a public figure noted for the mediocrity of the men surrounding him – had chosen one of the nation's leading academic lights to be his national security adviser.

Astute political commentators wondered aloud, however, whether the Kissinger appointment, coming as it did before the selection of either the Secretaries of State or Defense, was an auspicious sign. Indeed, at the formal announcement on 2 December 1968, the President-elect's perfunctory affirmation of his desire for a 'strong' Secretary of State did little to assuage the doubts of outside observers. The appointment of William P. Rogers, a former Attorney General with no previous experience in the realm of international politics, to the Secretaryship later in the month was merely regarded as further confirmation of the emerging executive (White House oriented) foreign policy *style* of the Nixon Administration. Though the precise institutional implications of this approach shall be explored in the next section, it is important to underscore that both Nixon and Kissinger assumed office with the conviction that the formulation of American foreign policy was pre-eminently a presidential function. Nixon candidly expressed this philosophy in a November 1967 interview: 'I've always thought this country could run itself domestically without a President. All you need is a competent Cabinet to run the country at home. You need a President for foreign policy; no Secretary of State is really important; the President makes foreign policy.'[5] In his celebrated interview with Italian journalist Oriana Fallaci, Kissinger, while rebutting the charge that he was Nixon's 'mental nurse,' articulated a similar view of presidential primacy in foreign policy decision-making and underscored the importance of 'style' in the relationship between President and adviser:

We mustn't forget that, before he ever met me, President Nixon had always been very active in matters of foreign policy. It had always been his consuming interest. Even before he was elected it was obvious that foreign policy mattered greatly to him. He has very clear ideas on the subject . . . I . . . am not at all so sure I could have done what I've done with him with another president. Such a special relationship, I mean the relationship between the President and me, always depends on the style of both men. In other words, I don't know many leaders . . . who would have the courage to send their aide to Peking without telling anyone. I don't know many leaders who would entrust to their aide the task of negotiating with the North Vietnamese, informing only a tiny group of people of the initiative. Really, some things depend on the type of president. What I've done was achieved because he made it possible for me to do it.[6]

Kissinger's choice of language is striking. For it suggests that the successful implementation of the Nixon–Kissinger strategy – that is, the creation of a 'stable structure of peace' – was predicated upon a unique fusion of style and substance. As shall be discussed in subsequent chapters of this study, this prerequisite of the new Administration's 'fresh approach' had two important implications on the domestic plane. First, the adoption of a rather more Byzantine, less ideological foreign policy approach, characterized by maneuver and manipulation, marked a fundamental shift in the American national style of conducting international affairs. Here, the close bond between style and substance is unequivocal as a transformation of the former led to one of the latter. This feature of the Nixon–Kissinger strategy made more problematic the task of forging a new domestic consensus (in Kissinger's own words, the 'acid test' of any foreign policy) and prompted observers to speculate whether the new balance which the Administration sought abroad would balance at home.

The second domestic implication of the new Administration's fresh approach stemmed from the first and centered upon the problem of institutionalization. In essence, the exceptional character of the Nixon–Kissinger foreign policy style, with its emphasis upon maneuver and manipulation, with its unprecedented centralization and secrecy (raising thorny constitutional questions of accountability), hampered, if not precluded, the process identified by Weber as 'routinization.' As one analyst observed in 1974:

If the Nixon–Kissinger machinery of foreign policy cannot be transmitted, then the diplomatic maneuvering required to make so complex a system manageable will become increasingly difficult to carry on. Style and substance are linked here, and any attempt to conduct a Kissinger-type diplomacy by pre-1969 methods might lead to disaster. A question is at least posed at to whether the Nixon Administration has left its successor a policy which only itself could work?[7]

Hence, the very characteristics which typified the Nixon–Kissinger approach had the net effect of turning the conduct of American diplomacy into a perpetual *tour de force* and thereby accentuating the traditional problem of institutionalization. This theme – the nature and implications of 'Kissinger's *apparat*' – shall be more fully explored in the following section.

Given the Nixon Administration's pledge to transform the theory and practice of American foreign policy, it would be useful at this juncture to examine the ideas which the President and his Assistant for National Security Affairs developed prior to their assumption of office. As reflected in the quotations cited above, Richard Nixon assumed stewardship of American diplomacy firm in the belief that it constituted the primary area of presidential responsibility. In both his final telecast to the nation on 8 August 1974 and his *Memoirs*, he expressed confidence that despite the taint of Watergate, history would judge his Administration kindly on the strength of its foreign policy achievements. It does not even appear to have occurred to the former President that this record too would be the focal point of much controversy and frequently bitter criticism.

At the time of his inauguration, Nixon was almost universally regarded as the quintessential cold warrior. His meteoric rise at home (from obscure lawyer to Vice President in six years) had been based upon his zealous espousal of the new anti-Communist orthodoxy – first, in the Congressional investigation of Alger Hiss (the case which propelled him to national prominence); later, in the Senate race of 1950 in which he dubbed his opponent, Helen Gahagan Douglas, the 'Pink Lady'; and finally, in the bitter presidential campaign of 1952 during which he charged that Adlai Stevenson was 'a graduate of Acheson's Cowardly College of Containment.' This inflammatory rhetoric, however, was not purely for domestic consumption: it genuinely reflected his analysis of the international situation and his perception of the pervasive monolithic threat which confronted the United States in the postwar period. His fervent advocacy of these beliefs later prompted his former speechwriter,

William Safire, to quip that Nixon's own *alma mater* was the 'John Foster Dulles school of international affairs.' Given this foreign policy orientation, it followed that Nixon regarded the global application of containment as an imperative and firmly believed in its logical corollary – the efficacy of American interventionary force.

To cite but two examples, these beliefs prompted Nixon, as Vice President, to urge US action during the Indochina crisis of 1954 (including the possible use of tactical nuclear weapons) and later, as a private citizen, to recommend that President Kennedy authorize a full-scale American assault on Cuba in the wake of the Bay of Pigs fiasco.[8] With respect to Vietnam, Nixon, like almost all American political leaders of the time, strongly supported the post-Gulf of Tonkin escalation of US involvement, although he seriously questioned (and, at times, ardently criticized) the Johnson Administration's choice of tactics. This criticism foreshadowed his own departures in policy after January 1969 (e.g. the shift from gradual escalation to massive and quick military action). In January 1966 the 'old' Nixon lashed out against Congressional proponents of an extended bombing pause, warning that Republicans would make a political issue of what he termed 'the soft line, the appeasement line.' In November of the same year he criticized the Manila Conference communiqué which included an American proposal for a mutual phased withdrawal of United States and North Vietnamese forces from the south. Ironically, this condition came to be the core of his own Administration's negotiating position – and indeed one which itself was quietly dropped in the final round of negotiations leading to the conclusion of the Paris accords.

The cautious, rather uninspired Nixon campaign for the Presidency in 1968 gave little indication of the foreign policy departures which the new Administration would initiate once in power. (The Nixon 'peace plan' was to remain a secret for fear of ostensibly prejudicing the ongoing negotiations with North Vietnam.) One sign of a possible shift in thinking, however, was evidenced in October 1967 when *Foreign Affairs* featured an article by Nixon, 'Asia after Vietnam.' While wrapped in much of the familiar rhetoric, the piece did anticipate two of his most important foreign policy initiatives: the enunciation of the Nixon Doctrine as a formula for politico-military retrenchment and the opening to China. The starting point of the article was an accurate reading of the change in psychological attitude on the domestic plane: the Vietnam debacle, having imposed severe strains on the United States (social and political as well as military and economic), had shattered the foreign policy consensus which, in turn, had sustained two decades of American globalism. As a result, 'if another friendly country should be faced with an externally supported communist insurrection – whether in Asia, or in Africa or even Latin America – there is serious question whether the American public or the American Congress would now support a unilateral American intervention, even at the request of the host government.'

In light of the prospective decline in American activism which the Vietnam experience portended, Nixon pointed to the nascent strength of regionalism as an alternative, more indirect means of channelling American influence. In language strikingly similar to that of the Nixon Doctrine, he asserted that the development of indigenous 'regional defense pacts' would permit a necessary reapportionment of the burdens of containment. In abandoning 'the role of the United States as world policeman,' Nixon maintained that the criteria governing the use of American interventionary force would invariably shift as part of the overall adjustment to new domestic and international realities. As under the Nixon Doctrine, he contended that the United States should only offer direct military assistance in situations where it would make a real difference in terms of political outcome and where it was in American interest to do so:

If the initial response to a threatened aggression, of whichever type – whether across the border or under it – can be made by lesser powers in the immediate area and thus within the path of aggression, one of two things can be achieved: either they can in fact contain it by themselves, in which case the United States is spared involvement and thus the world is spared the consequences of great-power action; or, if they cannot, the ultimate choice can be presented to the United States in clear-cut terms, by nations which would automatically become allies in whatever response might prove necessary. To put it another way, the regional pact becomes a buffer separating the distant great power from the immediate threat. Only if the buffer proves insufficient does the great power become involved, and then in terms that make victory more attainable and the enterprise more palatable.[9]

Though prescient in its anticipation of the change in criteria *vis-à-vis* the employment of American interventionary force along the periphery, the article reflected the central ambiguity which later came to surround the Nixon Doctrine. In failing to differentiate critically amongst the categories and levels of possible threat (given the changing and ambiguous nature of aggression), the criteria, never really made explicit either in the article or subsequently in the Nixon Doctrine itself, would not in practice make the choice for or against intervention any easier. For the 'good case' – an instance in which policy-makers regarded 'victory' to be 'more attainable and the enterprise more palatable' – would be precisely the kind which would not require a major assistance effort.[10] However, despite an overall reduction in American capabilities and the shift in criteria governing the use of American interventionary force, the validity of the nation's far-flung overseas commitments was universally re-affirmed as the first principle of the Nixon Doctrine. In thus maintaining the pre-existing Cold War structure of commitment as part of the Nixon–Kissinger strategy's pursuit of stability, American credibility was ostensibly called into question even in situations where its objective interests were not at stake and where the efficacy of American power to affect favorably the political outcome was dubious (e.g. the Cambodian 'incursion' of 1970, the Indo-Pakistan War of 1971, the Angolan Civil War of 1974–6.)

At the time of its enunciation (just as in 1967 at the time of its inception), the Nixon Doctrine was regarded as one of the new pillars of American foreign policy which would permit the effective reintegration of force and diplomacy in the post-Vietnam period. Yet, the very attempt to negotiate the transition from preponderance to 'military retrenchment without political disengagement' high-lighted the underlying ambiguity of its guiding strategy. And from the ambiguity arose the complications. The central thesis of this study is that American post-Vietnam foreign policy was premised upon the belief that the establishment of a new relationship with the United States' Communist great-power rivals would create the favorable political atmosphere so as to facilitate the orderly devolution of American power to incipient regional powers. The resulting stability along the periphery would, in turn, feed back into the central balance and thereby sustain the momentum of détente through the preservation of mutual trust. In this way, each component of the Nixon–Kissinger strategy – that is, détente and the Nixon Doctrine – would serve as the instrumentality for the achievement of the other.

In addition to its foreshadowing of the nature and scope of American politico-military retrenchment, Nixon's 1967 article in

Foreign Affairs also anticipated his Administration's precedent-breaking China initiative. Although advocating a change in American policy in order to 'come . . . to grips with the reality of China,' Nixon continued to regard the People's Republic as an implacable revolutionary power. It is interesting to note that, in many respects, his analysis reflected at least a tacit acceptance of the kind of dichotomy which Kissinger had underscored in his academic writings between 'revolutionary' and 'legitimate' international orders (see below). Hence, in Nixon's eyes, the essential prerequisite of a true Sino-American *rapprochement* would be evidence of China's transformation from a revolutionary power into a status quo oriented power:

The world cannot be safe until China changes. Thus our aim, to the extent that we can influence events, should be to induce change. The way to do this is to persuade China that it *must* change: that it cannot satisfy its imperial ambitions, and its own national interest requires a turning away from foreign adventuring and a turning inward toward the solution of its own domestic problems.[11]

At first glance, this approach would appear to have been fully in accord with the prevailing attitude of the time, namely that the United States could *impose* a pattern of stability upon the Chinese through the demonstration of the inefficacy of people's war, etc. Nonetheless, the familiar anti-Communist rhetoric – including the bizarre analogy that 'dealing with Red China is something like trying to cope with the more explosive ghetto elements in our own country' – belied the subtle shift towards a more flexible, more pragmatic approach *vis-à-vis* relations with China.

In the conclusion of the article, an explicit link was drawn between the regional devolution of American power and the containment of China. Nixon forcefully argued that the development of a strong indigenous regional security system in Asia would provide the most effective bulwark against Chinese expansionism, and thereby accelerate the transformation of China into a rational, status quo oriented power:

The primary restraint on China's Asian ambitions should be exercised by the Asian nations in the path of those ambitions, backed by the ultimate power of the United States. This is sound strategically, sound psychologically and sound in terms of the dynamics of Asian development. Only as the nations of non-communist Asia become so strong – economically, politically and militarily – that they will no longer furnish tempting targets for Chinese aggression, will the leaders in Peking be persuaded to turn their energies inward rather than outward. And that will be the time when the dialogue with mainland China can begin.[12]

Once in office, such language prompted observers to question whether the Nixon Administration had indeed embraced a new image of the international system ('the potential and the imperative of a pluralistic world') or rather, whether it sought new instrumentalities to achieve the familiar ends of American foreign policy (containment and orderly change) in the post-Vietnam period. Again, the thesis advanced within this study is that this question of rival perspectives and choice of image might best be viewed as reflecting perhaps the principal foreign policy dilemma to confront American decision-makers in the post-1969 period: the ongoing dilemma of reconciling continued (indeed revitalized) military bipolarity with the new conditions of global pluralism. As shall be examined in subsequent chapters, the feedback relationship which the Administration sought to forge between the twin policies of superpower détente and the Nixon Doctrine constituted its transitional response to this ongoing dilemma.

In this section, discussion so far has concentrated on the principal themes of continuity and change evidenced in Richard Nixon's thinking on foreign policy prior to his assumption of office. Attention shall now similarly focus upon the pertinent pre-1969 writings of Henry Kissinger. The importance of these works is obvious – for they provided the reference points upon which, to a large extent, the formulation and conduct of the Nixon–Ford foreign policy was to be based. Kissinger's ascent to power – his transition from scholar/ analyst to practitioner – came at the age of 45. For the previous two decades at Harvard, he had devoted much of his energies to the development of a sustained and detailed critique of American foreign policy. He had entered the academic world at the precise moment when the study of international relations in the United States was becoming a discipline in its own right. Indeed, the first wave of postwar writings (Morgenthau, Wolfers, Kennan, *et al.*) played the crucial role of providing policy-makers with the intellectual foundation and rationalization for the 'new' diplomacy.[13] However, whereas most of his fellow graduate students were absorbed with these questions of applied politics (Cold War tactics, etc.), Kissinger's own early work was devoted to the exploration of 'first-order' questions of political philosophy – those of power, order, and justice. An analysis of his undergraduate honors thesis, modestly entitled 'The Meaning of History,' reveals an ostensibly incongruous admixture as Kissinger coupled his espousal of conservative philosophy with an admiration for the metaphysical idealists, Kant and Hegel. His constant reference in subsequent works to the twin themes of 'limits' and 'will' reflected the profound influence of these diverse philosophical strands in the make-up of his world view.

Kissinger's doctoral dissertation, published interestingly enough in the wake of critical acclaim for *Nuclear Weapons and Foreign Policy*, utilized the Congress of Vienna system as a vehicle for continuing his enquiry into the nature of these 'first-order' questions of political philosophy. Although it remained largely ignored until his meteoric rise to power, it undoubtedly stands as Kissinger's most important work. Upon its completion, Kissinger, first at the Council on Foreign Relations and subsequently as Professor of Government at Harvard, concentrated upon specific problems of applied politics (e.g. such 'second-order' questions as American strategic doctrine, NATO, and East–West relations). However, the reference points – that is, the analytical framework which he employed and the criteria by which his moral judgments were made – were informed by a concealed philosophy of history derived from this earlier work.[14]

Remaining tacit, at best, Kissinger's philosophy of history is most accessibly approached by way of his concept of power. That, in turn, invariably brings one back to the two pervasive themes of his scholarly writings – 'limits' and 'will'. In *A World Restored*, praise is reserved for those post-Napoleonic statesmen, specifically Metternich and Castlereagh, who recognized and accepted the finite limits of their power and who subsequently chose diplomacy, buttressed by the adroit application of force, to achieve their objectives. Yet, a realistic acceptance of limits should not, in Kissinger's view, trap the statesman into a complacent assent to the status quo. Rather, the enduring challenge which, if taken up, propels the statesman to the limits of his possibilities is that of actually attempting to change 'external reality' through an act of internal will as manifested in creative diplomacy.[15] Hence, Kissinger's most damning criticism reserved for Metternich is that while acknowledging the limits of his power, he lacked 'the attribute which has enabled the spirit to transcend an impasse at so many crises of history: the ability to contemplate an abyss, not with the detachment of a scientist, but as a challenge to overcome – or to perish in the process.' Thus, for the statesman, the achievement of 'final greatness' can be secured only through 'the strength to contemplate chaos, there to find material for fresh creation.'[16] A decade later, Kissinger, writing in *The Troubled Partnership*, would strike the same theme within the context of a discussion centering upon the evolution of the Atlantic alliance and its leadership: 'There are two kinds of realists: those who use facts and those who create them. The West requires nothing so much as men able to create their own reality.'[17]

In practice, Kissinger's Sisyphean view of statecraft was to transform the conduct of diplomacy into a perpetual *tour de force*. Bismarck, of course, remains the supreme example of the enlightened statesman who was able to overcome the inherent tension between limits and creativity which Kissinger delineated, through the execution of a foreign policy based upon 'precise calculations of power.' In Kissinger's estimation, the true 'genius' of the Prussian chancellor lay in his ability to 'transcend' and so redefine the nature and objectives of conservative statecraft. In acting as though power provided its own legitimacy, Bismarck was able to '[create] a society in his image and a community of nations animated by his maxims in their dealings with one another.' However, Kissinger underscores that it was precisely because of Bismarck's 'magnificent grasp of the nuances of power relationships' that he 'saw in his philosophy a doctrine of self-limitation.' Having turned power into an instrument of self-restraint, Bismarck was left with the challenge of 'transform[ing] the personal act of creation into institutions that [could] be maintained by an average standard of performance.' The tragedy of Bismarck thus arose not from his inspired attempts to 'transcend' the limits of his power. Rather, it stemmed from the consequence of these attempts which revolutionized the prevailing norms of international conduct.

In the hands of lesser men – ones insensitive to the 'nuances of power relationships' – the perpetuation of Bismarck's methods (*Realpolitik* and the 'lightning war') was the prescription for disaster. This perception prompted Kissinger to conclude: 'The nemesis of power is that except in the hands of a master, reliance on it is more likely to produce a contest at arms than self-restraint.' Within this context, the inherent 'tragedy' of Bismarck's creative diplomatic activism was that he bequeathed a legacy of 'unassimilated greatness.'[18] A less charitable view of this heritage came from Sir Edward Grey, the British foreign secretary, in a 1907 assessment of the deteriorating international situation: 'It is the lees left by Bismarck that still foul the cup.'[19]

In light of the nature of Kissinger's own subsequent activities, it is especially interesting to note his appraisal of the statecraft of both Metternich and Bismarck. Indeed, once having assumed stewardship of American foreign policy, critics and commentators laboriously sought to liken the Kissinger diplomacy to that of either one or the other of his nineteenth-century predecessors. To many, the non-ideological approach of the new Administration with its emphasis upon maneuver and manipulation appeared to be clearly neo-Bismarckian in nature. To others, the manifestation of Kissinger's 'Spenglarian senescence,'[20] particularly in the wake of the multiple domestic and international shocks of 1973–4, reflected a Metternichian conservatism – a conservatism in which the certainty of the decline of one's relative position provides the starting point.[21] Yet, despite these assessments, it would be misleading, if not over-simplistic, to argue that the Kissinger diplomacy was *per se* either Metternichian or Bismarckian in conception. Certainly, as Bruce Mazlish sensibly concludes, neither taken alone can be said to have served as Kissinger's historical model. Rather, the ongoing challenge which confronts the statesman is that of fusing the limiting spirit of Metternich with the internal will and the creative activism of Bismarck to make the right combination. This dual theme – the acceptance and transcendence of limits – served as the motivating spirit underlying Kissinger's approach to statecraft. This was made explicit in a personally revealing interview with James Reston of the *New York Times* in October 1974:

When one looks at the process of growing up, it is largely a process of learning one's limits, that one is not immortal, that one cannot achieve everything; and then to draw from that realization the strength to set goals nevertheless. Now, I think as a country we've gone through this. We were immature in the sense that we thought the definition of goals was almost the equivalent of their realization . . . When you get to the recognition of your limits, then the question becomes whether you transcend them or wallow in them. That is a choice that is up to us.

Yet, the inherent tension which exists between the acceptance and transcendence of limits was never fully clarified either by Kissinger the scholar or statesman. In this respect, Kissinger's ambivalent attitude towards Bismarck is characteristic. For while the Prussian chancellor's iron will and creative activism permitted him to revolutionize the nature of diplomacy in his era, this act of transcendence led to the eventual abandonment of restraint and the collapse of an international order which had maintained stability for over a century. Thus, to Kissinger, Bismarck, though a genius for skillfully differentiating between self-restraint and tranquility, was ultimately to remain the 'white revolutionary.' Again, in the penetrating October 1974 interview cited above, Kissinger the statesman only hinted at the subtle interrelationship between will, limits, creativity and systemic evolution within the context of a discussion centering upon the demands and the possibilities of crisis diplomacy: 'If you act creatively you should be able to use crises to move the world towards the structural solutions that are necessary. In fact, very often the crises themselves are a symptom of the need for a structural rearrangement.'[22]

The question which remains shrouded in ambiguity, however, relates to the criteria by which one differentiates between a 'structural rearrangement' (i.e. the transcendence of limits via creative diplomacy) and a truly revolutionary challenge to the existing order. To state what would appear to be a paradox in Kissinger's own terms: would not the statesman who has achieved 'final greatness' – that is, a leader possessing 'the strength to contemplate chaos, there to find material for fresh creation' – invariably be one who has become, in effect, the 'white revolutionary' through the transcendence (or transgression) of limits. To the extent that Kissinger's pre-1969 writings do attempt to address this dilemma of statecraft, one must refer to his conception of legitimacy. For it is through this concept that the competitive demands of self-restraint (limits) and creativity (will) are ostensibly reconciled. Considerations of legitimacy, in turn, bring one to the concept to which they are inextricably linked – Kissinger's notion of orders with its attendant commitment to the pursuit of stability.

However, 'stability,' as he asserts in the Introduction to *A World Restored*, 'has commonly resulted not from a quest for peace but from a generally accepted legitimacy. "Legitimacy" as here used should not be confused with justice.' From this assessment, it is apparent that, to Kissinger, the most salient characteristic of 'justice' as a concept is that it is one which arises from the domestic structure of the nation-state. As such, notions of justice are held to be intrinsically both 'parochial' and absolute. Therein, however, lies the danger. For within this perspective, Kissinger argues, 'domestic legitimization' becomes the criterion by which policy is evaluated. This, in turn, may result in the fomentation of a 'revolutionary' situation as an individual state attempts to identify the legitimizing principle of the international system with a concept of justice derived from its domestic structure.[23] Given the absolute nature of values (as manifested here in the concept of justice), the claim of universal applicability is implicit. In this century, the presumption of certainty reflected in such appeals to universalism has resulted in the deaths of millions. Within this context of historical tragedy, Kissinger argues that the criteria for legitimacy arise not from the *domestic order*, but from the *international framework*.[24] It is interesting to note that this view was propounded by Kissinger at the precise moment when American analysts were forcefully arguing that the successful implementation of the containment doctrine was predicated upon a conscious acceptance of the 'lessons of Munich' – that is, the folly of attempting to appease a 'revolutionary' power. To Kissinger, one could not act upon the lessons of Munich without having first absorbed the more fundamental 'lessons of Versailles.'

In this light, one may appreciate the central importance which Kissinger attached to the concept of legitimacy within his theory of international relations. However, like his unelaborated philosophy of history, the normative implications of such an orientation were to remain tacit, at best, in his pre-1969 writings. Yet, it was the moral philosophy implicit within these principles of statecraft which came to be the motivating spirit underlying the Nixon–Kissinger strategy. One of the most important of these normative implications was evidenced in the manner in which the domestic structures of other nation-states were regarded by the new Administration. Informed by the concept of legitimacy elaborated by Kissinger prior to 1969, the critical characteristic of a specific regime in the Nixon–Kissinger schema was not how it behaved on the domestic level (e.g. human rights) but whether it constituted a pliable, working part of the international system.

In operational terms, these criteria for legitimacy comprised the intellectual bedrock upon which American support for various authoritarian regimes was rationalized during the Nixon–Kissinger tenure. For it was argued that within the context of the nuclear age, any direct challenge to the international order, whether revolutionarily-inspired or not, could conceivably precipitate Armageddon. Hence, the pursuit of stability – the driving force of the Nixon–Kissinger strategy – was held to be almost synonymous with the prevention of the *summum malum* (nuclear holocaust). As such, this goal, clearly derived from the interaction of Kissinger's concept of legitimacy and limits, was regarded almost in Kantian terms as the highest moral imperative. However, the pivotal importance of this principle transformed the Nixon–Kissinger diplomacy into 'the art of the possible, the science of the relative.'[25] When it is honestly believed that one's actions are contributing to the prevention of nuclear war through the bolstering of credibility, then almost any action taken below that level can be rationalized. The nature and development of the Nixon Administration's argument *vis-à-vis* credibility (specifically its importance in terms of the Nixon–Kissinger strategy's attempt to strike a new relationship between center and periphery) shall be examined in depth below. However, at this juncture, it is important to note that it was the tacitly expressed moral philosophy characterized above which permitted in certain contingencies the transformation of Kissinger's distinctive brand of *Realpolitik* into a brutal *Macht Politik*.

Related, though distinct from the moral implications, Kissinger's concept of legitimacy shaped his postwar perception of the Communist great powers. Writing in *Nuclear Weapons and Foreign Policy*, he observed: 'History demonstrates that revolutionary powers have never been brought to a halt until their opponents stopped pretending that the revolutionaries were really misunderstood legitimists.'[26] Again reflected here is the inextricable link which Kissinger perceived between the lessons of Munich and Versailles. In his early policy-oriented studies (the above-mentioned volume and *The Necessity for Choice*), the 'image' presented of the Soviet Union is that of a power whose 'revolutionary' status is confirmed by its quest for absolute security. Within this perspective, Kissinger expressed open scorn of those in the West who believed that a more forthcoming attitude towards the Soviet Union – a foreign policy premised upon 'goodwill' – would facilitate its transformation into a status quo oriented power. His criticism of the Eisenhower Administration's 'fatuous' summit diplomacy was based upon the belief that it generated a dangerously false atmosphere of euphoria and trust.[27] Ironically, a similar charge was levelled against his own management of US–Soviet relations following the May 1972 and June 1973 summit meetings.

In many respects, however, Kissinger's 'radical' critique of American Cold War policy represented little more at the time than a variation on the 'negotiation from strength' thesis. Although an outspoken critic of the Eisenhower approach, Kissinger did not, however, completely discount the efficacy of negotiations with the Soviets. Indeed, in his estimation, the special circumstances of the nuclear age strongly militated in favor of the achievement of a *modus vivendi* between the superpowers even during a revolutionary phase. However, the basis of this diplomatic accommodation, he warned, should be a mutuality of interests rather than the elaboration of a false structure of trust. Once again, the criticism brought by Kissinger the scholar is all the more striking in light of his activities as a statesman: the manifestation of 'trust' as a political concept underlying the Nixon–Kissinger strategy (and its critical bearing on the nature and development of the heated American domestic debate on détente in the aftermath of the October 1973 Middle East War) shall be fully explored in subsequent chapters of this study.

By the time of the publication of *The Troubled Partnership* in 1965, Kissinger's previous perception of the Soviet Union had undergone a major shift as a result of two major structural changes in the international system – the advent of strategic parity and the impact of nascent multipolarity. With the Soviet Union no longer regarded as an implacable revolutionary power, it became possible for him to think in the terms of the Nixon–Kissinger strategy with its avowed goal of establishing a 'stable structure of peace.' However, some of the very conditions which contributed to the altering of Kissinger's perception of the Soviet Union, and its role within the international system, were, ironically, precisely the ones which complicated, if not frustrated, the architectonic approach of the Nixon Administration. The precise nature of this dilemma shall be considered in the final section of this chapter, within the context of an appraisal of the turbulent conditions of the international environment in 1969 under which it was hoped that the Nixon–Kissinger strategy could be successfully implemented. In this section, the attempt has been made to delineate the principal themes developed in the pre-1969 writings of Nixon and Kissinger which had a bearing on their conduct of American foreign policy. Attention shall now focus upon the highly centralized and personalized decision-making structure which was regarded as the organizational prerequisite for the foreign policy innovations they hoped to effect.

The Nixon–Kissinger system: the decision-making framework

Richard Nixon assumed the Presidency in January 1969 with the avowed commitment to alter not only the theory upon which American foreign policy was premised, but also the nature of its practice. During the 1968 presidential campaign he had lashed out against the *ad hoc* procedures of the Johnson Administration, characterizing LBJ's semi-institutionalized 'Tuesday Lunch' sessions as 'catch-as-catch-can talkfests.'[28] To rectify the 'disorder' stemming from Johnson's handling of foreign affairs, Nixon asserted that it would be necessary to 'clean house.' The nature and scope of this planned reorganization was thus one of the major questions to be considered by Nixon and Kissinger in their preliminary meetings at the Hotel Pierre (New York) in the post-election period. Kissinger listened at one session as the President-elect forcefully argued that in order to 'give the people of this country the foreign policy they want,' it would be necessary to 'revitalize' the National Security Council (NSC) system and thereby shift the decision-making center of gravity from the bureaucracy to its rightful place in the White House's West Basement. As Kissinger was later recounting this discussion to one of his NSC aides, he simply smiled and added, 'I agreed.'[29]

The manner in which the Nixon–Kissinger strategy fostered a unique fusion of style and substance has been characterized above. The reorganization program initiated in late 1968 was but a recognition that this *style* (and hence the *substance* of the new Administration's foreign policy) necessitated a 'fresh,' innovative decision-making *structure*. The avowed goals of the new system – that is, the establishment of a centralized, White House oriented decision-making apparatus which would present the President with a coherent set of real options on any given policy question – were logically derived from two strong views which Nixon and Kissinger held in common. The first was a mutual antipathy towards the foreign policy bureaucracy – albeit one which had developed in each for quite different reasons. To Nixon, the federal bureaucracy, in particular the State Department, was to remain a suspect group staffed by eight years of Democratic functionaries. Quite irrationally, he feared that the anti-State Department activities of his early Washington career might lead 'them' to seek revenge through the internal sabotage of his Administration's foreign policy initiatives. His goal was thus to create a system which would make their role peripheral, if not irrelevant, to the policy-making process.

Kissinger's attitude towards the bureaucracy, like his conception of statecraft, was largely shaped by his pre-1969 studies of history at Harvard. Concluding his study of the Congress of Vienna system, he argued that the inherent tension between 'inspiration' and 'organization' remains 'the inextricable element of history.'[30] In *The Necessity for Choice*, Kissinger's language is still stronger: bureaucracy is there depicted as the bane of statesmanship as it obstructs creativity through its constant pursuit of safety. In advancing foreign policy responses which verge on the mechanical, creativity in planning is confounded with 'projecting the familiar into the future.'[31] Yet despite this critical assessment of bureaucratic performance, Kissinger could equally argue elsewhere that 'it is dangerous to separate planning from the responsibility of execution.'[32] In a prescient article published in 1968, Kissinger offered a candid solution to this apparent contradiction in terms quite similar to those of Nixon:

Because management of the bureaucracy takes so much energy and precisely because changing course is so difficult, many of the most important decisions are taken by *extra-bureaucratic means*. Some of the key decisions are kept to a very small circle while the bureaucracy happily continues working away in ignorance of the fact that decisions are being made, or of the fact that a decision is being made in a particular area. One reason for keeping the decisions to small groups is that when bureaucracies are so unwieldy and when their internal morale becomes a serious problem, an unpopular decision may be fought by brutal means, such as leaks to the press or to congressional committees. Thus, *the only way secrecy can be kept is to exclude from the making of the decision all those who are theoretically charged with carrying it out* [emphasis added].[33]

Like Nixon then, Kissinger's preferred solution to the dilemma of inspiration and organization was to isolate and thereby bar the foreign policy bureaucracy from any substantive role through the creation of a highly centralized and secret decision-making system. Their decision, thus, of late 1968, was not to reorganize the bureaucracy ('clean house'), but rather to 'revitalize' the NSC so as to work around and above it.

Complementing this NSC role, the Nixon–Kissinger system fostered the spectacular use of one particular 'extra-bureaucratic' method in the pursuit of its major foreign policy initiatives: personal diplomacy. The liabilities of this approach shall be explored below. Both detractors and defenders of its efficacy, however, acknowledged that it exemplified the Nixon Administration's unique fusion of style and substance. The image associated with personal diplomacy – the statesman, 'willing to stand alone', seeking to affect external reality through acts of will and creativity – was fully in accord with the Nixon–Kissinger view of history as the expression of personality.[34] In his extraordinary interview with Oriana Fallaci, Kissinger, who had once likened the statesman to 'one of the heroes in classical drama,' characterized his own role as the President's personal emissary in terms of a 'wild west tale':

[The main] element in the mechanics of my success . . . stems from the fact that I've always acted alone. Americans admire that enormously. Americans admire the cowboy leading the caravan [*sic*] alone astride his horse, the cowboy entering a village or city alone on his horse. Without even a pistol, maybe, because he doesn't go in for shooting. He acts, that's all: aiming at the right spot at the right time . . . This cowboy doesn't need courage. It's enough that he be alone, that he show others how he enters the village alone and does everything on his own. This romantic, surprising character suits me, because being alone has always been part of my style . . .[35]

This candid self-appraisal undoubtedly inspired Carter's choice of language when he criticized Kissinger's 'lone ranger' style of diplomacy during the 1976 presidential campaign.

The second attitude which helped to shape the character of the Nixon–Kissinger system was a mutual disdain for the predominantly Democratic foreign policy 'establishment.' For quite different reasons, both men stood apart from this elite group. With respect to Nixon, the 'politics of resentment' which he exemplified in his early career contained a deep vein of populism. Like McCarthyism, Nixon's meteoric rise to power (though more subtle and politically adept than that of McCarthy) may be regarded, in terms of its underlying basis, as a phenomenon of the 'everyman.' Indeed, his reputation was secured through the discrediting of Alger Hiss, patrician State Department official and one of the acknowledged leaders of the foreign policy establishment. Within this context, Nixon's assessment of Dean Acheson, and the elite group which he represented, is characteristic: 'In [the 1952] campaign . . . his clipped moustache, his British tweeds, and his haughty manner made him the perfect foil for my attacks on the snobbish kind of foreign service personality and mentality that had been taken in hook, line, and sinker by the Communists.'[36] The subsequent failure of this elite to manage effectively and resolve the Vietnam War was considered by Nixon to be one of the prime factors responsible for his electoral victory in 1968. Six years later, Nixon, in a moment of self-delusion, would lament to an aide that his difficulties over Watergate stemmed from this same group: 'The establishment is dying and they're trying to take us down with them.'[37]

Like Nixon (who did develop a working relationship with one exalted member of the elite, John Foster Dulles), Kissinger only penetrated the periphery of the foreign policy establishment. In a Council on Foreign Relations dominated by lawyers and businessmen with practical experience in the top echelon of government, he was judged to be a mere technician – an individual better left to the mundane task of translating rambling Council seminars into coherent studies. It was reflective of this implicit hierarchy within the foreign policy elite that few in 1968 considered Kissinger to be in line for the NSC post within a Republican Administration (despite his patronage relationship with Rockefeller). In office, Kissinger regarded himself to be an essentially non-establishment figure. In response to appeals from the (establishment) elders of the Democratic Party for a swift end to American involvement in Vietnam, he bitterly commented: 'If only the guys who got us into this would give us the chance to get out of it. I wasn't second-guessing Vance and Harriman in 1965 when I told them privately we couldn't win the war – instead, I asked them how I could help.'[38] Later, at the time of the Cambodian invasion, Kissinger angrily decried NSC staff resignations as yet another example of 'the cowardice of the Eastern establishment.'[39] Informed by this attitude towards the foreign policy elite, the Nixon–Kissinger system, as with the bureaucracy, denied that group the ready access and influence which they formerly enjoyed.

For the actual mechanics of reorganization, Kissinger turned to Morton Halperin, a former Harvard colleague who had served with distinction under Secretary of Defense Clark Clifford. Having received the President-elect's charge via Kissinger at the Hotel Pierre, Halperin, applying the techniques of systems analysis to the problem of foreign policy decision-making, completed a draft reform plan which was approved on Inauguration Day. In abstract, Halperin's reorganization proposal offered the promise of realizing the avowed ideals of the Nixon–Kissinger system (*viz.* the assertion of White House authority coupled with the presentation of a full range of options). The centerpiece of this apparatus was, of course, to be the NSC – an institution which, in the words of a 1960 Congressional report, is 'the President's instrument,' that 'exists only to serve the President.'[40] Contrasting the 'revitalized' NSC with the decision-making regimes of preceding Administrations, Kissinger asserted:

The orderly and regularized procedures which the NSC system provides have advantages which President Nixon prefers to exploit.

The more *ad hoc* approach of the 1960s often ran the risk that relevant points of view were not heard, that systematic treatment of issues did not take place at the highest level, or that the bureaucracies were not fully informed as to what had been decided and why . . .

At the same time, we have tried to avoid some of the problems of the NSC system of the 1950s. One such problem was that the papers which came to the President from the NSC system, and the decision papers based upon them, were often not specific enough to provide effective guidance to the bureaucracy. Incoming papers often reflected compromises reached among agencies at a lower level. The machinery gave too much emphasis to interdepartmental consensus and too little to the presentation of distinct points of view and distinct policy alternatives.[41]

A similar assessment, again reflecting what became the declared aspirations of the Nixon–Kissinger system, was candidly expressed by Kissinger at an academic gathering in 1968: 'The organizational problem seems to be to combine the procedural regularity of Eisenhower with the intellectual excitement of Kennedy. Whether that is possible, I do not know.'[42]

In order to support and consolidate White House management of foreign policy issues, Halperin successfully argued that a network of general inter-agency committees should be established below the NSC level. The ineffectual Interdepartmental Regional Groups (chaired by the Under Secretary of State) of the Johnson Administration were to be replaced by the Interdepartmental Groups (IG) and an Under Secretaries Committee (USC), respectively. The major departure in this action, however, lay not in the constitution of these committees, but in the manner of their accountability within the decision-making process. Whereas under the Johnson Administration these State-chaired groups normally only reported to each other, under the Nixon–Kissinger system they were placed under the firm direction of the NSC's Senior Review Group – a body chaired, not surprisingly, by the President's Assistant for National Security Affairs. In emphasizing the Administration's preference of 'policy' over 'operations,' the Interdepartmental Groups were to concentrate not on operational coordination, as under Johnson, but on supervising the drafting of NSSMs (National Security Study Memoranda). These completed memoranda, ostensibly reflecting intellectually honest, alternative perspectives on policy questions as opposed to the interplay of competitive bureaucratic interests, were to be presented to the full NSC via the Senior Review Group for consideration by the President. Upon NSC and presidential approval of a specific NSSM, responsibility for policy implementation ('review' and 'coordination') was theoretically to reside with the Under Secretaries Committee. In practice, the IG–USC system, resting as it did at the bottom of the NSC hierarchy, was never able to exert much actual influence over the policy-making process. Real power flowed from the *ad hoc* units created and dominated by Kissinger which overlay this formal committee structure.

In addition to the Senior Review Group noted above, Kissinger came to chair the following specialized committees through which the major foreign policy decisions of the Nixon Administration were derived:

1. *The Washington Special Actions Group (WSAG)*: established in April 1969 in the wake of North Korea's downing of an American EC-121 spy plane, this Under Secretary-level committee's designated function was to oversee crisis management and contingency planning (e.g. the Ussuri River crisis of 1969, the Jordanian crisis of 1970, and the Indo-Pakistan War of 1971);
2. *The Verification Panel*: originally created in July 1969 to establish an authoritative data base upon which to conduct strategic arms control negotiations with the Soviet Union, it subsequently became, in conjunction with the ultra-secret 'back channel' communications system with Soviet Ambassador Dobrynin, the institutional mechanism by which Kissinger directed American initiatives *vis-à-vis* SALT;
3. *The Intelligence Committee*: established to formulate general policy guidelines for the entire intelligence community (i.e. CIA (Central Intelligence Agency), NSA (National Security Agency), DIA (Defense Intelligence Agency), etc.);
4. *The '40 Committee'*: so named after the presidential directive which established it, this body was authorized to supervise covert intelligence operations;
5. *The Defense Program Review Committee (DPRC)*: an Under Secretary-

level committee whose declared function was to review 'the major
defense policy and program issues which have strategic, political,
diplomatic, and economic implications in relation to overall
national priorities';[43] in practice, this translated into jurisdiction
over the Pentagon budget;

6. *The Vietnam Special Studies Group (VSSG)*: established initially to
   monitor intelligence information 'on trends and conditions in
   the countryside in Vietnam,' it was subsequently utilized, like the
   Verification Panel with respect to SALT, as a clearing house for
   the Administration's negotiating initiatives.[44]

Through this highly centralized, hierarchical NSC structure (both
formal and *ad hoc*) Kissinger was able to secure what one observer has
identified as the two prerequisites of power in Washington – 'pro-
pinquity' and the 'power to execute.' The policy-making process
which stemmed from such a structure was succinctly characterized
by one of his NSC subordinates: 'Everyone reports to Kissinger, and
only Kissinger reports to the President.'[45] With surprising ease, the
organizational reform plan, as drafted by Halperin (and as
embellished by Kissinger), had become an institutional *fait accompli*.
The two cabinet officials most directly affected by the new NSC
approach, the Secretaries of State and Defense, do not appear to
have initially grasped its full implications: Rogers attempted to
assure worried aides that the formal decision-making structure was
irrelevant – 'I have a relationship with the President,' he confided to
one associate.[46] Laird's influence was limited as much by the role
which he chose to play as by the new structure; with the notable
exception of Vietnam, he acted as though he were merely the
adjudicator of competitive inter-service interests within the
Pentagon. As for the public perception, the recognition of
Kissinger's pervasive power gradually came with successive announce-
ments of his activities as the President's personal envoy (e.g. the Vietnam negotiations, the China initiative). In this capacity, Kissinger
was, in time, received by foreign governments as a plenipotentiary
fully equipped with presidential powers necessary to conduct the
requisite negotiations.

It was upon his record in this area that the Kissinger cult, and its
surrounding mythology, quickly developed: by early 1972, influential
journalistic admirers such as James Reston and Joseph Kraft were
referring to the President's National Security Adviser as a 'miracle
man' and 'the second most powerful man' in the world, while public

opinion polls placed him amongst America's 'most admired' men. And yet despite this public acclaim, Kissinger's White House activities were destined to remain outside the purview of public scrutiny and accountability. Although various Democratic members of the Senate increasingly decried the usurpation of the Secretary of State's powers after 1971, Kissinger was able to avoid testimony before Congressional committees owing to the principle of 'executive privilege' (a doctrine which Nixon invoked less successfully with respect to his aides' Watergate involvement). In March 1971, the *New York Times* sombrely assessed the operational consequences of the Nixon–Kissinger system: 'A *coup d'état* could hardly deprive the people's elected representatives more completely of their constitutional powers than this gradual process . . .'[47]

In addition to this problem of accountability, one which was to have important domestic implications examined below, the Nixon–Kissinger system suffered from three structural characteristics. First, the distinction which the new Administration had sought to restore between the functions of 'planning' and 'operations' proved impossible, given Kissinger's preferences, to maintain in practice. Nixon had announced the appointment of his Assistant for National Security Affairs with the comment: 'I don't want him to get down in the situation room in the White House and spend too much time going through cables.'[48] For his part, Kissinger assumed stewardship of the NSC, arguing that the new decision-making framework which he advocated would allow his White House command to concentrate solely upon 'conceptualized foreign policy germination.' Few Washington observers, however, accepted Kissinger's avowal at face value. The creation of WSAG within months of Inauguration Day is indicative of the extent to which Kissinger was intimately involved in day-to-day operations even at that early date.

The second structural problem associated with the Nixon–Kissinger system stems, in a sense, from the first and centers upon the presentation of 'options' within the context of NSC deliberations. Here, the emergence of Kissinger's 'operational' role invariably comprised his ostensible role of neutral inter-agency coordinator. I. M. Destler, in his important study of foreign policy decision-making at the presidential level, contends that Kissinger's elaboration of alleged options quite often constituted advocacy in more sophisticated guise, one real choice coupled with two or three straw men.[49]

This predicted emergence of the National Security Adviser as a potent policy advocate, in turn, highlights a third major problem which developed out of the Nixon–Kissinger system: the inordinate influence over the policy-making process which automatically accrued to Kissinger as a result of his control of the NSC's agenda. Directing a staff of 52 as of April 1971 (N.B. three times the size of the Bundy–Rostow at its peak), the selection of NSSM topics tended to correspond with Kissinger's own policy preferences. Through this mechanism, the criteria by which the relative salience of an issue was determined (i.e. whether or not it warranted an NSSM and full NSC consideration) became synonymous with the staff director's personal ones. An analysis of NSSM topics for the period 1969–71 is striking (and presumably reflective of Kissinger's assessment of their comparative importance): of 138 commissioned memoranda, only nine dealt with Latin America, four with sub-Saharan Africa and six with international economic topics (of which only one dealt with the nascent problem of American energy vulnerability).[50]

Under the cumulative impact of these structural characteristics, the Nixon–Kissinger system soon evolved into what has been characterized as a closed, 'two-man' system. Even by 1970, in sharp contrast to the lofty rhetoric of 1969, the two chief decision-makers were already tending to disregard or discount much of the advice they received from the broader government. It was from this kind of decision-making environment that such actions as the Cambodian 'incursion' of May 1970 arose. The authorization of this military action was perhaps the quintessential presidential decision of Nixon's first term – for it came in the face of opposition, often intense, from within the State and Defense Departments as well as the NSC staff itself. With the evolution of this centralized two-man system, the number both of commissioned NSSMs and full NSC meetings fell off sharply, particularly after 1972. Although this *de facto* Nixon–Kissinger system clearly suited the President's style, the deepening Watergate crisis of the following year necessitated a devolution of White House authority, even in the area of foreign policy, to the various executive departments. From Kissinger's point of view the move to Foggy Bottom, in addition to conferring *de jure* status to his pre-eminent policy-making position, had the major advantage of insulating him somewhat from a Chief Executive whose innermost circle was in disgrace (and, in many cases, under criminal indictment).

And yet, ironically, at the precise moment when Kissinger

assumed the Secretaryship – at the moment when he stood at the apex of his popularity even as his patron operated under the shadow of impeachment – forces, both internal and external, were calling into question the very 'stable structure' upon which his reputation had been secured. Within a month of his swearing-in, the center-piece of his foreign policy, US–Soviet détente, received a body-blow in the form of the October 1973 Middle East War – a setback from which many observers believe Soviet–American relations have yet to recover. At home, in the Autumn of 1973, open criticism was being voiced of a foreign policy whose prerequisites and criteria of 'stability' appeared to include a toleration of Soviet internal repres-sion and *carte blanche* arms transfer policy to nascent regional middle powers governed by clearly authoritarian regimes. Through feed-back, this substantive criticism of the Nixon–Kissinger strategy raised awkward questions of style. At his confirmation hearings in September 1973, Kissinger was hard-pressed by members of the Senate Foreign Relations Committee *vis-à-vis* his attitudes towards foreign policy accountability in general, and Congressional over-sight in particular. The Secretary of State-designate offered the Senators the usual *pro forma* assurances and, indeed, expressed the desire to institutionalize his foreign policy approach[51] or, as he put it in his study of Bismarck, to 'transform the personal act of creation into institutions that can be maintained by an average standard of performance'). But yet the maintenance of the Nixon–Kissinger strategy's stable structure was predicated upon a certain mode of foreign policy conduct from which it seemingly could not escape. Later asked to characterize this manner of policy-making, Daniel Moynihan quipped: 'Kissinger's own style was that of the Polit-buro.'[52] Ironically, it was precisely the nature of this style which ultimately denied the Nixon–Kissinger diplomacy its most impor-tant constituency – the American people and Congress.

The nature of the international environment

In retrospect, there can be little doubt that the Tet offensive of January–February 1968, through its precipitation of a major shift in strategy *vis-à-vis* the conduct of the Vietnam War by President Johnson in the following month, marked a fundamental turning point in American foreign policy. With such powerful images as the Vietcong capture of the United States embassy in Saigon flashed across millions of American television screens, both the *instrumentalities*, and by implication, the *ends* of American power were sharply called into question as never before during the postwar period. The 20-year road of undifferentiated globalism from the Truman Doctrine to Tet found a battered American diplomacy left, ironically, in a position of unprecedented immobility. Though there was a consensus of belief that the Vietnam debacle had 'arrested the growth of an implicit American universalism,' the future course of US foreign policy appeared far from certain.[53] But yet, with many other of the major elements of the international system in a simultaneous state of flux, this was clearly not a challenge which confronted American policy-makers alone. As Pierre Hassner observed at the time:

Every period is by definition a time of transition. Some periods, however, tend to give an illusion of permanence, others an expectation of utopia or doom. The peculiar feature of the present time is that it is almost impossible to escape the impression that we are entering a new period of international relations – and almost as difficult to agree on where we go from here. Our feeling of change is based on our witnessing the decay of the old, rather than many concrete fears or hopes about the emergence of the new. Indeed, sometimes sometimes seems as if a collective failure of imagination were at play, preventing us from seeing both how the present order could continue and by what it could be replaced.[54]

In accepting change itself as the 'starting point,' the Nixon Administration made clear its intent to develop 'a new approach to foreign policy to match a new era of international relations.'[55] It is to the nature of that new international environment – and the American response to it – that attention shall now focus.

Of the major qualitative changes reshaping the international political system at the end of the postwar era, perhaps the most fundamental was that *vis-à-vis* the nature and utility of power. The adverse outcome of the American intervention in Vietnam prompted a sharp revision of the *perceived* relationship between military means and political ends – specifically, a growing consensus in the utility of force's diminution.[56] In the case of Vietnam, the United States had and, under the Nixon Administration, continued to employ disproportionate means for the sake of a singularly modest political objective – the survival of a specific regime in Saigon. In the final analysis, however, the United States was unable to attain 'victory' in Vietnam, not for lack of will or material, but because the situation was unsusceptible to a purely military solution, and because, with an alien conscript army on a mission of imperial form (though certainly not content), the US could not substitute for Saigon in supplying the political conditions of success.[57]

At the time of the Nixon inaugural, statesmen and analysts alike were struck by the ostensible paradox of the United States' continuing preponderance of military power but yet its relative decline in political influence in the world. While in one sense this paradox is readily comprehensible in terms of the limitations of arms as a source of effective power, it also reflects a more fundamental transformation within the international system. As Joseph Nye observes: 'To understand what is changing, we must distinguish power over others from power over outcomes. What we are experiencing is not so much an erosion of our power resources compared to those of other countries (although there has been some), but an erosion of our power to control outcomes in the international system as a whole.'[58] Hence, while the United States clearly retained great capacity for favorably affecting the behavior of others (the classic definition of power), it no longer wielded the same magnitude of influence over the whole system. In accepting the reality of this new international environment, many would argue that the most profound challenge which confronted the United States at that historical juncture was the psychological one of negotiating the transition from preponderance to the rather ambiguous position of *primus inter pares*.

The dual transformation in the nature of power was, to be sure, the driving force behind many of these major qualitative changes within the international system. Of primary importance, the *diffusion* of power brought with it both an overall expansion in the number of relevant actors within the system and, *pari passu*, the assertion of a new foreign policy agenda (e.g. the North–South dialogue). Paradoxically, the development of these (often highly nationalistic) new centers of power resulted in a certain fragmentation of the system as a whole at the precise moment when diplomacy had indeed become truly global. The implications of this phenomenon subsequently gave rise to the regional emphasis of the Nixon Doctrine. The second change in the nature of power in the post-1969 period – one which further complicated the policy dilemmas stemming from the first – was its pronounced *diversification* into salient new forms. Together, these radical changes in the nature of power militated in favor of a system both more complex and less overtly hierarchical. This absence of a single, absolute hierarchy of inter-state power (one previously based largely upon military power) signalled the move towards a multihierarchical system reflecting the importance and utility of different kinds of power.

To Nixon and Kissinger, this transformation of the international political environment was to offer a fortuitous means of escape from the immobility which had increasingly entrapped American foreign policy with the escalation of its involvement in Vietnam. These new characteristics of the system were regarded as the prerequisites for a creative new diplomacy which would enable the United States to capitalize on the potential of a pluralistic world. This critical requirement of the Nixon–Kissinger strategy later prompted one observer to quip that had this system not naturally evolved, the new Administration would have had to have invented it. In giving substance to this close link between multipolarity and foreign policy creativity, Nixon and Kissinger invoked the concept of a pentagonal world.[59] Critics observed that such a notion of multipolar balance raised questions of categories as well as questions of level. Given the dominant, if no longer pre-eminent, American position across the various hierarchies of power (i.e. economic, political, military, etc.), the design (or at least the hope) was evidently for the United States to assume the role of central balancer in the mediation of relations between these rival heterogeneous power centers. Though no longer preponderant in terms of its leverage over the course of the international system as a whole, the United States could continue, under these new conditions, to assert its primacy through the maintenance of this favorable equilibrium.

As shall be evidenced in subsequent chapters, this pentagonal strategy was destined to founder in late 1973 under the multiple pressures which arose from the October 1973 Middle East War. It is clear that at bottom the problem lay in the nature of its three prerequisites. First, the success of this particular approach was predicated upon a rather optimistic assessment of the American ability to relate and efficaciously manage different kinds of power. In the final analysis, despite the intervening claims as to his creativity and intuition, Kissinger's failure to forge an effective correspondence between the various forms of power belied an essentially uni-dimensional view of power.

The second underlying assumption of this foreign policy orientation was, again, the rather optimistic premise that the other four 'poles' of the system could readily be co-opted into a stable structure of American design. In the language of Kissinger the scholar, such a shared notion of order would, of necessity, have to be based upon a common conception of *legitimacy*. However, in the absence of such a comprehensive accord of values and interests amongst the five great powers, it ultimately proved impossible to operationalize this kind of idealized pentagonal schema of world order.

Finally, in order to attain the requisite degree of flexibility and maneuverability, the third characteristic of this multipolar approach was a blurring of the distinctions between allies and adversaries. In one respect, this move may be regarded as a logical, if nonetheless flawed, extension of Kissinger's desire to remove overtly ideological considerations from the conduct of foreign policy. As the Nixon Administration's first 'State of the World' message proclaimed: '. . . the slogans formed in the past century were the ideological debate. Today, the 'isms' have lost their vitality . . .'[60]

Whereas the primacy of ideological criteria had immobilized American foreign policy through the promulgation of an undifferentiated global posture, the obverse strategy of non-ideological maneuver and manipulation, as practiced by Nixon and Kissinger, was to create quite different problems both abroad and at home. Allies, by and large, were resentful of the new American approach as they viewed it, not without good reason, to be both one-sided and hypocritical. Indeed, the same Administration which expressed alarm over independent overtures to the Soviet Union (e.g. *Ostpolitik*) later presented the Europeans and the Japanese with the *fait accompli* – the 'shocks' – of Summer 1971: the ultra-secret China initiative in July and the combative economic program engineered by Treasury Secretary John Connally in August. Like the allied response to this distinctive new form of *Realpolitik*, the American domestic reaction reflected considerable disquiet with an approach which, to paraphrase Stanley Hoffmann, had the net effect of treating traditional friends like competitors and traditional competitors like friends. With increasing fervor, domestic critics expressed this concern through the advancement of 'trilateralism' as an alternative organizing principle to that implicit within the Nixon–Kissinger design. By 1976, this concept, with its basis in the consonance of 'core' values and interests held by North America, Western Europe, and Japan, was explicitly embraced by the Democratic candidate for the Presidency as part of the attempt to 're-Americanize' American foreign policy.[61]

While espousing the virtues of the new pluralism, the second major qualitative change in the international environment – the emergence of the Soviet Union as a truly global power coupled with its attainment of strategic parity – presented American decision-makers with a rather different set of policy imperatives. Paradoxically, as has been noted above, this development of Soviet power and the nature of its subsequent actions reinforced and so conferred an ostensibly new legitimacy to the image of bipolarity during a period in which its relevance across the spectrum of issues was clearly waning. Once again, the ironic, if not tragic, element in these developments was that they occurred at the very moment when the United States was psychologically prepared to cast off the admittedly defective bipolar image which had sustained two decades of undifferentiated globalism in favor of one which reflected the implications of multi-polarity. As Kissinger noted in a 1968 essay entitled 'Central Issues of American Foreign Policy': 'In the year ahead, the most profound challenge to American policy will be philosophical: to develop some concept of order in a world which is bipolar militarily but multipolar politically.'[62] In this light, the Nixon–Kissinger strategy (i.e. the establishment of an efficacious relationship between the twin policies of US–Soviet détente and the Nixon Doctrine) may be regarded as a *transitional* response to the on-going dilemma of reconciling continued (indeed revitalized) military bipolarity with the new conditions of global pluralism. As noted above, this confluence of contending images required the design of policies to harmonize (1) the necessity of containing the new realities of Soviet power with (2) the imperative of post-Vietnam politico-military retrenchment (with its logical implication of a devolution of responsibility in favor of nascent regional centers of power).

With the relative decline of American globalism, the central purpose of the Nixon–Kissinger strategy was evidently to forge a new, more indirect policy link between the center and periphery. During the period preceding the October 1973 Middle East War, the twin strategies of détente and devolution were defined as being not only compatible, but symbiotic. To varying degrees, each was to serve as the instrumentality of the other. Within this context, superpower détente ('linkage' policy, etc.) was regarded as a means of creating the stable regional conditions which would facilitate an orderly devolution of power to emerging 'middle power.' Likewise, a superpower-managed stability along the periphery would maintain the political atmosphere and the structure of trust upon which new functional agreements (e.g. SALT, grain sales, MFN trade status) between the United States and Soviet Union could be based. Again, such, at least, was the design. The purpose of this chapter has been to examine the historical, political, organizational and intellectual background of the Nixon–Kissinger strategy. The focus of subsequent chapters will be the operational nature of this foreign policy approach and those forces (both domestic and international) which militated for or against it.

3. THE NIXON–KISSINGER STRATEGY:

1. DEFINING THE 'LIMITED ADVERSARY RELATIONSHIP,' 1969–1973[1]

The principles to which we agreed in Moscow are like a road map. Now that the map has been laid out, it is up to each country to follow it.

President Richard M. Nixon
in his post-summit address to the Congress, 1 June 1972[2]

The nature and requirements of Kissinger's 'Stable structure'

In a 1968 essay addressed to the challenges confronting American statecraft at the end of the postwar era, Henry Kissinger observed:

The greatest need of the contemporary international system is an agreed concept of order. In its absence, the awesome power is unrestrained by any consensus as to legitimacy; ideology and nationalism, in their different ways, deepen international schisms. Many of the elements which characterized the international system in the nineteenth century cannot be re-created in the modern age. The stable technology, the multiplicity of major powers, the limited domestic claims, and the frontiers which permitted adjustments are gone forever. A new concept of international order is essential; its stability will prove elusive.

The problem is particularly serious for the United States. Whatever our intentions or policies, the fact that the United States disposes of the greatest single aggregate of material power in the world is inescapable. A new international order is inconceivable without a significant American contribution. But the nature of this contribution has altered. For the two decades after 1945, our international activities were based on the assumption that technology plus managerial skills gave us the ability to reshape the international system and to bring about domestic transformations in the 'emerging countries.' This *direct* 'operational' concept of international order has proved too simple. Political multipolarity makes it impossible to impose an American design. *Our deepest challenge will be to evoke the creativity of a pluralistic world, to base order on political multipolarity even though overwhelming military strength will remain with the two superpowers* [emphasis added].[3]

A year later, the 'stable structure' – or, in the earlier language of *A World Restored*, the new 'legitimate order' – advanced by Kissinger (as the President's Assistant for National Security Affairs) sought to reconcile the demands of residual strategic bipolarity with those presented by the new conditions of politico-economic multipolarity. The inherent difficulties of this effort were compounded by the decidedly different foreign policy agenda implicit in each.

In the realm of policy-making, the challenge was primarily of a conceptual nature; for whereas the realities of strategic management clearly continued to militate in favor of a system marked by superpower predominance, the notion of multipolarity (later expressed by Kissinger as 'interdependence') implies the emergence of a multihierarchical system embodying a greater number of relevant actors. In terms of the nature and utility of power, the prospect of such a diverse, multipolar system raised complex questions both of categories and levels.

With so much of the early rhetoric of the Nixon Administration addressed to 'the potential and the imperative of a pluralistic world,'[4] it would be useful to explore the exact nature of the 'new pluralism' upon which the Nixon–Kissinger schema of international order was predicated. Again, as Kissinger expressed it in 1968, 'political multipolarity, while difficult to get used to, is the precondition for a new period of creativity.'[5] Within this context, multipolarity was perceived as a means of overcoming the immobility which had beset American foreign policy as a result of the Vietnam debacle. The ostensible downgrading of ideological concerns was the natural complement to this foreign policy stance. Together, they implied a fundamental shift in American attitude towards both allies and adversaries. Yet significantly, the pluralism to which Nixon and Kissinger referred in 1971–2 was quite different from the phenomena with which they had to contend in the post-1973 period (e.g. OPEC, the North–South dialogue, etc.). Rather, the pluralism which was invoked in order to restore some degree of maneuverability to an immobile American foreign policy was that of the pentagonal model first alluded to by President Nixon during a rambling press conference in Kansas City on 6 July 1971. In view of pronounced disparity both in kind and magnitude among the five power centers which the President named, as well as the revolutionary impact of events in 1973–4 on the international economic system, this neo-classical model quickly disappeared from American policy statements.

At the time of its inception, however, this type of multipolar schema of international order offered the hope not only of restoring flexibility and maneuverability to American diplomacy through the blurring of distinctions between allies and adversaries, but also of maintaining the United States' predominant international position, given its commanding rankings across the various hierarchies of power. And yet its successful application was predicated upon an overly optimistic assessment of the American (*viz.* Kissinger's) ability to relate adroitly various forms of power to each other. That this traditional model of pentagonal balance was either premature or irrelevant was made evident in 1973 when Kissinger was compelled to address the agenda of quite a different form of pluralism. However, even then, the exigencies of the 'new pluralism' (labelled interdependence) were regarded by Kissinger as tangential to the main concerns of US policy.

The reasons for this had much to do with the nature and conditions under which the Soviet Union emerged as a truly global power in the late 1960s – and the perception in Washington of that emergence. Again, one must return to the theme of contending images and the policy dilemmas which were to arise from their confluence. The precise nature of this phenomenon has been characterized in previous sections of this study. In recapitulation, it has been argued that the underlying irony of American foreign policy during the Nixon–Kissinger era was that at the precise moment when the United States was prepared to shift away from an undifferentiated bipolar image of international order in favor of one which reflected the implications of multipolarity, the former image was ostensibly being reconfirmed by events within the new context. The cumulative impact of the latter developments (*viz.* Soviet attainment of strategic parity) prompted the Secretary of State to assert that 'the problem of our age is how to manage the emergence of the Soviet Union as a superpower.'[6]

A decade earlier, Kissinger had written that 'the ultimate test of statesmanship' is 'the act of choice.'[7] Within the circumstances of 1969, the choice involved was that of differentiating between rival, and ostensibly equally valid, perspectives of the evolving international system. This question was at the heart of the controversy which later ensued between Kissinger and his Assistant Secretary of State for African Affairs (and later Congress) at the time of the Angolan Civil War (*viz.* whether to regard the conflict primarily within its local/regional context or as part of the ongoing East–West competition along the Afro-Asian periphery). During his tenure in office, Kissinger was inexorably drawn towards a Soviet-centric image of the international system for three major reasons. First, despite the demands of the new pluralism, there remained the imperative of achieving a *modus vivendi* with the Soviet Union given the global nature of the US–Soviet engagement. Such a relationship clearly did not exist with any other existing or nascent power center. With respect to the nature of Sino-American competition, for example, Kissinger observed: 'We do not impinge on each other as countries on a global basis the way we do with the Soviets.'[8]

The second reason for Kissinger's attraction to a revised bipolar image of the international system stems from the first and centers upon his perception of the nature and utility of power in the post-Vietnam period. Given the inherent difficulties of relating the various categories and levels of power implicit in a truly pluralistic approach, it is probable that Kissinger, in view of the nature of his academic studies prior to 1969, felt more at ease with a foreign policy stance premised upon a largely uni-dimensional view of power extrapolated from the Cold War experience. In his eyes, questions of a non-politico-military nature (e.g. the international monetary system, GATT, energy, etc.) were regarded as technical, 'mercantile' subjects which he seigneurially despised and attempted to ignore – at least until the revolutionary events of 1973–4.[9]

Third, and perhaps most important, the predication of the Nixon–Kissinger strategy upon a predominantly bipolar image of the international system was sustained by the belief that only the Soviet Union posed a pervasive threat to international stability. Given its ability to precipitate a nuclear holocaust, Kissinger, like the practitioners of the Congress of Vienna system, was led to regard the attainment of a Soviet-American *modus vivendi* as a moral exercise through the identification of value with order.[10] Within the Nixon–Kissinger schema, it was tacitly assumed that the primary role of domestic structures was to serve as pliable, working parts of a stable international order – for to challenge the prevailing order would be to invite holocaust. The normative implications of this approach – most notably, its disguised preference for the status quo – was to become a major focal point of Administration critics.

In sum, the elaboration of Kissinger's stable structure, with its emphasis both upon bipolar strategic management (the special role of China within this system shall be considered below), was perceived not in terms of its efficacy in coping with the agenda of the new pluralism (however compelling), but rather as an attempt to fashion a new legitimate order addressed to the inescapable legacy of the Cold War. In Kissinger's view, this exercise, designed as it was to avert the *summum malum* during a period of ascendant Soviet power, was regarded as the most profound moral imperative. As he put it in a March 1973 interview:

What this administration has attempted to do is not so much play a complicated nineteenth-century game of balance of power, but to try to eliminate those hostilities that were vestiges of a particular perception at the end of the war and to deal with the root fact of the contemporary situation – that we and the Soviet Union, and we and the Chinese, are ideological adversaries, but we are bound together by one basic fact: that none of us can survive a nuclear war and therefore it is in our national interest to try to reduce those hostilities that are bureaucratic vestiges or that are simply not rooted in overwhelming national concerns.[11]

By 'hostilities . . . not rooted in overwhelming national concerns,' Kissinger presumably was referring to the continuing pursuit of unilateral advantage along the periphery by the superpowers. Here, Kissinger's perception and memory of events was to become somewhat selective: while, for example, condemning in the strongest language the pursuit of unilateral advantage by the Soviet Union *militarily* in Angola during 1975–6, he seemingly disregarded the fact that the United States had been doing much the same *diplomatically* in the Middle East in the aftermath to the October 1973 War. And yet, however one-sided Kissinger's interpretation and opposition to this concept of 'selective' détente, it was from that premise a short intellectual step to an acceptance of its obverse – namely, the notion of an 'indivisible' détente. In the following section this theme will be explored within the context of a discussion centering upon the evolution of 'linkage' politics. But, in anticipation of that argument, the focus of analysis shall shift at this juncture to an examination of the precise nature of the relationship between the concepts of credibility, commitment and interests within the Nixon–Kissinger schema.

As a starting point for this discussion, it is necessary to return briefly to the rationale underlying American involvement in Vietnam during the Kennedy–Johnson period. In chapter 1, it was argued that the terms of US involvement shifted dramatically in early 1966 as a result of the subtle Sino-American dialogue to avoid an escalation of the war. With the containment of China no longer regarded as the *raison d'être* for an American presence in Indochina, the reasons why the United States was fighting in Vietnam were thus transformed. In the initial period of large-scale involvement prior to 1966, the US 'commitment' had been justified in the terms of American universalism. Thereafter, and in particular during the Nixon–Kissinger tenure of office, it was asserted that the American commitment to a specific regime in South Vietnam, whatever its original bases for existence, had assumed the proportion of an important interest in and of itself. Thus, in a 1968 article written prior to his entry into government service, Kissinger baldly asserted that 'the commitment of 500,000 Americans has settled the issue of the importance of Viet Nam.'

Within this context, a decision-making process which had long sustained a commitment originally undertaken for the defense of American core values (the 'indivisibility of peace') became transformed into one in which the validity of that specific commitment was maintained through the identification of value with order. Here it should be noted that a necessary prerequisite to such an approach was the perpetuation of credibility as the criterion of American commitment. Again, as Kissinger observed in that highly suggestive article which anticipated his own conduct of the Vietnam negotiations:

However fashionable it is to ridicule the terms 'credibility' or 'prestige,' they are not empty phrases; other nations can gear their actions to ours only if they can count on our steadiness. The collapse of the American effort in Viet Nam would not mollify many critics; most of them would simply add the charge of unreliability to the accusation of bad judgment. Those whose safety or national goals depend on American commitments could only be dismayed. In many parts of the world . . . stability depends on a confidence in American promises. Unilateral withdrawal, or a settlement which unintentionally amounts to the same thing, could therefore lead to the erosion of restraints and to an even more dangerous international situation. No American policymaker can simply dismiss these dangers.[12]

Given the general direction of American foreign policy in the aftermath of the Tet offensive, in conjunction with the nature of evolutionary trends reshaping the international system as a whole, this position was to yield paradoxical results. In light of it, one can, for example, make sense of the Nixon Administration's avowal within the first State of the World message that 'We are not involved in the world because we have commitments; we have commitments because we are involved. Our interests must shape our commitments rather than the other way around.'[13] On one level, this formulation may be taken, as Hans J. Morgenthau characterized it in his critique of the Nixon–Kissinger 'strategy for peace,' as a patently specious syllogism: 'involved' is simply a synonym for having interests.[14]

During the post-1969 debate over the nature and timing of United States disengagement from Southeast Asia, critics of Administration policy hotly contested the Kissinger view that American credibility was at stake in Vietnam. In digesting the 'lessons' of that divisive conflict, they asserted that as the original commitment had been misconceived, it was therefore possible to envision the swift extrication of American forces without any significant international repercussions. Within that perspective, it was thought that Nixon could disengage the United States from Vietnam in much the same way as De Gaulle had skillfully engineered French decolonization in Algeria. But whereas the nature of the problem was perhaps analogous – in short, how to manage defeat abroad while contending with a volatile domestic environment – the United States, unlike France, remained a global power whose actions invariably carried broader international implications. Thus, the continuing American commitment to the defense of the Saigon regime was to be justified and perpetuated within the Nixon–Kissinger strategy not, as previously, in the value terms of American Cold War policy, but rather in terms of the symbolic importance which cumulative, even marginal, power shifts along the periphery might have *vis-à-vis* the validity of emerging understandings about the center. Kissinger's concern was that new political and military precedents on the periphery (e.g. the victory of a Soviet client, as in Vietnam, or more direct Soviet intervention in a country far from its traditional area of interests, as in the case of Angola) might lead to the undermining of the regime of restraints which maintained the stability of the center (e.g. SALT). Such an erosion of the central balance on the perceptual level, he argued, would complicate the task of bipolar strategic management through the heightened danger of uncontrolled escalation in a crisis situation.

Informed by this attitude, Kissinger offered a characteristic response to Congressional critics following the fall of Saigon in April 1975, when he declared: 'Given our central role, a loss in our credibility invites international chaos.'[15] Administration recriminations in the wake of Saigon's fall served as a prelude to its forceful advocacy of American support for the anti-Soviet factions in Angola.[16] Though somewhat paradoxical in its implications, the link between the Vietnamese and Angolan cases is highly suggestive. For while the Vietnam commitment was depicted by the Administration as an anomaly – a burdensome legacy of the previous period, whose quick termination on honorable terms was to pave the way for a 'new period of creativity' in the realm of foreign policy – the very manner and favorable conditions under which it sought to liquidate that residual commitment was to become the basic paradigm of the Nixon–Kissinger strategy.

The discussion above has centered on the nature of Kissinger's new legitimate order in terms of its international requirements. Attention now shall focus briefly upon its domestic prerequisites – and their implications. Here, it is possible to delineate three sets of domestic considerations which were to assume particular significance. First, as discussed in the preceding chapter, the successful application of the new Administration's distinctive brand of *Realpolitik*, with its emphasis upon diplomatic maneuver and manipulation, was contingent upon a high degree of domestic quiescence – that is, non-interference by either the Congress or the American public in the conduct of foreign policy. Yet, despite an earlier commitment to a conception of order with 'deeper purposes than stability,'[17] the ultimate failing of the Nixon–Kissinger strategy was manifested in its inability to coalesce domestic support – the 'acid test of a policy' – for the task which it set forward. Here again, style and substance fused in such a way as to raise disturbing questions about both in the public mind.

In the past, 'internal security,' not without good reason, has been regarded as the domestic corollary of 'national security.' In light of the rather expansible conception of national security implicit within the Nixon–Kissinger strategy, it is perhaps not surprising that it too had such a domestic component. This second domestic prerequisite of the new Administration's foreign policy orientation emerged largely out of the events of 1969–71. During that period, the Administration suffered successive public disclosures of classified documents and internal deliberations: most prominent amongst these were William Beecher's revelation of the Administration's 'secret' bombing campaign in Cambodia in May 1969,[18] Daniel Ellsberg's 'leaking' of the 'Pentagon Papers' to the *New York Times* and *Washington Post*, and Jack Anderson's disclosure of the Administration's covert decision in June 1971 to 'tilt' in favor of Pakistan at the height of the 1971 conflict while publicly avowing a position of neutrality. Following a meeting with Kissinger, Attorney General John Mitchell, and FBI Director J. Edgar Hoover in the Oval Office on 25 April 1969, Nixon authorized a 'leak-plugging' program which eventually produced 17 wiretaps and four cases of physical surveillance of White House aides, journalists, and a senior Pentagon official. It remains a matter of contention whether Kissinger initiated this series of national security wiretaps under a broad presidential mandate or, as he has steadfastly maintained since, merely supplied the names of targets for the FBI to monitor. Whatever the case, Kissinger both approved of the wiretaps and believed them to be legal.[19] His support for this limited program of domestic surveillance (the more grandiose Huston Plan was vetoed by none other than J. Edgar Hoover) was rationalized in terms of the danger which leaks posed to the Administration's conduct of foreign policy. Amidst the storm following public disclosure of the wiretaps program, Kissinger struck this theme in defense of his actions. Thus, during an emotional press conference in Vienna on 11 June 1974 at which he threatened to resign, Kissinger declared it impossible 'to conduct the foreign policy of the United States when the credibility of the Secretary of State is at issue . . .'[20]

The third domestic prerequisite of the Nixon–Kissinger approach stems from the first and again centers upon the particular post-Vietnam problem which the new Administration confronted of maintaining domestic support for a continuing American global role. Indeed, given the close interrelationship which Nixon and Kissinger perceived between developments of the periphery and the center, this was regarded as an essential pre-condition and support for the stable structure which they sought to put into place. Yet, cognizant that the driving force behind the middle-class revolt in 1967–8 against the Vietnam intervention had been conscription and high casualty rates, the Nixon Administration recognized that the *form* of American involvement was to be perhaps the prime determinant of domestic support. As shall be discussed in the following chapter, the underlying purpose of the Nixon Doctrine was thus to devise the new, and presumably efficacious, instrumentalities of American power which would allow the nation to remain 'involved' at a sustainable domestic price. However, the nature of this doctrinal accommodation to new domestic realities bred its own contradictions. In essence, how was the strategy of politico-military retrenchment and the reduction of American capabilities to be reconciled with the continuance of commitments (as evidenced in the first principle of the Nixon Doctrine)? Again, to return to the central thesis of this study, the Administration's hope to bridge this contradiction was predicated upon the symbiotic relationship which it sought to effect between the Nixon Doctrine and superpower détente. Thus, it was envisioned that post-Vietnam retrenchment with its logical corollary of a less overt American role was to take place within the context of a radically altered political environment. Such, at least, was the design – and the hope. That it did not so transpire may be attributed largely to the manner in which the détente process evolved – specifically, the Soviet ability to compartmentalize its relationship with the United States.

Détente and the evolution of 'linkage' politics

The picture to emerge out of the preceding analysis is that of an increasingly reactive American foreign policy adjusting to the multiple challenges posed by the evolution of the Soviet Union into a truly global power. This development was regarded by Kissinger as the dominant and inescapable fact of international life in the post-1969 period. The power of this perception made the attempt to achieve a global *modus vivendi* with the Soviet Union the centerpiece of the Nixon–Kissinger strategy. But yet the nature of the emergence of Soviet power suggested both the limits and the possibilities of such an endeavor. As Helmut Sonnenfeldt articulated it in his now famous background briefing to an assembled group of American ambassadors in London in December 1975:

The reason we can today talk and think in terms of dealing with Soviet imperialism, outside of and in addition to simple confrontation, is precisely because Soviet power is emerging in such a flawed way. This gives us the time to develop and to react. There is no way to prevent the emergence of the Soviet Union as a superpower. What we can do is to affect the way in which that power is developed and used. Not only can we balance in the traditional sense, but we can affect its usage – and that is what détente is all about.[21]

Sonnenfeldt's use of the word 'flawed' to characterize the nature of the emergence of Soviet power is striking – for it suggests that this uneven, irregular pattern of development was to provide the underlying basis of the Administration's 'linkage' approach *vis-à-vis* the moderation of Soviet behavior. Towards this end, it was hoped that a favorable American international position – somewhere between preponderance and *primus inter pares* – might be maintained through the adroit exploitation of the asymmetries which existed between the United States and Soviet Union across the various hierarchies of power. These pronounced differences, again raising questions of categories as well as questions of levels, were to provide the material basis for the network of incentives and penalties at the heart of the 'linkage' approach. In a sense, this approach was a clear reflection of Soviet weakness. For whereas the United States, despite its major political and psychological setback in Indochina, retained an impressive panoply of power, Soviet status as a superpower was confirmed almost solely on the basis of its military capabilities. Hence, the uni-dimensional character of Soviet power was indicative of inadequacies in other spheres of activity, and it thereby underscored the indeed 'flawed' nature of the Soviet Union's emergence as an 'imperial power' (again to use Sonnenfeldt's language).

Given the chronic nature of Soviet domestic economic deficiencies, it was thought possible in the initial phase of Administration policy to influence favorably Soviet behavior through the elaboration of a network of functional agreements. Indeed, by 1972 some 20 such agreements (including SALT, the 1975 space rendezvous program, grain sales, etc.) were signed, in the American hope that the development of a strong bond of mutual interests at the core of the US–Soviet relationship might be broadened into a more comprehensive *modus vivendi*. To many observers, particularly in Western Europe and China, the form of this attempted global accommodation hinted at the possibility of 'superpower condominium.' However, the Administration's perception was that it both embodied a realistic approach to the problem of ascendant Soviet power and underscored the fact that strategic management, despite the rhetoric of the new pluralism, would continue to be negotiated within a bipolar context. Yet this accommodation was to encompass more than what political scientists would characterize as a shift from a zero-sum to multiple-sum game. Given Soviet economic requirements and the flawed (uni-dimensional) nature of its emergence as a global power, an implicit assumption of the linkage approach was that effective diplomacy could permit the United States to translate the power asymmetries which it enjoyed *vis-à-vis* the Soviet Union into political advantage – that is, a favorable balance of power as opposed to mere equilibrium. Again, such an approach would require a diplomatic style of maneuver and manipulation so as to frustrate Soviet attempts to compartmentalize the relationship. This approach to the management of the US–Soviet relationship brings to mind Kissinger's characterization of 'the essence of the 'Metternich system;' the policy of enmeshing the opponents by his own moves, of frustrating him with invisible bonds, and dependent on the myth that the "rules of the game" prevented the adversary from sweeping the web away in a moment of impatience . . .'[22]

Yet Metternich operated within an international system premised upon a common conception of *legitimacy*. The perceived transformation of the Soviet Union from a 'revolutionary' to a status quo oriented power led Nixon and Kissinger to believe that under the new conditions and exigencies of the 1970s it would be possible to co-opt this emergent 'imperial power' into a new 'legitimate order.' In providing the intellectual starting point of the Nixon–Kissinger strategy, this perception subsequently fostered the attempt to forge a symbiotic relationship between the twin policies of superpower détente and the Nixon Doctrine. These strategies of détente and devolution (as so defined) were thus regarded *ab initio* as being much more than compatible: to varying degrees, each was to serve as the instrumentality of the other. Within such a context, superpower détente was viewed as a means of creating the stable regional conditions which would militate in favor of a less overt American role through the devolution of power and responsibility to nascent middle powers (see chapter 4). Likewise, the maintenance of stability along the periphery would reinforce the validity of understandings about the center and sustain the favorable political atmosphere in which the US–Soviet relationship might further develop.

Though remaining tacit, the underlying basis of this approach was to be what might be characterized as a structure of *trust*. By way of feedback, it was assumed that if one could 'trust' Soviet behavior on the periphery (as manifested, for example, in what Washington hoped would be a more forthcoming attitude *vis-à-vis* the negotiations concerning Vietnam and the Middle East), then one could trust in them to act in such a way as to maintain the stability of the center as well. This false structure of trust was perhaps the major motivating factor behind the public euphoria for détente evidenced during the period between the summits of May 1972 and June 1973. As shall be discussed in chapter 5, the stable structure itself threatened to come apart in the wake of the October 1973 Middle

East War when Soviet behavior along the periphery raised disturbing questions about the stability of the center (e.g. the charge of Soviet 'cheating' on the SALT I accords; the claim that détente had become a 'one-way street'). Confusion and eventual disillusionment, at least in the public mind, was to result from the mistaken belief that the creation of an expanding network of *functional* agreements with the Soviet Union reflected a broader consensus in terms of shared *values* – in other words, a common conception of international legitimacy. The ultimate inability to translate the Nixon–Kissinger strategy into an operational system of international order (Kissinger's 'stable structure') underscored that the elaboration of a 'seamless web' of functional accords did not automatically confer Soviet acceptance of American-inspired rules of engagement. In the absence of a shared notion of legitimacy, this pursuit of stability – what might be regarded as a kind of modified *pax Americana* – proved unable to constrain the Soviet drive for unilateral advantage along the periphery.

The reasons for this failure are complex, but fall roughly into three categories. First, despite the rhetoric of devolution and politico-military retrenchment surrounding the Guam (only later the Nixon) Doctrine, the Nixon–Kissinger strategy grossly underestimated the importance of local actors in the determination of political outcomes along the periphery. The net effect of this orientation was an exaggerated assessment of the impact of the triangular great-power relationship, and the 'high politics' agenda which it implied, on the rest of the world. With respect to the Vietnam negotiations, for example, this perception sustained the belief within the Administration that 'the road to Hanoi' lay through Moscow or Peking.

Second, the translation of the developing 'web' of functional agreements into a 'stable structure of peace' (*viz.* the establishment of a global *modus vivendi*) would have required a profound transformation in the form of the debate with the USSR – that is, a shift from a solely interests-oriented discussion towards a dialogue on values. Though such an attempt was evidenced, for example, in the Declaration of Principles that emerged from the Moscow summit of May 1972, the central paradox underlying the US–Soviet relationship remained. For while the notion of détente ostensibly implied the acceptance of a *structure* of international relations, at least in terms of the stabilization of threat at the center, the evident goal of both superpowers continued to be that of favorably affecting changes in the nature of that structure by way of cumulative shifts along the periphery. Thus, the continuing pursuit of unilateral advantage, reflecting the absence of a common conception of international legitimacy, frustrated the architectonic approach advanced by the Nixon Administration and seriously complicated the problem of strategic management.

Third, and finally, the efficacy of the Nixon–Kissinger strategy was predicated upon an overly optimistic assessment of the American ability to wield the incentives and sanctions at its disposal so as to moderate Soviet behavior. Once again, this calculation was the result of the new Administration's perception of the flawed, uneven pattern of the development of Soviet power – and the diplomatic possibilities which might accrue to the United States as a conse-quence of it. The Administration's desire to exploit these existing asymmetries across the various hierarchies of power for the sake of political advantage led to the promulgation of the linkage approach to relations with the Soviet Union. It is to the nature and application of that rather problematical theory that the focus of analysis shall now shift.

Ironically, the term 'linkage' was first employed by United States diplomats in the mid-1960s to object to the Soviet Union's connec-tion of the American bombing of North Vietnam to the develop-ment of détente elsewhere.[23] During the 1968 presidential campaign, the concept was invoked by candidate Nixon on several occasions. The context, almost invariably, was Vietnam with the Republican candidate expressing the view that the Soviets could, if appropriately motivated, exert decisive influence upon the Hanoi regime to adopt a more forthcoming attitude towards the Paris negotiations. At his initial press conference as President, Nixon's response to a question concerning SALT suggested the new approach upon which the Administration sought to base the development of relations with the Soviet Union:

It is a question not only when but the *context* of those talks. The context of those talks is vitally important because we're here between two major . . . guidelines. On the one side there is the proposition advanced by some that we go forward with talks on the reduction of strategic forces on both sides. We should go forward with such talks clearly apart from any progress on political settlement and on the other side the suggestion is made that until we make progress on political settlements, it would not be wise to go forward on any reduction of our strategic arms even by agreement with the other side . . . What I want to do is to see to it that we have strategic arms talks in a way and at a time that will promote, if possible, progress on outstanding political problems *at the same time*, for example, on the problems of the Mideast, on other outstanding problems in which the United States and the Soviet Union acting together can serve the cause of peace [emphasis added].[24]

Kissinger, while referring to 'linkage' on a background basis to journalists, reportedly opposed Nixon's public enunciation of this strategy at such an early stage for fear that the Soviets might interpret it as a direct challenge – a mere variation on the Cold War theme of 'negotiation from strength.'[25] In spite of Kissinger's eloquent elaboration of the mutual advantage of the linkage approach to Soviet Ambassador Dobrynin at their initial White House meetings in early 1969, this, in fact, was the Soviet reaction to the new American theology.

The *New York Times*, anticipating some of the difficulties which later beset the linkage approach, voiced its editorial opinion that it was 'unfortunate' that the President had explicitly linked the long-awaited SALT negotiations with superpower behavior in the Middle East as both sides had such an overriding mutuality of interest in the former.[26] The editorial position of the *Washington Post* was perhaps more reflective of the general public reaction to Nixon's enunciation of the linkage strategy *vis-à-vis* the development of US–Soviet relations: 'It is an idea easy enough to defend, or to criticize, in the abstract; the specific application of it will be what counts . . .'[27] Contradictory statements emanating from within the Administration during the first half of 1969 underscored that on an operational level the ambiguous concept could be easily mishandled and misunderstood. While Secretary Laird, for example, stated that Moscow would have to produce 'signs of progress' on Vietnam and the Middle East 'before' Washington would enter into SALT, Secretary Rogers, somewhat eschewing the linkage concept, remarked that there were no barriers to the negotiations and expressed the hope that 'they [would] go forward very soon.'[28] The Secretary of State attempted to undercut further Kissinger's policy of linkage when, upon the White House announcement of 25 October 1969 that negotiations with the Soviets would commence on 17 November, he declared that SALT was 'not conditional in any sense of the word. We haven't laid down any conditions for those talks.'

Kissinger, as always sensitive to the delicate signaling process, recommended a prompt rebuttal of the Rogers line as a means of resuscitating linkage. The White House press spokesman accordingly told reporters that 'these talks cannot take place in a vacuum. The President's feeling is that there is a certain relation between SALT and outstanding political problems.'[29] With respect to the specific application of the linkage approach, Kissinger appears to have wanted to steer a diplomatic course somewhere between the alternatives reflected in the initial positions taken by Laird and Rogers – that is, neither the adoption of rigid prerequisites to negotiations nor the complete decoupling of those discussions from considerations of the general political environment. What was imperative in Kissinger's view was the mutual perception of the importance of the milieu in which negotiations were conducted. This position was made clear in the Administration's first 40,000-word State of the World message published in February 1970: an 'essential in successful negotiations is an appreciation of the context in which issues are addressed. The central fact here is the inter-relationship of international events. We did not invent the inter-relationship; it is not a negotiating tactic. It is a fact of life.'[30]

As discussed in the previous section, this newly articulated linkage approach to relations with the Soviet Union was regarded as perhaps the primary means by which it would prove possible to operationalize the stable structure implicit within the Nixon–Kissinger strategy. It was hoped that its successful application would permit the achieve-ment of the feedback relationship which the Administration sought to effect between the twin policies of superpower détente and the Nixon Doctrine. Within this context, the essential importance of linkage as a foreign policy orientation is evident. The intended relationship between the dual strategies of détente and devolution was one in which each was to serve as the instrumentality for the realization of the other. Linkage was to sustain this feedback process via its function as both pivot point and catalyst *vis-à-vis* the two. In this way, a mutually reinforcing 'structure of stability' was to be forged between the center and periphery.[31] The creation of this stable structure was thus predicated upon the efficacy of linkage diplomacy (*viz.* the frustration of Soviet attempts to compartmentalize the relationship) as buttressed by the new modalities of American power reflected in the Nixon Doctrine. The hope was clearly that together they would allow the United States to maintain at least transitionally its predominant international position at a sustainable domestic price during the post-Vietnam period.

Running through the Administration's elaboration of the linkage approach to US–Soviet relations was a continuing and overriding preoccupation with American credibility. Indeed, the preservation of credibility was regarded as a vital prerequisite to the maintenance of the 'emerging structure of peace.' For one of the major precepts of the Nixon–Kissinger strategy was that the erosion of stability along the periphery through the creation of new politico-military precedents would invariably result in the undermining of the stability of the center. Moreover, in view of the omnipresent danger of escalation, it was argued that even ostensibly 'limited' conflicts on the periphery could have unforeseen consequences. In Nixon's analysis, this was to account for what he considered the somewhat 'ambivalent' Soviet policy towards the Middle East and Vietnam. While noting with disquiet the massive Soviet arms transfer operation to both these areas, the President observed that, at the same time, 'the Soviet Union recognizes that if these *peripheral areas* get out of control . . . the result could be a confrontation with the United States' (emphasis added).[32] Indeed, it was this perception of the inextricable link between the stability of the periphery and center which motivated Administration attempts to somehow co-opt the Soviet Union into an American-inspired global *modus vivendi* (the new 'legitimate order') as embodied in the Nixon–Kissinger strategy. This, of course, was to hinge upon the efficacy of the new theology of linkage. In his assessment of the Nixon–Kissinger diplomacy, Stanley Hoffmann characterized the intended process as follows: 'The bear would be treated like one of B. F. Skinner's pigeons: there would be incentives for good behavior, rewards if such behavior occurred, and punishments if not. It may have been a bit pedantic, or a bit arrogant; it certainly was rather theoretical.'[33]

An analysis of the nature and evolution of the Administration's linkage strategy is perhaps best approached by way of an examination of its responses to those crises which arose in 'peripheral areas', but yet were perceived in terms of their effect upon the central US–Soviet relationship. Washington's management of the episodes considered below reflected the transitional nature of the Nixon–Kissinger strategy as a response to the challenge of reconciling the contending demands of nascent multipolarity (the 'new pluralism') and revitalized bipolarity. Within the context of this background, the focus of analysis shall now shift to a consideration of the four major regions on the periphery – the Middle East, Latin America, South Asia, and Indochina – in which the perceived interactions between local and extra-regional actors prompted the Administration to assume an active American politico-military role during the period preceding the May 1972 summit meeting.

While Vietnam was without doubt the most immediately pressing international problem to confront the new Administration in January 1969, the Middle East remained the most potentially explosive. In that region, American and Soviet interests intersected in a manner and magnitude of importance that they clearly did not in Southeast Asia. From the outset of their tenure of office, both Nixon and Kissinger instinctively viewed the Arab–Israeli conflict in terms of the ongoing global engagement between the United States and the Soviet Union. In Kissinger's reading of events, the Soviet Union, having originally seized upon the Middle East conflict as a means of penetrating the region, was now attempting to exploit further that conflagration so as to establish predominance in the area. The logical implication of this analysis was that the USSR and its new clients in the region could be deterred only through firm American support for Israel.

In contrast, the State Department forcefully argued that undifferentiated support for Israel not only undercut American allies in the Arab world, particularly Saudi Arabia, but further facilitated Soviet penetration into the region. As reflected in the Rogers Plan of 1969–70, they recommended that the Administration pursue an 'evenhanded' policy in the Middle East, thereby establishing some distance between the United States and Israel.[34] The backdrop to this internal American policy debate was, of course, the steadily escalating 'war of attrition' along the Suez which had been initiated by Nasser in March 1969. With casualties already exceeding the level of those of the Six Day War, the Israeli government decided in December to launch deep-penetration air strikes against targets in Egypt. With an embarrassed Nasser secretly threatening to resign in favor of someone who could seek a settlement through the United States, the Soviet Union responded quickly to the Egyptian demand for a comprehensive air defense system to counter the Israeli 'raids in depth.' In one strike, the arrival of Soviet crews in February–March 1970 to man both SAM-3 missile batteries and MiG-23 fighters dramatically changed the complexion of the war of attrition and, in so doing, presented the Nixon Administration with its first superpower crisis. During his press conference of 21 March, the President, noting the recent infusion of Soviet military personnel into the UAR, warned that 'if the USSR, by its military assistance program to Israel's neighbors, does essentially change the balance of power, then the United States would take action to deal with that situation.'[35]

At the end of March, Soviet-manned MiG-23s scrambled for the first time to intercept Israeli fighters headed for a mission in the vicinity of Cairo. Facing the specter of a Soviet–Israeli military confrontation, the Administration decided to resurrect the Rogers Plan – a ceasefire proposal whose unanimous rejection the previous autumn by the concerned parties was undoubtedly connected with the lukewarm support that it had received from the Nixon–Kissinger White House. Diplomatic movement proceeded on two fronts during the ensuing period. In Washington, the talks between Secretary Rogers and Ambassador Dobrynin, resumed as a result of the secret correspondence between Nixon and Premier Kosygin during January–February 1970, centered upon the immediate problem of restoring the ceasefire. Not surprisingly, the Soviet Union, in view of the uni-dimensional nature of its relationship with the Arab 'confrontation states,' refused to broaden the scope of the negotiations to include the consideration of limitations on arms transfers into the region. Concomitant to this superpower dialogue in Washington, the Administration entered into discussions with the Egyptian government in order to develop the framework of a possible 'Rogers Plan II.' American officials were encouraged by the fact that Nasser's continuing public intransigence belied a more pragmatic and flexible attitude evidenced during the private diplomatic exchange with him in April. At the end of the month, with the White House engrossed in the international and domestic repercussions of the Cambodian 'incursion,' the State Department began to prepare a 'standstill' ceasefire proposed as part of a broad negotiations formula. By 19 June 1970, when Secretary Rogers transmitted the completed American proposal to the involved parties, the war of attrition had reached new and even more fearful proportions.

Though the immediate danger lay in the spiraling escalation of fighting along the Suez battle zone, Nixon and Kissinger were equally concerned that the presence of a 15,000-man combat/advisory force in the UAR was creating a new reality in the Middle East. Kissinger's remarks concluding a 26 June background briefing at San Clemente reflected the growing fear that Soviet actions were undermining the tacit regime of restraints governing superpower behavior on the periphery: 'We are trying to *expel* the Soviet military presence, not so much the advisers, but the combat pilots and the personnel, before they become so firmly established' (emphasis added).[36] Five days later, the President, when asked to comment upon Kissinger's candid description of American goals, took the opportunity to reaffirm forcefully the importance of American credibility for the maintenance of international order (the 'stable structure').[37] With the Israeli and American governments unclear as to the precise level which the Soviets were prepared to involve themselves, the tough statements by Nixon and Kissinger may be regarded as part of a carefully orchestrated deterrence policy. By early July, the steady extension of the Soviet–Egyptian air defense network, having previously ended the damaging and embarrassing cycle of deep-penetration raids, now brought Israeli Phantoms under intense fire over the Suez battle zone itself for the first time. The loss of several Israeli aircraft in the first week of the month prompted officially inspired press reports that it might become necessary for Israeli ground forces to invade the west bank of the canal in order to neutralize the missile sites.

Such was the developing situation when Nasser arrived in Moscow on 30 June for a meeting with the Soviet leadership (as well as medical treatment). While the Egyptian President pushed for an even more overt Soviet role so that he might enter into negotiations from a position of strength, his Russian hosts reportedly expressed concern that the rapidly escalating war of attrition held the danger of strong counter-measures from an increasingly desperate Israel, perhaps with the full support of the United States.[38] With the Soviet Union unwilling to escalate further the level of its involvement, a bitter Nasser returned from Moscow on 17 July with no other alternative than to accept the terms of the Rogers Plan II. Under heavy American pressure, the Israeli government, which detested the limited nature of the ceasefire with no promise of direct negotiations, was compelled to do likewise on 31 July.

Though the ceasefire came into effect on 8 August 1970, there were immediate Israeli charges that the Soviet Union and Egypt were 'massively' and systematically violating the accord. This situation, however, was soon overshadowed by disturbing developments in Jordan. Following months of intermittent fighting with Palestinian guerrillas seeking to use the country as a base of operations against Israel (thereby prompting savage Israeli reprisal raids against Jordanian positions), King Hussein decided to take defensive action against the *fedayeen* on 15 September. When the CIA reported that Syrian armored vehicles with Soviet advisers were moving towards the Jordanian frontier, Kissinger convened an *ad hoc* WSAG meeting in the White House 'Situation Room' to consider the American response. During a presidential trip to Chicago on the following day, Nixon gave a background briefing to reporters in which he stated that the United States would consider direct intervention if the Syrians and Iraqis with Soviet backing threatened the Amman regime.

Once again, Nixon and Kissinger used the American press to signal their disapproval of Soviet actions and to reaffirm the Administration's will to resist such fundamental changes in the status quo. In response, the Soviet leadership privately conveyed to the American government that it was doing its utmost to restrain its clients from intervening in the Jordanian civil war. Nonetheless, on 19 September, one hundred Syrian tanks crossed the frontier into Jordan – an action which the White House believed would spark another major war in the Middle East. The crisis came to a head on 20–21 September when Jordanian reverses on the ground prompted a remarkable request from King Hussein for Israeli air cover. While the Israeli cabinet feverishly debated the Jordanian request, Nixon continued the signaling process to Moscow and Damascus by ostentatiously placing American airborne divisions in North Carolina and West Germany on alert and adding an additional carrier task-force to the Sixth Fleet.

The Israeli government's decision to accede to Hussein's request came on 21 September when President Nixon unequivocally promised that if the Egyptians or the Soviets intervened, the United States would intervene against both. Fortunately, it was not necessary for the Israelis to fulfill their pledge, for by the afternoon of 22 September it was apparent that the Jordanians had skillfully repulsed the Syrian armored attack.[39] Having been checked on the ground and under the threat of Israeli Phantoms, Syrian forces broke into full retreat. In the ensuing period, Hussein was able effectively to turn his forces against the Palestinian military concentrations near Amman, thus ending the immediate crisis.

Yet, coinciding with the Jordanian episode, the Administration was confronted with what it perceived as another disturbing Soviet attempt to erode the tacit regime of restraints governing superpower behavior on the periphery. In early September 1970, a U-2 photo-reconnaissance mission over Cuba revealed that new barracks, communication facilities and SAM batteries were under construction near the southern naval base of Cienfuegos. As this site included a soccer field (the Cuban national sport is baseball), CIA photo interpreters concluded that it was being prepared for the Russians. At the same time, intelligence reports indicated the presence both of a 900-ton Urga-class submarine tender (with two barges in tow designed to handle radioactive wastes from reactors) and a Soviet nuclear submarine in the vicinity of Cienfuegos. The ominous conclusion drawn by the intelligence community and presented to Nixon by Kissinger on or around 10 September was that the Soviets, in strict violation of the 'understanding' reached between the two countries in 1962, were intending to base an offensive weapons system in Cuba. Kissinger made oblique reference to this new evidence at the same 16 September background briefing in which the President issued a warning with respect to the developing Jordanian crisis. Several meetings with Soviet Ambassador Dobrynin resulted in official 'assurances' on 27 September that the USSR was not constructing an offensive military installation in Cuba.[40]

Although Nixon and Kissinger subsequently regarded the Cuban crisis as a triumph in 'preventive diplomacy,'[41] several outside observers seriously questioned both the timing and nature of the crisis. In an investigative report published in the *New York Times* following the Cienfuegos affair, Tad Szulc revealed that, during the deliberations over the crisis, senior State Department officials had been somewhat skeptical of Kissinger's analysis and expressed opposition to this attempt to translate ambiguous evidence into a major crisis. One theory advanced from within the Department was that Kissinger had wanted both to utilize the Cuba issue to put pressure on Moscow *vis-à-vis* the Jordanian crisis (as part of the global signaling process) and, with respect to American domestic opinion, to relate the dangers inherent in Castro's Cuba to the dangers in Chile if Allende were confirmed by its Congress as President.[42]

In the absence of internal NSC memoranda, this hypothesis regarding Kissinger's application of the linkage approach, though plausible, cannot be substantiated. Yet it is known that Chile was a major preoccupation of his during the Summer of 1970. At a 27 June 1970 meeting of the 40 Committee, convened to consider the consequences of Allende's electoral victory and possible American responses, Kissinger is reported to have remarked: 'I don't see why we have to let a country go Marxist just because its people are irresponsible.'[43] This statement is wholly consistent with the conception of *legitimacy* to emerge from Kissinger's academic writings prior to 1968 (see the discussion in chapter 2 above) in which domestic considerations are subordinated to the maintenance of the international framework. A similar assessment of the impact of peripheral shifts on the central balance was made by Kissinger to Jiri Hajek, Alexander Dubcek's foreign minister, several months prior to the Soviet invasion in August 1968; according to Hajek, Kissinger 'confirmed that the existing division of the world was regarded by both sides as an element of stability based on peaceful coexistence. And that every disruption of the equilibrium would have to lead to unfathomable consequences.'[44]

In the year following the Jordanian and Cuban episodes, it was this perception of the inextricable link between 'disruptions' on the periphery and the preservation of the stable structure which motivated Administration policy *vis-à-vis* the dispute between India and Pakistan. The development of the crisis witnessed the expression of concern by Nixon and Kissinger not so much with regard to its horrific domestic consequences (the pattern of systematic repression in East Bengal) as in terms of its possible international ramifications. In this respect, it should be noted that the Administration's celebrated tilt towards Pakistan, in fact, predated the outbreak of hostilities by many months. This tacit shift in American policy may be attributed to three major considerations. First, the conclusion of the Indo-Soviet Treaty of Peace, Friendship and Cooperation on 9 August 1971, despite its inclusion of a specific clause reaffirming India's non-aligned status, reinforced the image of a tacit alliance between the two powers. Second, in light of the vital role played by President Yahya Khan in the Administration's ultrasecret China initiative, both Nixon and Kissinger were loath to alienate the Pakistanis. Third, and perhaps uppermost in the minds of American policy-makers, there was the strong incentive not to antagonize the Chinese in the few months preceding the Peking summit meeting.

Occurring less than half a year after the major breakthrough in the Sino-American relationship, the Indo-Pakistan War of December 1971 dramatically highlighted the importance of the nascent 'triangular' great-power relationship *vis-à-vis* the dynamics of strategic management. From the American perspective, the *rapproche-*

ment with China had two underlying rationales. First, despite repeated Administration claims to the contrary, it furnished the United States with a powerful lever to assist in its ongoing attempt to moderate Soviet behavior. It is interesting to note that this was clearly the Chinese perception of American motivations at the time. As Premier Chou En-lai put it during a confidential briefing in December 1971: 'When the US got stuck in Vietnam, the Soviet revisionists embraced the opportunity to extend vigorously their sphere of influence in Europe and the Middle East. The US imperialists cannot but improve their relations with China to combat the Soviet revisionists.'[45] Second, and equally important in terms of the Administration's pursuit of stability, the improvement of relations with China was regarded as the logical corollary to the application of the Nixon Doctrine in Southeast Asia. For it was envisioned that the development of a comprehensive Sino-American *rapprochement* would contribute to the creation of the stable regional conditions which would permit the orderly devolution of American power (politico-military retrenchment). This was the essence of the Nixon–Kissinger strategy.

As in most of the international crises which the Nixon Administration faced, its actions during the Indo-Pakistan War were primarily reactive. The multiple demands of the Vietnam negotiations and the China initiative on Kissinger's time meant that the developing crisis in South Asia was accorded secondary priority until November 1971 when it was apparent that both sides were preparing for war. At that late date, American efforts at mediation and 'preventive diplomacy' were doomed to failure. In light of the rapidly deteriorating situation in East Bengal, the Indian government felt compelled to move militarily on 3 December. Its forces, supporting the Bangladesh guerrilla forces, were able quickly to overrun the former East Pakistan, trapping 90,000 Pakistani soldiers. In the west, though the conflict was more balanced, the Indians were able to capture some territory in Kashmir.

At the first WSAG meeting on the morning of the outbreak of hostilities, Kissinger made clear the President's attitude towards the conflict: 'I am getting hell every half-hour from the President that we are not being tough enough on India. He has just called me again. He does not believe we are carrying out his wishes. He wants to tilt in favor of Pakistan. He feels everything we do comes out otherwise.'[46] Four days later, on 7 December, Kissinger misleadingly told reporters during a background briefing that press stories that the Administration was 'anti-Indian' were 'totally inaccurate.'[47] The WSAG meeting on the next day (8 December) was devoted almost entirely to the developing situation in West Pakistan. CIA Director Richard Helms reported that prior to their acceptance of a ceasefire, the Indians intended to attempt to 'eliminate' Pakistan's armor and air force capabilities as well as to 'straighten out' the southern border of Azad Kashmir. Kissinger observed that this would amount to turning West Pakistan into a 'client state' and went on to comment 'that what we may be witnessing is a situation wherein a country equipped and supported by the Soviets may be turning half of Pakistan into an impotent state and the other into a vassal. We must consider what other countries may be thinking of our actions.'[48] Once again, one finds Administration policy expressed and rationalized in terms of the demands of American *credibility* and the maintenance of stability. Thus, in the State of the World message published less than two months after the termination of hostilities, the Administration declared:

The global implications of this war were clear to the world community. The resort to military solutions, if accepted, would only tempt other nations in other delicately poised regions of tension to try the same. The credibility of international efforts to promote or guarantee regional peace in strife-torn regions would be undermined. The danger of war in the Middle East in particular would be measurably increased. Restraints would be weakened all around the world.[49]

At the WSAG meeting of 8 December 1971, Kissinger's analysis of Indian intentions was vigorously contested by Assistant Secretary Joseph Sisco, who noted that fighting was confined largely to the disputed area of Kashmir. Upon the questionable strength of the CIA intelligence reported cited above, the Kissinger line was sustained by the President. On 9 December a naval task force of eight ships, led by nuclear aircraft carrier *Enterprise*, was ordered to sail from the Gulf of Tonkin to the Bay of Bengal as a clear signal to both New Delhi and Moscow. The implication, not outrightly denied by the White House, was that the United States would actively intervene if the Indians, having subdued East Bengal, launched an all-out attack on West Pakistan. During the course of a background briefing to reporters on 14 December, Kissinger (again engaging in an explicit form of linkage politics) sought to underscore the impact of peripheral disruptions on the center when he baldly warned that unless the Soviet

Union began to exert an immediate 'restraining influence' on the Indian Government 'the entire US–Soviet relationship might well be re-examined.'[50] When a ceasefire was declared two days later ending the war, Kissinger claimed that it had been his veiled threat to cancel the Moscow summit which had prompted the Soviets to exert decisive influence on the Indian government to cease their reckless attempt to 'dismember' West Pakistan. While the State Department remained skeptical that this had ever indeed been the Indian intention, both Nixon and Kissinger regarded the episode as but further confirmation of the efficacy of the Administration's linkage approach to US–Soviet relations.[51]

In April 1972, this central relationship was again put to a severe test when the North Vietnamese launched a large-scale offensive designed to crush the ARVN (Army of the Republic of Vietnam) prior to a negotiated ceasefire. Two years earlier, the American 'incursion' into Cambodia (considered in chapter 4 below) had, amongst other things, served to reveal the rather one-sided conception of linkage politics emerging within the Administration. At the height of the crisis, for example, the Soviet Union and China were explicitly warned not to link American behavior in Cambodia with the development of bilateral relations – the clear implication being that linkage was a singularly American prerogative. Later, following the withdrawal of United States forces from Cambodia, Kissinger maintained that the episode had greatly assisted the Administration's global strategy through the reinforcement of American *credibility*. This same overriding concern for the United States not to appear 'a pitiful, helpless giant' underlay the Administration's forceful response to the North Vietnamese offensive of April–May 1972.

The initial American military reaction, approved by the President over the objections of Rogers and Laird, was to expand the air war to Hanoi and Haiphong (including the use of B-52 heavy bombers). Kissinger believed that this strategy of 'compellence' (to use the concept developed by Thomas Schelling in *Arms and Influence*) would both prompt Hanoi to adopt a more forthcoming attitude at the Paris negotiations and signal to Moscow that its continuing massive assistance to North Vietnam might jeopardize the May 1972 summit meeting. On the evening of 19 April, Kissinger secretly departed for the Soviet capital – a trip which had been originally planned to prepare the ground for the Nixon visit (e.g. SALT) instead was taken up largely by the developing crisis in Vietnam. The ritualistic pattern of policy affirmation was broken by Kissinger when he revealed a major departure in the American negotiating position: the United States was henceforth willing to accept a ceasefire-in-place in return for a North Vietnamese pledge to withdraw those forces which had entered the South since the start of the offensive on 31 March.[52] Though successive American proposals had hinted at increased flexibility on the thorny question of 'mutual withdrawals' (cf. the American peace proposals of November 1969 and October 1971), this was the first explicit reference to the agreed presence of northern forces in South Vietnam after the termination of hostilities. It was characteristic of the Nixon–Kissinger approach (*viz.* the perception of North Vietnam as a Soviet 'client') that this major American concession was put forward in Moscow rather than Paris. Six months later, it served as the basis of agreement between the two parties.

By the time of Kissinger's return to Washington, it was clear that the situation in South Vietnam had severely deteriorated and the nature of the policy debate within the Administration shifted accordingly. With the fall of Quang Tri on 1 May 1972, basic agreement was reached between Nixon and Kissinger on the decision to mine Haiphong harbor – a move previously rejected by the Johnson Administration on political grounds, but here thought an appropriate response to the North Vietnamese offensive when considered against the 'generous' American proposal conveyed to Brezhnev. On 5 May, this decision was confirmed by the full NSC over the objections of Secretary Laird (who challenged it both on political and operational grounds) and the assessment of Kissinger that there was a 50-50 chance that the Soviets would cancel the summit. Several days earlier, following a barbecue held at the Texas ranch of Treasury Secretary John Connally (the strongest advocate of retaliation), the President had again reaffirmed the importance of Vietnam in terms of the impact of peripheral developments on the center and the maintenance of American credibility:

In the event that one country like North Vietnam, massively assisted with the most modern technical weapons by two Communist superpowers . . . is able to invade another country and conquer it, you can see how the pattern would be repeated in other countries throughout the world – in the Mideast, in Europe, and in others as well. If, on the other hand, that kind of aggression is stopped in Vietnam, and fails there, then it will be discouraged in other parts of the world. Putting it quite directly then, what is on the line in Vietnam is not just peace for Vietnam, but peace in the Mideast, peace in

Europe, and peace not just for [the] years immediately ahead of us, but possibly for a long time in the future . . . What is really on the line here, of course, is the position of the United States . . . as the strongest free world power, as a constructive force for peace in the world.[53]

As during the Cambodian episode two years earlier, Nixon warned in his 8 May 1972 address announcing the mining decision that the Soviet government would bear ultimate responsibility for the consequences if it chose to link American behavior in Indochina with outstanding bilateral issues:

Let us not slide back towards the dark shadows of a previous age . . . We, the United States and the Soviet Union, are on the threshold of a new relationship that can serve not only the interests of our two countries, but the cause of world peace. We are prepared to continue to build this relationship. The responsibility is yours if we fail to do so.[54]

At his press conference on the morning after the President's speech, Kissinger defended the decision to mine Haiphong harbor and asserted that it did not impose an unacceptable risk of confrontation with the Soviet Union:

The judgment was that it did not involve an unacceptable risk, especially compared to the risks of the situation where for the second time since the summit meeting was arranged [the Indo-Pakistan war being the first] Soviet arms fueled a military upheaval, and no one has pretended that this decision was lightly arrived at. The judgment has been, obviously, that the risks were not unacceptable.

Underlying Kissinger's statement that the Soviet Union had supplied but did not plan the April–May 1972 operation, there was a strong hint that they had privately expressed anger over the timing of the offensive and were becoming increasingly impatient with Hanoi's intransigence at the negotiating table: 'What we face here is one of the problems great powers have in dealing with their client, that the client looks at problems from its own regional or national perspective, while the great powers [must] take actions in a much wider one.'[55]

Unlike the U-2 incident of 1960, Brezhnev refused to seize upon the mining of Haiphong harbor as an excuse for canceling the Moscow summit. The available evidence would suggest that the Politburo's decision to proceed with the summit was motivated principally by the desire to check diplomatically the nascent Sino-American relationship as well as to secure the expansion of trade relations (e.g. credits, MFN status, etc.). With the military situation having stabilized in South Vietnam, the President departed for Moscow on 20 May secure in the belief that the efficacy of his Administration's particular variety of *Macht Politik* had been confirmed by the events of the preceding weeks. In its full effect (Nixon's self-laudatory assessment aside), the Indochina crisis of Spring 1972 again served to underscore the paradoxical status of Vietnam within the policy-making process. On the plane of internal American decision-making, the broad scope of considerations brought to bear (e.g. the theme of credibility) established its paradigmatic importance *vis-à-vis* the Nixon–Kissinger strategy. Yet, at the same time, the shared perception of Vietnam as an anomalous, peripheral vestige of the Cold War permitted it to be largely decoupled from the development of détente and the triangular relationship.

The Moscow–Washington accords and the evolution of strategic management

In the detailed and sustained critique of US foreign policy developed prior to his entry into government service, Kissinger reserved some of his strongest language for the American approach to negotiations (e.g. the 'fatuous diplomacy' of the Eisenhower Administration). Beyond his overriding belief that the realities of the nuclear age had prompted the transformation of the Soviet Union from a revolutionary into a status quo oriented power, Kissinger was little concerned, at least on the surface, with the question of Soviet intentions. Indeed, he forcefully argued, as in *The Necessity for Choice*, that the continuing American emphasis upon the underlying forces motivating Soviet behavior only contributed to the dangerous oscillation in political atmosphere which characterized superpower relations. Though the Administration's summit diplomacy of 1972–3 generated its own unwarranted sense of euphoria, Kissinger similarly warned against any undue preoccupation with Soviet intentions during the vociferous domestic debate over détente which developed in the aftermath of the October 1973 War:

To the extent that our attention focuses largely on Soviet intentions we create a latent vulnerability. If détente can be justified only by a basic change in Soviet motiviation, the temptation becomes overwhelming to base US–Soviet relations not on realistic appraisal but on tenuous hopes: a change in Soviet tone is taken as a sign of a basic change of philosophy. Atmosphere is confused with substance. Policy oscillates between poles of suspicion and euphoria.[56]

In contrast, the Nixon–Kissinger strategy was premised upon the belief that greater predictability and restraint might be infused into the 'limited adversary relationship' through the elaboration of a network of mutual interests, not unlike Kissinger's depiction of the 'Metternich system.' As suggested above, this rather architectonic approach – the new theology of linkage – was regarded as perhaps the primary means by which it would be possible during a period of ascendant Soviet power to maintain the equilibrium of the emerging stable structure.

The global nature of the US–Soviet engagement sustained the perception of a close interrelationship between developments at the periphery and center within the Administration. As during the Cold War period, this Soviet-centric image of the international system was utilized as the basis for proclaiming the *indivisibility* of détente. Such was the new ideological universalism of the Nixon–Kissinger strategy. At the time, much was said of the claim that order within this schema was no longer defined in overtly ideological terms, but rather was viewed more traditionally as a balance of power. As Kissinger observed in 1968 as the United States reaped the bitter harvest of two decades of undifferentiated globalism: 'Part of the reason for our difficulties is our reluctance to think in terms of power and equilibrium.' The clear implication was that having discarded the ideological baggage of the Cold War period, it would thus be possible to move towards a more discriminatory foreign policy premised upon a less expansive conception of the American national interest. Prior to his entry into government service, Kissinger therefore maintained that a return to the traditional criteria governing inter-state behavior would allow a new American Administration to confront 'the challenge of relating our commitments to our interests and our obligations to our purposes.'[57] Yet, in contrast to the overtly ideological concerns which dominated the Cold War period, the globalist foreign policy approach of the Nixon–Kissinger period was justified in terms of the importance of American credibility *vis-à-vis* the maintenance of the emerging stable structure.

From this perspective, the domination of the Moscow summit agenda by the twin issues of SALT and Vietnam was fitting and symbolic. For although there was no effort explicitly to link the two issues in view of the overwhelming mutuality of interest in the former, their coincidence did function on the perceptual level ostensibly to reinforce the underlying premise of the Nixon–Kissinger strategy (i.e. the vital interrelationship between developments of the periphery and center). SALT, motivated as it was by the mutual desire of the superpowers to maintain the stability of the central balance, was regarded as the quintessential exercise in strategic management. The Administration's goal, *pari passu*, of somehow implicating Moscow in the settlement of the Vietnam War reflected the broader belief (or hope) that it might prove possible to expand the 'structure' or network of agreements governing the center into a rather more comprehensive *modus vivendi* encompassing the periphery.

The prerequisites of such a global accommodation, however, were twofold. First, given the Nixon–Kissinger strategy's implicit identification of value with order, its successful implementation would have required a fundamental transformation in the nature of the dialogue with the Soviet Union. That is, at some stage in the evolving relationship, a basically functional approach to détente centering upon the creation of a seamless web of mutual interests would have to be supplanted by one which less obliquely addressed the fundamental questions of international order. In the absence of such a shift, negotiations would potentially yield a series of disparate agreements operating outside of any shared notion of *legitimacy*. Within this context (and the circumscribed definition of détente which it implied), the maintenance of stability would hinge almost solely upon the efficacy of linkage politics – the second prerequisite of the Nixon–Kissinger approach.

To a larger extent, the successful application of linkage across the various categories of bilateral issues was contingent upon the American ability to frustrate Soviet attempts to 'compartmentalize' the relationship. Given the nature of the emerging 'structure,' this had the net effect of reducing diplomacy to a perpetual *tour de force* as Kissinger sought to out-maneuver Soviet interests on a tactical basis. In spite of the intervening rhetoric manifested in successive State of the World messages, the Nixon–Kissinger approach ultimately proved more manipulative and 'acrobatic' than architectonic. In part, the tactical character of the Administration's actions derived from the nature of linkage politics itself. For the relatively unstructured quality of most policy interactions indicates that linkages do not exist *ab initio*; they are made and, indeed, operate as much on the psychological plane (the mind of the policy-maker) as on the material. Moreover, while the goal remains that of favorably affecting the behavior of one's adversary, the very process of establishing a close interrelationship across categories of issues more often than not firmly places the onus upon the party which seeks to create the linkage: witness Kissinger's contradictory statements at the time of the Angolan Civil War.

In the case of the search for a negotiated settlement to the Vietnam War, the United States sought what the Soviets clearly could not produce. At their initial series of secret White House meetings in 1969, Soviet Ambassador Dobrynin reportedly sought to persuade Kissinger that Moscow 'simply did not have the clout to deliver North Vietnam.'[58] The implications of this conclusion no doubt ran contrary to Nixon's instinct for downgrading the importance of local actors in the determination of regional outcomes. The Administration's determined but chimerical pursuit of an imposed great-power settlement in Southeast Asia led to the exclusive devotion of four separate negotiating sessions to the question of Vietnam at the Moscow summit in May 1972. Characterizing the American actions of April–May 1972 as 'barbaric,' Brezhnev reiterated the compartmentalized Soviet view of détente. With the development of bilateral relations proceeding apace, the American delegation was severely castigated for permitting a clearly peripheral issue to escalate to the point where it potentially jeopardized the long-awaited breakthrough in superpower relations. Having rationalized the continuing commitment to the Saigon regime in terms of the demands of US credibility, the Administration now found the Soviet leadership paradoxically echoing the persistent assertion within NATO circles that American credibility was not at stake in Vietnam.

With both allies and adversaries refusing to endorse the Nixon–Kissinger claim that the stabilization of threat at the center was contingent upon the credibility of American commitments on the periphery, why did the Administration so fiercely resist any critical re-evaluation of the relative importance of Vietnam? Here the record is highly suggestive. In terms of the avowed goals of the Nixon–Kissinger strategy, an acceptance of this perception of the Vietnam conflict (with its logical corollary of an explicit dichotomy between the periphery and the center) would have implied a concomitant acquiescence to the kind of minimalist/compartmentalized conception of détente which the Administration sought to eschew. With SALT the undisputed centerpiece of US–Soviet relations, there was the dangerous temptation to identify détente narrowly as a category of deterrence (here again defined as the stabilization of threat at the center). Given the Administration's perceived linkage between the stability of the center and periphery, the central challenge to emerge was that of working towards 'rules of engagement' for contested areas so as to keep the ongoing political competition between the superpowers within reasonable and safe bounds.

The conclusion of the Basic Principles of Relations and the Agreement on the Prevention of Nuclear War at the May 1972 and June 1973 summit meetings, respectively, was regarded by the Administration as the initial step in the long-term process of translating a functional network of relations into a global *modus vivendi*. To many observers caught up in the euphoria of the US–Soviet summit meetings, the agreement between the superpowers on a set of 'basic principles' appeared to militate in favor of the Nixon–Kissinger 'structure of peace' – the new 'legitimate order.' From the Soviet position, the dialogue in and of itself served a useful function as it sustained what previously had been rather less the reality than what one observer has characterized as an 'ascriptive courtesy': the status of the Soviet Union as a full-fledged superpower. On the perceptual level, the aforementioned accords of 1972–3 were regarded as important symbolic affirmations of the Soviet Union's attainment of global political parity *vis-à-vis* the United States. Yet beyond these lofty political statements, it was SALT – universally held up as the quintessential example of bipolar strategic management (or superpower condominium) – which confirmed parity in terms of that most familiar of material measures of postwar strategic power.

The American response to the advent of rough parity (assessed in terms of numbers of 'strategic nuclear delivery vehicles') was striking. Most of the analysis which ensued focused essentially upon the technical implications of the Soviet development program. Significantly, scant attention was paid to either the political implications of strategic parity or, indeed, the political context in which any American Administration would envision the use of nuclear weapons.[59] For the United States, the new condition of numerical parity required a profound psychological readjustment, since in the public mind the long-standing American numerical advantage had somehow implied 'superiority' even after the acquisition of an 'assured destruction' capability by the Soviet Union. Confusion, however, was not confined to the general public. On the very heels of

President Nixon's enunciation of the concept of strategic sufficiency at his initial press conference, Secretary of Defense Laird inserted the qualification that the use of the term 'sufficiency' should in no way be taken to suggest that the United States had given up 'the idea of superiority.'[60] Within a context of 'mutual assured destruction,' such pronouncements appeared both hollow and potentially destabilizing.

While the Soviet Union's attainment of numerical parity satisfied perhaps the major prerequisites for the beginning of SALT, it had the additional effect of heightening the American sense of vulnerability within a strategic relationship whose stability, paradoxically, was contingent upon the maintenance of mutual vulnerability. To many, the *theoretical* threat which Soviet SS-9s posed to the American *Minuteman* force was taken as incontrovertible proof that the Soviet Union was bent on achieving a first-strike capability against the United States. This concern over *Minuteman* vulnerability within the Administration fostered the policy-making environment in which the decisions to deploy the ABM and MIRV systems were taken. The process which governed these responses to the build-up of Soviet forces reflected both the inherent problem of intellectual residue in American strategic thinking (i.e. negotiating the transition from superiority to parity) as well as the difficulty in overcoming the inertia of bureaucratic interests once vested in a given development program.

The use of the term 'parity,' when characterizing the post-1969 strategic balance, is a misleading one to the extent that it implies that a plateau had or has somehow been reached. Indeed, the onset of MIRV and the steady upgrading of warhead accuracies during the period under consideration augured the rise of qualitative improvements as the new focal point of strategic arms competition. This ominous development prompted many observers to conclude that the 1972 SALT I agreement owed its success largely to an accident of history when the nuclear arsenals of both superpowers allowed easy comparison and when verification depended merely on the ability to count launchers. The subsequent difficulties of negotiating SALT II within a context of asymmetrical force development (e.g. the cruise missile/*Backfire* bomber controversy of 1975–6) underscored the extent to which SALT I – and the stabilization of threat at the center – was contingent upon this fortuitous, albeit transient, convergence on the technological plane. With both parties on the threshold of major qualitative improvements not covered by the SALT I framework, the net effect, despite numerical constraints on launchers, was to make the process of mutual deterrence increasingly complex.

A belated recognition of this trend was reflected in the Administration's marked shift in perception *vis-à-vis* multiple warhead systems. The original decision to develop and deploy MIRVs had been rationalized in terms of their utility to penetrate the Soviet *Galosh* ABM system then under construction. In this role as an ABM penetrator, it was hailed by the Administration as a cost-effective and stabilizing response to the Soviet defense effort. Senatorial critics of the MIRV program contended that the hard target/counterforce capability derived from the wedding of increased numbers of warheads with improved accuracies would render precisely the opposite results. The Defense Department, noting the smaller intended yield of US warheads, attempted to downplay the counterforce potential of the American program while stressing the inherently destabilizing effect which Soviet MIRV systems would have when deployed.[61] Unlike the controversy over ABM, the decisions to deploy MIRVs failed to generate a heated domestic debate. Within the Administration, scant attention evidently was paid to the impact of a quantum increase in the number of available warheads on the stability of the central balance. At the time of the signing of the Vladivostok accord in 1974, this belated recognition prompted Kissinger to acknowledge: 'I would say in retrospect that I wish I had thought through the implications of a MIRVed world more thoughtfully in 1969 and 1970 than I did. What conclusions I would then have come to I don't know.'[62]

Within the politically charged atmosphere of US–Soviet relations following the October 1973 War, the theoretical vulnerability of land-based missile forces resulting from major qualitative improvements outside the purview of SALT I (e.g. MIRV deployments, warhead accuracy improvements) served to redirect American attention to the ongoing challenge of projecting a credible system of extended deterrence. As shall be discussed in chapter 5, concern centered upon the possibility that a perceived, albeit marginal, asymmetry in the central strategic balance could politically influence the outcome of crises along the periphery. In 1972 this problem appeared less immediately pressing for two reasons. First, as suggested by Kissinger's subsequent assessment cited above, the implications

of the new weapons technologies *vis-à-vis* the minimum requirement of strategic stability had not been fully explored. Second, and
perhaps more significant, on the political plane, it was envisioned
that the presumed efficacy of the Nixon–Kissinger strategy (that is,
the harmonization of the twin strategies of détente and politico-
military retrenchment) would generate a favorable relationship between the stability of the center and the periphery.

The May 1972 Statement of Basic Principles and the June 1973
Agreement on the Prevention of Nuclear War were regarded as
important contributions towards this end. Whereas the former
stipulated the renunciation of the pursuit of unilateral political
advantage, the latter obligated the parties to consult with each other
in those situations in which there existed the danger of escalation.[63]
As Kissinger characterized their importance during the Washington
summit:

The principal goal of the foreign policy of this administration ever since
1969 has been to set up what the President has called a structure of peace, by
which we mean an international system less geared to the management of
crises, less conscious of constant eruptions of conflict, in which the principal
participants operate with a consciousness of stability and permanence . . .
[In our negotiations with the Soviet Union] we have attempted to develop
certain principles of conduct by which the two great nuclear countries could
guide their expectations and by which both in relations to each other and in
their relations to third countries, they could calm the atmosphere and
replace purely military measures by a new attitude of a cooperative international system.[64]

The lofty nature of these basic principles, as well as their presentation, implied a degree of consensus on the bases of international
order which, in retrospect, was clearly exaggerated. That is not,
however, to conclude that these accords were merely an exercise in
'fatuous diplomacy' (to borrow Kissinger's caustic assessment of 'the
spirit of Camp David' in *The Necessity of Choice*). Their symbolic
importance, at least on the aspirational level, as an initial step in the
process of establishing a set of rules of engagement to moderate
superpower behavior in contested areas, should not (as many
Kissinger critics have done) be glibly dismissed. Yet, when presented
as part of the Administration's domestic attempt to sell politically
the concept of détente, they undoubtedly contributed to the generation of that unwarranted sense of euphoria which came to pervade
US–Soviet relations in the year following the Moscow summit. It was

during this brief period that, from the Administration's perspective, there existed at least some of the preconditions for the co-optation of the Soviet Union into a global *modus vivendi*.

Complementing SALT and the stability of the central strategic balance, the symbiotic relationship forged between superpower détente and the Nixon Doctrine – Kissinger's seamless web of relations – was viewed as facilitating the orderly post-Vietnam devolution of American power by providing the Soviet Union with a major incentive for the maintenance of regional stability. These (admittedly excessive) American hopes were shattered under the momentous impact of the events of October 1973. As will be considered at length in chapter 5, that dangerous episode in US–Soviet relations – one from which détente has really yet to recover – served to highlight the central paradox of the Nixon–Kissinger strategy. For while the American conception of détente, as it came to evolve after 1969, assumed the mutual acceptance of the new legitimate order (the stable structure of peace), the reality of superpower behavior continued to underscore the concomitant and unswerving drive by each to alter favorably that very structure through the pursuit of unilateral advantage on the periphery.

4 . THE NIXON–KISSINGER STRATEGY: 2. THE LIMITS OF POLITICO-MILITARY RETRENCHMENT

There are lessons to be learned from our Vietnam experience – about unconventional warfare and the role of outside countries, the nature of commitments, the balance of responsibilities, the need for public understanding and support. But there is also a lesson *not* to be drawn: that the only antidote for undifferentiated involvement is indiscriminate retreat . . . The Nixon Doctrine will enable us to remain committed in ways that we can sustain. The solidity of domestic support in turn will reverberate overseas with continued confidence in American performance.

Richard Nixon, 1 March 1971

It's his doctrine and he can damned well do what he wants with it.

Attributed to Henry Kissinger, 29 January 1971[1]

The Nixon doctrine and the evolution of American regional security policy

With American 'globalism' having foundered on the shoals of Vietnam, the premier foreign policy challenge facing the Nixon Administration in January 1969 was that of arriving at the new terms under which a continuing and active American involvement system could be sustained. To be sure, the Tet offensive of the previous year, like no other single postwar episode, had sharply called into question both the *instrumentalities* and the *ends* of American power. In the absence of the kind of domestic consensus which for two decades had ensured the continuity and coherence of US foreign policy, there were legitimate fears that the aftermath of the Vietnam debacle would witness a resurgence of American isolationism.[2] In December 1968 *The Economist*, reflecting overseas concern, was prompted to comment: 'It will be no small thing if America's enemies come to the conclusion that the Americans abandoned a major policy because they could not stand seeing what war looks like on television.'[3] It was within the context of these domestic and international exigencies that the newly-installed Administration sought to revitalize American foreign policy as the nation approached the post-Vietnam period.

Although the immediate problem remained that of the disengagement of US combat forces from Indochina, the more general one was posed by the global over-extension of American commitments. Hence, the post-1969 foreign policy debate, as it came to evolve, focused not just upon the ways (as it were) of managing defeat in Vietnam, but upon the nature and scope of American politico-military retrenchment along the periphery. Here, again, a large part of the analytical confusion arose from the paradoxical status accorded the Vietnam question within that debate. To a growing segment of the American public, the Vietnam conflict was perceived as an anomalous vestige of the Cold War from which American forces should be quickly extricated. The Administration, acknowledging the immobilization of American diplomacy which stemmed directly from the military impasse in Vietnam, accepted the logic of disengagement, but forcefully argued that the *manner* in which it was accomplished was of critical importance.

Though American involvement in Indochina was no longer rationalized in the language of John Foster Dulles or the Kennedy inaugural address, the overriding preoccupation with the maintenance of 'credibility' dictated that the United States could not (as the President liked to characterize pejoratively the position of his domestic critics) simply 'bug out'. As a result of this perpetuation of credibility as the criterion of American commitment, the exceptional nature of the 'commitment' to Saigon was discounted by the Administration. The chorus of appeals from American allies affirming that US credibility was not at stake in Vietnam fell upon deaf ears. Guided by the central premise of the Nixon–Kissinger strategy, it was argued that the erosion of stability on the periphery owing to a failure of American will would, by way of the subtle and complex feedback process discussed in chapter 3, invariably undermine the stability of the central balance itself. Thus, in terms of the Administration's ongoing attempt to operationalize its conception of international order – Kissinger's 'stable structure' – the process of disengagement from Vietnam was, paradoxically, to assume paradigmatic importance. With the perception of the close inter-relationship between the developments of the periphery and the center as a kind of intellectual backdrop, the central purpose of the Nixon Doctrine was to devise the new instrumentalities of American power which would permit a new, less overt US role in Third World regions.

There has been a tendency to regard Nixon's October 1967 article in *Foreign Affairs*, 'Asia after Vietnam', as the direct antecedent to the major policy pronouncement he subsequently made as President on Guam in July 1969. Although wrapped in much of the familiar Cold War rhetoric, the article has since been heralded for its anticipation of two of the major policy departures of the Nixon Administration: the China initiative and the Nixon Doctrine's emphasis upon the development of indigenous regional security systems.[4] Yet with respect to the latter, there is some evidence that, under the cumulative impact of events in Southeast Asia, the Johnson Administration was itself moving in the direction of a Nixon Doctrine-type approach by mid-1968. A report drafted during that period within the 'Senior Interdepartmental Group' on foreign internal defense policy advanced four policy prescriptions strikingly similar to those of the Nixon Administration a year later: (1) the United States, for a number of political, military, and economic reasons, will find that occasions will arise in the future when basic national interests will make it extremely undesirable that a given foreign insurgency succeed; (2) although not all internal instability arising from disruptive modernization is a threat *per se*, the United States cannot remain indifferent to subversion supported by a foreign power; (3) if direct intervention is deemed both important and feasible, the United States should seek to mount a multilateral effort of concerned allies; and (4) unilateral American action should be considered only as a last resort.[5]

In a similar exercise to that of the Nixon–Kissinger NSC in 1969–70, the Johnson Administration's SIG on foreign internal defense policy had sought to explore the new means of implementation by which it would prove possible to maintain American commitments during the post-Vietnam period. The question was framed somewhat differently within the legislative branch. Reflecting the volatile shifts of American public opinion during this period, Congressional attention focused not solely upon the implementation of American commitments, but, indeed, upon the continued desirability and utility of those security obligations. With the Nixon Administration in office less than two weeks, the Senate Foreign Relations Committee announced plans for a far-ranging investigation into the power of the executive and the military to dictate or influence foreign policy as part of a general review of American security commitments.[6] This action was followed in March (the month coincidently in which the

Senate approved the Non-Proliferation Treaty) with the passage by the Senate Foreign Relations Committee, over the objections of the State Department, of a National Commitments Resolution calling upon the Executive not to enter into further security obligations without the concurrence of Congress.[7]

These sentiments were not simply a reflection of Congressional disaffection with the Vietnam War. Rather, there was the firm belief amongst senior members of the Senate Foreign Relations Committee (most notably its chairman, Senator J. William Fulbright) that if the 'end of the postwar era' had indeed ushered in a new period of 'pluralism', then the United States should critically reassess its global network of security commitments. Increasingly, this expansive structure of commitments was regarded as but part of the ideological baggage of the Cold War period.

By the time of the Nixon inaugural, the slogan 'no more Vietnams' had already become an abstraction within the American political context. Although this attitude clearly shaped the milieu in which the Nixon Doctrine was formulated, it would be inappropriate to judge the Guam pronouncement as merely a belated presidential acceptance of the old 'never again' military beliefs that the United States should not again become involved in a land war on the Asian mainland. Part of the analytical problem in assessing the nature and impact of the Nixon Doctrine is that it did present itself on two separate levels. To be sure, it did offer, first and foremost, a concrete *strategy* for the disengagement of American forces from Indochina (*viz*. Vietnamization). Yet beyond that immediate objective, it sought to satisfy the intellectual and diplomatic prerequisites for the development of a wholly new *philosophy* to govern American security policy towards the Third World during the post-Vietnam era. Explicitly portrayed as a transitional policy, the Nixon Doctrine embodied the commitment to maintain regional military balances as a key means of maintaining stability and a substitute for direct American intervention.

In assessing the Nixon Doctrine, it is possible to delineate two distinct phases of its implementation. During the period immediately following its enunciation (1969–73), the Nixon Doctrine's emphasis, not surprisingly, was upon the disengagement of US combat forces from Indochina and the more general task of retrenchment in East Asia. The ensuing phase (1973–6) was shaped by three sets of events whose cumulative impact was to prompt a marked shift in the orientation of the Nixon Doctrine: first, the termination of direct American involvement in Southeast Asia as made possible by the conclusion of the Paris accords and the cosmetic success of Vietnamization; second, the deterioration of US–Soviet relations in the aftermath of the October 1973 Middle East War; third, and perhaps most important in terms of its overall effect on the international political economy, the so-called 'oil revolution'.

Under the profound influence of these events, the Nixon Doctrine was simultaneously pushed in two ostensibly compatible directions. The first consequence of the tumultuous events of 1973 was to create an even greater American reliance upon conventional arms transfers as an instrument of policy. This move was dictated to a considerable extent by the economic necessity of eliminating potentially massive balance of payments deficits through the 'recycling' of 'petrodollars' – hence the primary focus of the Foreign Military Sales program (outside the NATO geographical area) on the Persian Gulf.[8] And yet, significantly, this more pronounced emphasis of the Nixon Doctrine on conventional arms transfers to nascent regional powers was regarded as being wholly consonant with the political consequences of the October 1973 War *vis-à-vis* the state of US–Soviet relations. The net effect of that crisis had been to underscore dramatically the inability of the Nixon–Kissinger strategy to engineer regional stability through the feedback relationship which it sought to create between the twin strategies of détente and politico-military retrenchment. It was thus in the politically charged atmosphere following the fourth Middle East War that the utility of conventional arms transfers to regional 'middle powers' was increasingly justified by the Administration in terms of the necessity of containing the emergence of Soviet power. With the completion of this brief overview of the Nixon Doctrine, attention shall now focus more closely upon the first phase of its formulation and implementation.

During the period preceding Nixon's Asian tour of July 1969, considerable discussion within the Administration focused upon the nature and scope of American security assistance to the region following the extrication of American forces from Vietnam. Although the immediate context was Southeast Asia, the deliberations were regarded as having much wider implications. Here, the question of the limits of American politico-military retrenchment became fused with that of the proper role of the United States within the international system. On 18 July Kissinger outlined the

Administration's philosophy for post-Vietnam Asia during a White House background briefing:

The issue of the nature of commitments in the United States often takes the form of a discussion of legal obligations. But on a deeper level . . . the relationship of the United States to other countries depends in part, of course, on the legal relationships but more fundamentally on the conception the United States has of its role in the world and on the intrinsic significance of the countries in relationship to overall security and progress.

What we do want to discuss is . . . how these countries visualize their own future because, as one looks ahead to the next decade, it is self-evident that the future of Asia . . . will have to depend not only on prescriptions made in Washington, but on the dynamism and creativity and cooperation of the region.

We remain willing to participate, but we cannot supply all the conceptions and all the resources. The initiative has to move increasingly into that region. For that reason, it is important that we consider our view of their future.[9]

A week later, Nixon, much to the apparent surprise of his senior aides, elaborated upon these themes in an informal background briefing to the press on 25 July in the US officers' club on Guam. By the time of the President's Vietnam address of 3 November 1969, the 'Guam Doctrine' had been elevated by the White House to the loftier, more personalized status of the 'Nixon Doctrine' and distilled into three key points:

1 The United States will keep all its treaty commitments.
2 We shall provide a shield if a nuclear power threatens the freedom of a nation allied with us, or of a nation whose survival we consider vital to our security and the security of the region as a whole.
3 In cases involving other types of aggression we shall furnish military and economic assistance when requested and as appropriate. But we shall look to the nation directly threatened to assume the primary responsibility of providing the manpower for its defense.[10]

Under the rubric of 'Peace through Partnership' in its first self-described State of the World message, the attempt was made by the Administration to expand upon the general application of these principles:

[The] central thesis [of the Nixon Doctrine] is that the United States will participate in the defense and development of allies and friends, but that

America cannot – and will not – conceive all the plans, design all the programs, execute all the decisions and undertake all the defense of the free
world. We will help where it makes a real difference and is considered
in our interest.[11]

As characterized above, the political prerequisites of the Nixon
Doctrine necessitated a fundamental change in perception of the
American domestic and international environments. On the
military plane, its enunciation was complemented by two major
departures from US security policy of the previous decade. First, the
military expression of the change in political perception of the international system (the nature and level of potential threat) was a modest
scaling down of American capabilities. By 1971, defense spending,
taken as part of GNP, reached its lowest level since 1951: 7 percent –
a figure down from the Vietnam high of 9.5 percent in 1968. In his
first defense posture statement to Congress in February 1970, Secretary Laird justified this reduction both in terms of the demands of
combatting domestic inflation and the altered character of plausible
threats which American forces should prudently be designed to
counter. With respect to the latter, for example, it was argued that
the implications of the Sino-Soviet split should be incorporated into
American defense planning. As the possibility of a combined operation in Europe and Asia against the Western alliance appeared
extremely remote into the foreseeable future, Laird asserted that the
Administration's posture of strategic 'sufficiency' would permit the
reconfiguration of American forces from a 2½ to a 1½ war-fighting
capability.[12] Closely aligned to this restructuring scheme was the
second major departure in defense planning advanced as part of the
Administration's 'strategy of realistic deterrence'. Under that
strategy's 'total force' concept, the magnitude and effectiveness of
allied capabilities were to be more explicitly integrated into the
future planning and allocation of American defense forces.[13] The
obverse of this shift in attitude *vis-à-vis* the role of indigenous forces
was a renewed commitment to military assistance and foreign
military sales.

Paradoxically, the central feature of the Nixon Doctrine – its
ambiguity – was to be a source both of praise and criticism. To the
Administration and its supporters, ambiguity would permit American
diplomacy to regain the initiative and flexibility which the presumed
certainties of the Cold War had taken from it. Mindful of the
ramifications of the 1950 Acheson defense perimeter speech, Nixon

and Kissinger were determined to exploit the Nixon Doctrine's underlying ambiguity so that maneuver (and the ability to discriminate between cases) would not become a prisoner of declaratory policy. To American allies, ambiguity was depicted as a sign of maturity – the logical outgrowth of 'partnership' and 'dialogue':

We recognize that the Doctrine, like any philosophic attitude, is not a detailed design. In this case ambiguity is increased since it is given full meaning through a process that involves other countries. When other nations ask how the Doctrine applies to them in technical detail, the question itself recalls the pattern of the previous period when America generally provided technical prescriptions. The response to the question, to be meaningful, partly depends on them, for the Doctrine's full elaboration requires their participation. To attempt to define the new diplomacy completely by ourselves would repeat the now presumptuous instinct of the previous era and violate the very spirit of our new approach.[14]

Under this guise, the Nixon Doctrine, and the strategy of politico-military retrenchment that it implied, was to permit the Administration to engage in the kind of diplomacy of maneuver and manipulation made necessary by a world of nascent multipolarity. In this respect, the Nixon Doctrine was clearly intended by the President to be 'his doctrine' – one which could potentially address any number of contingencies. Under its avowed terms of reference, the 'test case' mentality which had previously promoted indiscriminate American involvement was to be supplanted by that of the new flexibility. Henceforth, the perceived interest which the United States would have in intervening in any particular case was itself to be subject to change. And yet, ironically, as part of the Administration's concerted attempt to cope with the implications of revitalized bipolarity, the demands of 'credibility' under the Nixon–Kissinger strategy would have the net effect of fostering its own test cases (as in Angola).

Critics of the Nixon Doctrine contended that it was a dangerously flawed policy which failed to provide either a vision or coherent framework for the conduct of US foreign policy.[15] In many quarters, it was forcefully argued that both the Nixon Doctrine's undisguised preference for the status quo – the rhetoric of 'stability' – and its underlying ambiguity – its supposed sensitivity to altered international circumstances and domestic conditions – would potentially transform the execution of American diplomacy into a perpetual *tour de force*. In so doing, this process served to heighten the unique fusion of style and substance within the Nixon–Kissinger strategy.

Again, it was this salient feature which contributed to the erosion of domestic support for the Administration's diplomacy.

Critics of the Nixon Doctrine focused upon two related aspects of policy. First, in failing to provide more tangible and rigorous *criteria for intervention*, the Nixon Doctrine's three principles were regarded by many as an inadequate guide for future American policy. The Administration's position, as affirmed in successive State of the World messages, was that in moving toward a posture of truly flexible response it would henceforth be prepared to act in those cases in which American 'interests' were 'involved' and where the proposed intervention would make a real difference. This policy formulation, however, appeared to side-step many of the disturbing and ongoing questions which directly stemmed from the US involvement in Vietnam. While reiterating an American willingness to assist directly those nations threatened by overt external aggression, the criteria of the Nixon Doctrine offered less substantive guidance when the matter was one of potential intervention on behalf of an ally threatened by internal subversion. The Vietnam debacle had underscored both the dangers of undertaking the commitment to preserve a specific national regime and the difficulties within the American political context of disengaging once the decision to intervene had been implemented.

While the third guideline of the Nixon Doctrine (with its emphasis upon the 'primary' role of indigenous forces) was hailed by the Administration as a major post-Vietnam adjustment in American regional security policy, the question remained as to how the United States would respond if that local effort should prove insufficient in the face of internal subversion (perhaps encouraged and aided from the outside). Given the Administration's reluctance to reappraise critically the structure of American commitments, interests and alliances within the context of politico-military retrenchment, the supposed virtues of ambiguity were given a skeptical hearing. This skepticism was of two sorts: conceptual criticism of the Nixon–Kissinger schema for international order – the new stable structure, and political criticism of the effects of Administration policy. It was argued that the continued maintenance of credibility as the criterion of American commitment (*viz.* Vietnam) confounded the Administration's avowed goal of moving towards a strategy of selective engagement.

This consideration leads to the second focal point of criticism which came to surround the Nixon Doctrine – namely, the ostensible contradiction between capabilities and commitments within the Nixon–Kissinger strategy. Despite Administration claims, critics contended that the underlying reality of the Nixon Doctrine was a policy of 'mechanistic force substitution' designed to provide political cover for the highly dubious Vietnamization program.[16] As Earl Ravenal argued in the January 1971 issue of *Foreign Affairs*:

> And so the 'balance' promised in the new security policy is achieved – but not by adjusting our commitments, restricting our objectives or modifying our conception of the interests of the United States. Rather, budgetary stringencies inspire a reduction in force levels; a '1½-war strategy' is tailored to fit the intractable realities; and a series of rationalizations is constructed to validate the new strategy – rationalizations that simply stipulate a reduced threat, count heavily on subsidized and coerced allied efforts at self-defense, and suggest an early nuclear reaction if our calculations prove insufficiently conservative.[17]

How then did the Nixon Administration hope to reconcile the continuance of American commitments with the requisite post-Vietnam contraction of US military capabilities? Once again, one must return to the Nixon–Kissinger strategy and the symbiotic relationship which the Administration sought to effect between the twin policies of superpower détente and the Nixon Doctrine. As discussed above, to varying degrees, each was to serve as the instrumentality of the other. Thus, the policy of superpower détente was viewed as a means of creating and ensuring the stable conditions along the periphery which would allow for an orderly devolution of responsibility to incipient regional powers. In effect it was hoped that the rhetoric of commitment, as evidenced in the first guideline of the Nixon Doctrine, could continue because the reality of détente would allow the commitments to remain unimplemented. The purpose of this section has been to examine the conceptual evolution of the Nixon Doctrine and its relation to the policy of superpower détente during the period prior to the October 1973 Middle East War. With this as background, attention shall now focus upon the record of its application in the region which supplied the initial political impetus for its formulation.

Vietnamization and the role of the Nixon Doctrine in Asia

The paradoxical status accorded the Vietnam question within the post-1969 foreign policy debate is striking. While on one level acknowledged as an anomalous vestige of the Cold War, the position that it ultimately assumed *vis-à-vis* the Nixon–Kissinger strategy conferred upon it paradigmatic importance. Thus it was that the scope of considerations brought to bear over Vietnam in 1969–70 proved identical to those subsequently advanced by the Ford Administration at the time of the Angolan Civil War. As discussed in chapter 3, the paradoxical status of the Vietnam question stemmed from the central emphasis placed upon the role of credibility within the Nixon–Kissinger strategy. As during the previous period of Cold War diplomacy, Administration officials continued to regard it as the criterion of American commitment. Within this context, the policy of disengagement pursued by the Nixon Administration after 1969 may be viewed as having been derived from many of the very same conceptual roots which had, in fact, initially fostered the American involvement in Vietnam.

Upon assuming office in January 1969, Kissinger sought to deflect liberal criticism of the Administration's handling of Vietnam with the plea: 'Give us six months.' During testimony before the Senate Foreign Relations Committee on 21 March, Secretary of Defense Laird was subjected to tough questioning as anti-war politicians began to break their silence. The committee's chairman, Senator J. William Fulbright of Arkansas, lectured: 'You've got to do something radical to change this war or we're going down the drain. Soon it will be Nixon's war, and then there will be little chance to bring it to an end. It is time to de-escalate and settle it.'[18]

Prior to inauguration, Kissinger, working out of the Hotel Pierre in New York, had assembled a special task force to prepare an 'A to Z' options paper on Vietnam (i.e. from the gradual and complete withdrawal of American forces to their indefinite presence). This study was complemented by a 28-question survey which was distributed to various agencies within the bureaucracy (the State and Defense departments; the CIA; the Military Assistance Command, Vietnam (MAC/V); and the American embassy in Saigon) on the day following the Nixon inaugural ceremony. The comments and replies to the questionnaire, submitted separately by each governmental branch so as to avoid the kind of useless pre-arranged cross-bureaucratic consensus which had plagued the Johnson Administration, were received by Kissinger on 21 February and provided the basis for the NSC's first major policy study, designated NSSM-1.

Two of the generally pessimistic findings contained within this document take on added significance when viewed in light of the methods by which the Nixon Administration continued to pursue the war while simultaneously seeking the extrication of American ground forces.[19] From the CIA came the report that the sustained air campaign of interdiction strikes in Laos and Vietnam had neither seriously affected the flow of men and supplies from the North nor significantly eroded Hanoi's determination to persist in the war. Equally disturbing in view of the Administration's desire to quickly de-Americanize the war (the term 'Vietnamization' was coined shortly thereafter by Melvin Laird) was the conclusion from the Office of the Secretary of Defense that it was unlikely that the ARVN (Army of the Republic of Vietnam) could ever be built up to match militarily the Viet Cong.

Despite the serious reservations expressed in NSSM-1 as to their efficacy, the Administration decided to move in both of these policy directions simultaneously. That is, it acted to escalate significantly the air war at the same time as it endeavored to forge the ARVN into an effective indigenous fighting force. Although taken virtually in tandem, the factors which motivated each of these decisions were to a large extent quite separate. The eventual increase in bombing to levels of unprecedented intensity was wholly consistent with the Nixon–Kissinger belief that fruitful diplomatic activity would only occur within the context of decisive military action. In their view, that the limited air campaign conducted by the Johnson Administration had proved ineffectual was an indictment of the previous strategy only insofar as it indicated that a quantum increase in bombing would be necessary in order to effect the desired political outcome. It is significant to note that within three weeks of the receipt of the reports from the bureaucracy which comprised NSSM-1, the NSC recommended that the President accept the long-denied request of the JCS and begin the 'secret' bombing of Viet Cong/NVA sanctuaries in Cambodia.[20]

Even before the Administration's formal enunciation of the Vietnamization program, there was a growing constituency within the Pentagon advocating a major revision in American military doctrine. Indeed, by the end of 1968 it was clear that General William Westmoreland's 'search and destroy' strategy was unworkable and needed to be supplanted by a more defensive one which emphasized American air and logistical support for the ARVN. The prime exponent of Vietnamization was Secretary of Defense Laird who regarded it as the centerpiece of the Nixon Doctrine and the necessary complement to the Administration's diplomatic efforts. Although Laird, former House Republican leader, was keenly aware of the domestic political dividends of Vietnamization, it is evident that he accepted the proposition that the ARVN could be transformed into a credible fighting force as an article of faith. While testifying before a House subcommittee in October 1969, Laird went so far as to claim that Vietnamization 'in itself could lead the way to military victory in the sense of the South Vietnamese being able to defend their country, even against North Vietnam.'[21] Laird's optimistic assessment was neither widely shared within the Administration nor the bureaucracy at large. Those familiar with the state of the ARVN argued that a realistic program of Vietnamization would take years (witness the effort in South Korea) and that the kind of short-term strategy advanced by Laird's working group at the Pentagon would be perceived by Hanoi as little more than a cloak for unilateral American withdrawal.

Kissinger harbored his own doubts, believing that Vietnamization was an opportunity which, if it ever existed, had been 'lost' by his predecessors.[22] Rather, he favored a two-pronged negotiating strategy designed to make the continuation of the war appear increasingly 'less attractive' to Hanoi while simultaneously seeking somehow to implicate the Communist great powers in a negotiated settlement. In adopting this approach, however, it remained uncertain as to what the precise relationship between Vietnamization, bombing and negotiations was to be. The tension which existed between using bombing both as a framework for Vietnamization and as a spur to negotiations was never fully resolved. It has been reported that Kissinger initially valued Vietnamization insofar as it ensured that once a peace accord was concluded, Saigon would be unable to argue that it was premature. At a later stage in the negotiations, Kissinger was concerned that the perception of a strong South Vietnamese regime stemming from the Vietnamization program might, in fact, inhibit Hanoi's willingness to sign an agreement.[23]

In order to erode Hanoi's will to persist in the war, Kissinger advanced a number of major departures from the Johnson strategy which Nixon readily embraced. Leslie Gelb and Richard Betts in their important study of the Vietnam decision-making process argue that this radical shift in the American conduct of the war reflected the whole-hearted acceptance of what they term the 'instrumental lesson' of Vietnam (*viz.* that the war was fought in the wrong way).

The three components of the Johnson strategy were: (1) gradual escalation; (2) a highly restrictive list of permissible operations (no mining of harbors, no bombing of population centers in North Vietnam, no large-scale conventional cross-border operations, etc.); and (3) a declaratory policy that sought to assure Hanoi and its allies that the United States had no intention of threatening the existence of North Vietnam.

In sharp contrast, the strategy adopted by the Nixon Administration in 1969 was one anchored to massive and rapid military action, to a much less restricted bombing target list, and coupled with a declaratory policy that was ominously silent about what might happen to the North Vietnamese regime if it persisted.[24] These features of the Administration's 'fresh approach' (as applied to the Vietnam conflict) prompted many observers narrowly to identify the Nixon Doctrine as but a grandiose rationale for the implementation of an 'off-shore' posture with emphasis on American air and naval power. The excessive claims made on behalf of the Vietnamization program when judged against the uneven if occasionally disastrous performance of the ARVN (e.g. in response to the North Vietnamese offensive of April–May 1972) did little to dispel this image.

The Administration justified its adoption of a policy of quick and massive escalation by the failure in Vietnam of the elegant theories of controlled and gradual escalation propounded by American strategic thinkers in the 1960s. Elliot Richardson, the then Under Secretary of State who enjoyed a close working relationship with Kissinger, publicly articulated the rationale underlying this shift: 'The large powers have found it increasingly difficult to determine the appropriate response to small-power provocation. The strategic concept of a graduated response has been undermined by the Vietnam experience. If the large power voluntarily abstains from using its full power or feels the strategic situation to be such that it cannot do so, it in effect loses the advantage of being a big power.'[25] Kissinger privately expressed the same point to his NSC aides in much more blunt terms: 'I refuse to believe that a little fourth-rate power like North Vietnam doesn't have a breaking point. The Johnson Administration could never come to grips with this problem. We intend to come to grips.'[26]

The failure of the North Vietnamese to adopt what the Administration considered a more forthcoming attitude following its peace proposal of May 1969 (complemented by secret meetings in Paris with Xuan Thuy) and the announcement of American troop withdrawals prompted Kissinger to initiate a new study of possible military options in Vietnam at the beginning of October. In order to ascertain Hanoi's breaking point, Kissinger assembled a select NSC/ Pentagon study group to consider the form that a 'savage blow' against North Vietnam might take. The military scenario depicted was that of massive air strikes and mining staggered with pauses to give Hanoi time to respond diplomatically in some way. In the end, the study group – primarily influenced by the civilian analysts – recommended against the implementation of the savage blow on both *technical* and *political* grounds. This finding sustained the CIA's conclusion earlier expressed in NSSM-1 that bombing would not significantly decrease the capability of North Vietnam to wage a major offensive in the South and which predicted that such an escalation in the war would spark significant American domestic disturbances. On the strength of this analysis, Kissinger recommended that the President opt to defer the implementation of the military options outlined in the savage-blow study. Although its resurrection came at the time of the North Vietnamese offensive in April 1972, it is significant to note that the air and naval actions announced by Nixon on 8 May were coupled with an important shift in the American negotiating position.

American activities in Cambodia and Laos were regarded collectively by the Administration as an important complement to the Vietnamization program wholly consistent with the spirit of the Nixon Doctrine. The Cambodian incursion of May 1970 was publicly justified in terms of the ongoing threat which the NVA/Viet Cong forces operating out of that country posed to the success of Vietnamization and the safe extrication of American forces. The immediate goal of the attack was to locate and destroy the legendary COSVN (Central Office for South Vietnam), described by Nixon in his address to the nation as 'the headquarters for the entire Communist military operation in South Vietnam.'[27] Likened, as one observer quipped, to some kind of Pentagon East made of reinforced concrete and buried 29 feet underground with a staff of 5,000, COSVN was, in reality, a myriad of free-floating Communist base camps. The impression conveyed by the Administration was that the Ho Chi Minh trail was the major, if not sole, conduit for Communist arms from the PRC into South Vietnam. In fact, this had only recently become the case: for the four years prior to the ouster of Prince

Sihanouk, it was the Cambodian port bearing his name which had primarily served in this function. Upon his ouster in March 1970, the Lol Nol regime moved quickly to close the port to Communist shipping. In so doing, the overall significance of the Ho Chi Minh trail was enhanced. It was within this context then that the various arguments advanced in favor of the interdiction of this route by South Vietnamese and, if necessary, American ground forces gained ascendancy within the Administration. The net effect of the May 1970 incursion, however, was to push Communist guerrillas further into the Cambodian interior, thus complicating the Lon Nol regime's own insurgency problem.

At the pre-invasion briefing to senior White House officials, Kissinger justified the action in terms which went beyond the immediate battlefield concerns in Indochina to the very essence, as he saw it, of the US–Soviet relationship: 'Look, we're not interested in it not being used as a base . . . We're trying to shock the Soviets into calling a conference, and we can't promote this by appearing weak . . . Anyone who wants to negotiate a peace must hang tough.'[28] Nixon's speech again emphasized the importance of the credibility of American commitments and ended on a characteristically hyperbolic note: 'If when the chips are down, the world's most powerful nation . . . acts like a pitiful helpless giant, the forces of totalitarianism and anarchy will threaten free nations and free institutions throughout the world.'[29] A year later, the President, acknowledging the reliance of the Lon Nol regime upon American airpower and military/economic assistance in its confrontation with the Khmer Rouge, characterized Cambodia as 'the Nixon Doctrine in its purest form.'[30]

The Cambodian incursion was repeated on a smaller scale in February 1971 when South Vietnamese forces penetrated 4–5 miles into Laotian territory in an attempt to sever the Ho Chi Minh trail. Unlike the Cambodian operation of the previous Spring, no American ground personnel were sent into Laos; US involvement was limited to the ferrying by helicopter of ARVN forces and the provision of tactical air support. The initial reports of ARVN gains in the Laotian 'panhandle' were hailed by the Administration as a vindication of its Vietnamization program. Given the heavy concentration of B-52 raids in that area, the ferocity of the North Vietnamese Army's combined armored/infantry counter-assault in the last week of February took the ARVN by surprise. By the middle of March, the South Vietnamese were in complete disarray and on the verge of virtual annihilation. Though the Administration steadfastly contended the ARVN's withdrawal from Laos constituted an 'orderly retreat', the contrasting image left with the American public was that of South Vietnamese Rangers clinging to the skids of US helicopters as they were evacuated to safety. Though the immediate American response to the Laotian debacle was a significant increase in the intensity of bombing so as to camouflage the deficiencies of Vietnamization, the implications of it were more profound and long-lasting. As Roger Morris, a former NSC aide to Henry Kissinger, concludes:

The paper victory of Lam Son 619 [code name of the Laotian operation] was a psychological blow to the South Vietnamese army from which it never recovered. The defeat was, in a critical sense, the parent of the final collapse of 1975. But in the Spring of 1971 the cover up of the disaster continued for all the familiar bureaucratic reasons of outward deceit and inner self-deception that accompanied the war in both Saigon and Washington. Most important in ignoring the reality was that Kissinger began that May the final, twisting diplomatic sequel that led to a settlement. And Kissinger and Nixon were to abandon Saigon much as their forerunners originally had become ensnared in the country, in a weary, expedient blindness to the truth of what they were doing.[31]

After the dramatic announcement of 15 July 1971, the perception of Asian nations to the Nixon Doctrine was dominated not so much by the new, less overt security role that the United States was assuming in Indochina as by the altered state of its relations with the PRC. Prior to that, allied reaction, like that of American domestic critics of the Nixon Doctrine, centered upon the apparent contradiction between the contraction of capabilities and the maintenance of commitments. Given the Nixon Doctrine's ostensible similarity to the Eisenhower Administration's New Look, there was concern that the implementation of the former, like that of the latter 15 years earlier, would lead to a greater reliance upon tactical nuclear weapons. Following the Peking summit meeting there was heightened sensitivity in both countries to the complex interrelationship between the triangle of great power relations and local stability. As inhabitants within a potential theater of conflict, the South Koreans, in particular, were concerned that their country might well become the focal point of tensions arising from this new constellation of power.

The American pursuit of a *rapprochement* with China was regarded by Nixon and Kissinger as the necessary complement to their policy of politico-military retrenchment in Asia. Indeed, it could be argued that the kind of global *modus vivendi* that they were attempting to forge with the Soviet Union via the harmonization of the twin policies of détente and the Nixon Doctrine was precisely what they were hoping to replicate in this regional context with the PRC.[32] Thus, the improvement of relations on the great power level, in this case China, was perceived as fostering the stable regional conditions so as to permit an orderly devolution of American power to nascent 'middle powers'.

In East Asia, the logical candidate for a devolution of American responsibility within the terms of the Nixon Doctrine was Japan. Though an economic superpower, Japan had abstained from a more active regional role during the postwar period – particularly in the realm of security – for fear of provoking hostile domestic and regional reaction. With the change in political atmosphere resulting from the negotiation of the return of Okinawa in 1969, however, it appeared as though Japan might be prepared to move in the direction of such a role. These hopes were dashed by two sets of 'shocks': first, the Nixon pronouncements of July–August 1971 (i.e. the China initiative and the Administration's 'New Economic Policy') which eroded Japanese confidence in the United States as a reliable partner; and second, the oil revolution of 1973–4 which served to underscore Japan's vulnerability within the international economy. The combined effect of these events was to inhibit the development of a more dynamic Japanese foreign policy. Indeed, it was not until August 1977 with the first visit of a Japanese Prime Minister to the ASEAN states that one could detect the cautious beginning of a transformation in that nation's regional role which many analysts had anticipated since the turn of the decade.

The pattern of American policy towards Japan during the period under consideration is clearly one of missed opportunities and a certain disregard of Japanese sensitivities. In retrospect, it is striking that the Nixon Doctrine refrained from transferring regional security responsibilities to Japan – the one center of allied power that could discharge such responsibilities in East Asia.[33] Here, as one observer quipped, part of the answer may rest in the fact that the United States was becoming friendlier with its traditional competitors (*viz.* China) at the same time as it was becoming more competitive with its traditional friends (e.g. the problem of Japanese–

American trade relations). Yet, the question was not solely one of American reluctance. To be sure, the Japanese themselves were resistant to any prospective change in their bilateral relationship with the United States which entailed the adoption of a more activist regional security role.

This type of disjunction between American policies and those of its regional partners invariably raised broader questions about the efficacy of the Administration's approach to politico-military retrenchment. A devolution of American power to whom and for what ends? Would there necessarily be a coincidence of interests between patron and client? What of indigenous sources of instability? Would the Nixon–Kissinger approach to regional security with its emphasis upon the role of preponderant local powers prove more effective than previous policies in coping with such internally generated threats to allied regimes? Although the Administration clearly viewed the Nixon Doctrine's underlying ambiguity as a major asset providing it scope for diplomatic maneuver, the inevitable consequence was the persistence of such concerns to American allies.

The Nixon Doctrine and the role of regional 'middle powers'

The successful implementation of the Nixon–Kissinger strategy rested upon a fundamental shift in American attitude toward both allies and adversaries. A reflection of this change was the President's 1972 foreign policy report to Congress which, for the first time, openly proclaimed that American alliances were 'no longer addressed primarily to the containment of the Soviet Union and China behind the American shield'.[34] Through the adroit application of linkage, it was hoped that the expanding web of relations between the United States and the Soviet Union could serve as a means of influencing, and hopefully, mitigating, Soviet behavior. Closely related in Administration thinking to this effort to stabilize the superpower relationship was the development of regional 'middle powers' under American auspices. These pivotal, locally preponderant states were to be the recipients, as it were, of American devolution and become increasingly responsible for the promotion and maintenance of regional stability. Paradoxically, the emergence of these new centers of different kinds of power resulted in a certain *fragmentation* of the international system as a whole during a period when diplomacy had become truly *global*.

The Administration's initial moves in the area of regional security policy (especially the Nixon Doctrine and its surrounding rhetoric of local self-sufficiency) were widely seen as embodying a genuine American acceptance of the implications of nascent multipolarity – the so-called 'new pluralism'. The clear hope of Nixon and Kissinger was that a modest devolution of American power on the periphery could be accomplished without any concomitant gain for either of its Communist great power adversaries. The feedback relationship that the Administration sought to effect between the twin policies of superpower détente and the Nixon Doctrine through the various mechanisms of linkage politics was regarded as one way of coping with the apparent contradiction between the reduction of capabilities and the maintenance of commitments. The local efforts suggested by the Nixon Doctrine were not narrowly conceived as an adjunct to the global *modus vivendi* achieved on the superpower level. Rather, they were to serve as a kind of regional safety-net, presumably consonant with American interests, should there develop a local crack in the stable structure.

Despite the Nixon Doctrine's emphasis upon the development of regional middle powers, it is striking that the Administration refrained from transferring regional security responsibilities to the two centers of allied power which were indeed capable of assuming such a role – Japan and Western Europe. The case of Japan – and the ambivalent attitude toward it – has been considered in the previous section's analysis of American politico-military retrenchment in East Asia. With respect to the Nixon Doctrine's application in Western Europe, one detects the same kind of ambivalence in American policy. There, on the central front, the 'sharing of responsibilities' implied by the Nixon Doctrine was held in Washington to be virtually synonymous with the policy of economic 'burden-sharing' within the Atlantic alliance (e.g. offset payments for the stationing of American forces in West Germany, etc.). While seeking to link advantageously security and economic issues in this way, the Administration resisted both independent European diplomatic initiatives (e.g. *Ostpolitik*) and domestic demands for a reduction of American forces in Europe (as embodied in the Mansfield amendment). Through these actions (notwithstanding the intervening rhetoric of Kissinger's ill-fated 'Year of Europe' speech in 1973),[35] the circumscribed nature of Administration plans for a devolution of US security responsibilities in Western Europe, as part of the general post-Vietnam contraction of American power, was made evident.

American ambivalence, however, was matched by European doubts and disunity. Both factors hindered US efforts to deal with Western Europe as a coherent entity. While desirous of maintaining maximum scope for diplomatic maneuver, the European allies were concerned that a genuine devolution of American power would translate into much higher defense expenditures and an erosion in the credibility of the American commitment. This latter factor reflected residual European fears that the Nixon Doctrine was a sign of US neo-isolationism. Moreover, though 'the end of the postwar era' had been proclaimed, such a process also threatened to upset delicate continental political sensitivities. Indeed, it was widely acknowledged that any prospective transfer of American security responsibility to 'Europe' meant, in effect, West Germany. In the absence of a concerted European defense effort under these circumstances there was concern that, over time, the continent might become politically dominated under the shadow of Soviet military preponderance. American analysts ominously warned of the dangers of 'Finlandization' in Western Europe.

On the periphery, the transitional and ambiguous nature of the Nixon Doctrine was evidenced in the awkward, uncoordinated manner in which the Administration conducted relations with those countries which were nominally targeted to be the recipients of any regional devolution of American power – Brazil, Zaire, Iran and Indonesia. Although this tentative, *ad hoc* approach to regional security questions might be attributed to the general state of flux within the international system, it is also evident that these matters were considered of secondary importance relative to the Administration's major diplomatic undertakings – the Vietnam negotiations, the opening to China, and SALT.

The manner in which the confluence of contending images characterized above impacted upon the policy-making process (specifically, the traditional dilemma of integrating force and diplomacy) will be considered in the concluding section of this chapter. In the present discussion of the role of regional middle powers under the Nixon Doctrine, perhaps the most salient aspect of the Administration's approach was a perpetuation of the overly optimistic assumption that a long-term consonance of interests could be sustained between the United States and its various regional champions. In so doing, the Nixon–Kissinger approach failed to differentiate critically amongst contending conceptions of security both *within* and *between* regions. Here, the analytical problem is twofold. First, within a region there is often no common perception of threat and its definition. Second, what one means by security – that is, the criteria themselves – may significantly vary from region to region.

For the Administration, regional security, particularly after the October 1973 Middle East War, was viewed in terms of the containment of Soviet power on the periphery. This perception, however, was not always shared by its ostensible regional partners. In the case of Indonesia, for example, there was the widespread belief that President Suharto would adopt a regional posture compatible with American interests (as he had led the military coup in 1965 which overthrew the markedly pro-Communist regime of President Sukarno). These hopes were dashed when the Indonesian President, visiting Washington four weeks after the onset of the Cambodian operation, reaffirmed his country's non-aligned status and castigated the American incursion into that neutral country in the strongest terms.[36]

Relations with Brazil posed similar problems of contending security perspectives both within and between regions. That the Administration regarded Brazil as the focal point of its regional security policy in that area was made manifest during the state visit of Brazil's authoritarian President, General E. G. Medici, to Washington in early December 1971. In praising 'the Brazilian miracle' and the Medici record at the White House banquet in the visiting President's honor, Nixon remarked that Washington would continue to orient its regional policy around Brazil 'because we know that as Brazil goes, so will go the rest of that Latin American continent . . .'[37] Though Brazil – the locally preponderant power both strongly anti-Communist and favorably disposed toward US investors – appeared to satisfy the criteria of the Nixon Doctrine, the Administration's tendency to frame security questions in geopolitical terms prompted it to miscalculate regional reaction to the preferential treatment accorded the Medici regime. The interventionary role implied by the very notion of an American devolution of power – albeit disguised in the rhetoric of 'shared responsibilities' – was viewed within the region as but further confirmation of Brazil's desire for expansion at the expense of its neighbors. Clearly Argentina, a nation with a history of seeking to unite the smaller Spanish-speaking countries against either US or Brazilian hegemony, felt slighted by the preferential treatment accorded Brazil by the Administration.

As in other specific regional contexts, the application of the Nixon Doctrine in Latin America suffered from the problem of contending security perspectives. This reaction ran contrary to the concepts of 'total-force' planning and regionalism underlying the Nixon Doctrine in which it was assumed that there would be a consonance of regional interests sufficient to bind a diverse group of countries both to the United States and to each other. In the Latin American case, the Administration miscalculated both the degree to which a convergence of interests with Brazil was possible (witness the often acrimonious exchange between the two over Brazil's unilateral claim to 200-mile territorial waters) and the hostile perception of that special security relationship by the adjoining states in the area.

Though in many respects an exceptional case, the evolving American relationship with Iran after 1969 was hailed by the Administration as a paradigmatic application of the Nixon Doctrine. From the late 1940s the United States had been intimately involved in the development of Iran's various military programs. Yet significantly, in light of subsequent events, even in the immediate postwar period there was an evident discrepancy between the Shah's perception of Iran's security requirements (as manifested in military procurement) and that of the United States. The psychological dependency of the Iranian leadership on Washington increased markedly after the American-assisted restoration of the Shah in 1953. This was complemented by a real material dependency on US grant and budgetary assistance until 1967. At that time, the revenues generated by its burgeoning oil industry permitted it to move from grant-aid to credit-purchases from the United States.

The announcement in 1968 of the British intention to withdraw from positions 'East of Suez' by 1971 found the US unprepared and disinclined to substitute its presence for that of Britain's in the Persian Gulf. The State Department's country director for the Arabian Peninsula bureau of Near Eastern and South Asian affairs publicly confirmed this stance in an October 1968 address: 'Local leaders must and will carry on after the end of Britain's historic role. The United States will continue to do what it can to help, but there can be no question of any "special role" in Gulf affairs.'[38] Two weeks prior to the enunciation of the Nixon Doctrine on Guam, Kissinger ordered the NSC staff to begin a study of the Persian Gulf situation. Designated NSSM-66, the NSC report concluded that Iran, militarily and economically supported by the United States, could fill the vacuum left by the British. In terms of the Nixon Doctrine, Iran was, at least ostensibly, the ideal case of a state whose leadership was psychologically prepared and materially capable of assuming a preponderant role within an evolving regional security system.

Though stressing the apparent congruence of its interests with that of the West, Iran's shift from grant-aid to credit-purchases in the late 1960s provided it with an unprecedented scope for maneuver in its relations with the United States. This was manifested in early 1969 when the Shah indicated his opposition to the continuation of an American presence in Bahrain after 1971 as part of his more general opposition to any attempt by the superpowers to fill the vacuum created by the British withdrawal. Seeking 'to make the Persian Gulf a closed sea,' he believed that such an American course of action would invariably trigger a more activist and destabilizing Soviet policy with regional foci in Iraq and South Yemen.[39] Significantly, this call by the Iranian leader for the exclusion of non-littoral powers from the Persian Gulf antedated Nixon's pronouncement on Guam. During his state visit to Washington in October 1969 the Shah met ranking members of the Senate Foreign Relations Committee and advanced a plan under which Iran would annually allocate a $100 million oil quota for the United States in exchange for American arms on favorable terms. It was argued that this oil for arms relationship would be both economically beneficial to the United States (given its chronic balance of payments deficits and increasing dependence on imported oil) and consonant with the self-help philosophy of the Nixon Doctrine. Though the Administration eschewed such an explicit linkage across issue areas in 1969–70, it was unwillingly propelled in that direction three years later in the wake of the 'oil revolution'.

The failure of the United States adequately to support Pakistan during its December 1971 conflict with India influenced the Shah's thinking in two ways. First, it further eroded what was an already debased estimate of the value of an American treaty commitment (in spite of the glowing reaffirmation embodied in the first principle of the Nixon Doctrine); and second, it reinforced his belief in the necessity of creating a regionally preponderant, militarily self-sufficient Iran. This dual lesson was reiterated by the Iranian Prime Minister, Abbas Hoveyda, who concluded that while CENTO remained a nice 'club' – a practical forum in which to develop economic projects and to discuss ideas – it could hardly be characterized 'an effective alliance.'[40]

Following the 'dismemberment' of Pakistan, Iranian anxiety was further heightened with the conclusion of a Treaty of Friendship and Cooperation between Iraq and the Soviet Union on 6 April 1972. This provided the immediate security context for discussions between the Shah and Nixon on 30–31 May 1972 following the Moscow summit. Though with the Nixon Doctrine the United States clearly ceased to be a brake on Iranian arms purchases as it had arguably been during the 1960s, it was at the time of the May meeting that Nixon and Kissinger accepted the concept of an open-ended, so-called *carte blanche* arms transfer program for Iran. To be sure, the momentum of American arms sales to Iran was increased as a result of the Tehran meeting. Within a year, the Shah was able to confirm to an interviewer that 'we are getting anything and everything non-atomic that the US has.'[41]

The nature and timing of the Nixon Administration's *carte blanche* pledge to the Shah is noteworthy in several respects. First, by the time of the Tehran meeting in May 1972, Iran's definition of security had expanded beyond merely the defense of its own territorial integrity to include the Strait of Hormuz and its approaches in the Gulf of Oman. With that broadening of the Iranian conception of security – admittedly a change facilitated by its declining material dependence on the United States – came what was less a new sensitivity to its regional environment than a renewed confidence in its ability to shape that environment.[42] Over time, this fostered a more activist, occasionally interventionist, Iranian regional role. A manifestation of this expanded security conception was the despatch of Iranian forces by the Shah to Oman to assist in the suppression of the Dhofar rebellion.[43] Second, complementing this broadened regional security role was an increased tendency on the part of Iran to assess its defense needs and to configure its armed forces with specific reference to those adjacent to it in the Soviet Union. This correspondence between Soviet capabilities and Iranian procurement requests is striking: MiG-25 overflights of Iran triggered an extraordinary request by the Shah for the ultra-secret American air reconnaissance craft, the SR-71; the Iranian decision to push for the purchase of British *Chieftain* tanks rather than additional American M-60s was justified solely in terms of the former's much better match-up against the new generation of Soviet armor;[44] Soviet tactical air superiority in the region precipitated the Iranian request for advanced American aircraft, such as the F-14A long-range interceptor and the E-3A AWACS (Airborne Warning and Control System).[45]

Third, and finally, given the conclusion of the Nixon–Kissinger agreement with the Shah prior to the quintupling of oil prices and following the regional developments noted above, it could be argued that the pre-1973 transition of the United States from restraining patron to acquiescent partner was motivated less by a desire to expand American arms sales than from a congruence of geo-strategic perspective. Kissinger subsequently asserted:

On all major international issues, the policies of the United States and the policies of Iran have been parallel and therefore mutually reinforcing. Those countries which have represented the greatest threat to the security of Iran are also those countries whose domination of Iran would have a profound effect on the global balance of power or on the regional balance of power, and would therefore have profound consequences for the United States. In all the years of our cooperation, Iran has never gone to war or threatened to go to war for any purpose which would not have been parallel to our own. And this cooperation has been all the more significant because it grew out of a leadership that is clearly independent and that pursues its conception of its own national interest based on a history of 2,500 years of Iranian policy.[46]

From the Administration's perspective, the development of a special arms relationship with Iran was an important political signal consonant with its evolving 'twin-pillars' approach[47] to Persian Gulf security. It is significant to note that prior to the May meeting in Tehran the Pentagon remained unreconciled to the Nixon–Kissinger line on arms transfers to Iran. Questioning the ability of the Iranian armed forces to absorb advanced American military technology, the Pentagon specifically advised the White House on the eve of the Nixon trip against making a firm commitment to the Shah to sell Iran the F-14 or F-15.[48] This as well as other conventional arms transfers within the FMS program was politically justified by the Administration through reference to the Nixon Doctrine and the philosophy of military assistance which it implied.[49]

Quite apart from promoting Iran's transition into a middle power for reasons of regional stability, Washington perceived Iranian defense needs *vis-à-vis* the more traditional criteria of a state which shared a 1,300-mile frontier with the Soviet Union. The increasing tendency of the Shah to configure his armed forces with an eye toward the nature and disposition of Soviet capabilities was thus not inconsistent with the American conception of Iranian defense requirements. As before the Nixon Doctrine, the development of an Iran less prone to succumb to potential Soviet pressure was seen to be clearly in the American interest. Indeed, when the Nixon Doctrine became a more overt component of the American strategy to contain the expansion of Soviet power in the period following the October 1973 War, this interest was viewed in even more heightened terms.

In assessing the development of the US–Iranian *security* relationship between 1969 and 1976 the record is clear. In three respects – the containment of Iraq, the establishment of a working relationship with Saudi Arabia, and the suppression of the South Yemen-assisted Dhofar rebellion in Oman – the role which the Shah assumed in the Gulf (with explicit reference to the Nixon Doctrine) did enhance the region's overall stability. From the time of the British announcement in January 1968, American and Iranian security interests began to converge.[50] Yet the *carte blanche* agreement of May 1972 did not create this interdependent relationship. It was, rather, a reflection of it. On the Iranian domestic plane the perception of this congruence of security interests completed the process set in motion in 1953. With it, the future of US interests in Iran became inextricably linked with the Shah's fate.[51] As a result of this subtle process, the Nixon Doctrine, like its Cold War precedents, fostered an American decision-making environment in which the security of the 'nation' – in this case Iran – was increasingly held to be synonymous with the security of a specific 'regime'. The demise of the Nixon Doctrine and the system of regional middle powers which it sought to promote ostensibly came with the Iranian Revolution. The impact of this development on the American debate over regional security questions will be assessed in the concluding chapter of this study.

Force and diplomacy after Vietnam

Throughout this study of the Nixon–Kissinger diplomacy, the focus of analysis has invariably returned to two unifying themes: first, the question of 'image' in international politics and its influence upon the decision-making process; and second, the special difficulties of integrating force and policy in the nuclear age. In chapter 1, it was argued that during the Cold War – a period in which the United States pursued what has been characterized as a foreign policy of 'undifferentiated globalism' – there was extreme resistance to any reappraisal of the prevailing bipolar image of the international system. Results not fully consonant with the implications of that image (such as the credibility problems of massive retaliation or the Sino-Soviet rift) prompted not a re-evaluation of the validity of the underlying premises of American policy. Rather, these circumstances precipitated a search for more efficacious means to achieve objectives upon which there was a continuity of Cold War consensus. Successive Administrations asserted that the image of anti-Communist global engagement remained fundamentally valid, but that it was the insidious nature of the *threat* which had become diversified. They contended that it was necessary for the United States to differentiate critically amongst the means at its disposal so as to enable it, in any given crisis situation, to differentiate adroitly the type of reciprocal threat (from all-out nuclear to counter-insurgency) which could be credibly brought to bear. Strategic doctrine was thus subject to alteration in order to ensure the maintenance of the prevalent American image of the international system. In retrospect, this process of deftly discriminating between the categories and levels of threat – the differentiation of means within the Cold War context – belied a tacit differentiation of ends or commitments.

In shattering the domestic consensus which had sustained two decades of postwar policy, the Vietnam debacle sharply called into question both the instrumentalities and ends of American foreign policy. As never before, the United States was politically and, perhaps more significantly, psychologically prepared to cast off an admittedly defective bipolar image in favor of one which reflected the implications of multipolarity – what Kissinger hailed as the new pluralism. And yet, as discussed above, the emergence of the Soviet Union as a fully-fledged global military power (through the attainment of strategic nuclear parity with the United States and the dramatic expansion of its conventional capabilities), in conjunction with the unfolding nature of the détente process, had the net effect of conferring an ostensibly new legitimacy to the image of bipolarity during a period in which its relevance across a broad spectrum of issues was clearly waning. It was from this confluence of contending images – and the competitive demands which they reflected – that the post-1969 policy dilemmas largely arose. Whether the issue was Vietnam or Angola, the debate itself took the form of a clash in perspectives. While proponents of the geopolitical school were prone to regard Third World sources of instability within the East–West context of global US–Soviet engagement, those of a regionalist perspective advocated policies which underscored the importance of indigenous circumstances and were thus held to be consonant with the implications of the new pluralism.

Though the Administration seized upon the rhetoric of pluralism in successive State of the World messages, its actions over time appeared to be animated rather more by an image of the international system which, at least in military terms, remained essentially bipolar. Within this context, pluralism became a virtual synonym for the Kissinger diplomacy of maneuver – a foreign policy approach which tended, as noted above, to blur the distinction between allies and adversaries. Given the commanding American position across the various hierarchies of power, it was thought that pluralism (as so defined) would liberate the Administration from the rigidities of Cold War policy by permitting it to establish a favorable set of relations with the emerging new centers of different kinds of power. With the general downgrading of ideological considerations in its calculations, the Administration's hope of assuming the rather mercurial role of central balancer within a nascent multipolar system was tantamount to a kind of American Gaullism. Though this may have been its long-term goal, the concomitant – albeit 'flawed' emergence of the Soviet Union as a superpower militated against the adoption of such a foreign policy orientation.

Over time, the manner in which this confluence of contending images was internally reconciled within the decision-making process resulted in the shift in emphasis of Administration policy from the new pluralism to the 'new containment'. This process, whose roots may be traced to the superpower crises of 1969–71 (Cuba, Jordan, and the Indian subcontinent, etc.), was given added impetus by the events of October 1973 and the dramatic impact which that episode had on the Administration's assessment of Soviet intentions. Thus, whereas the Nixon Doctrine was originally hailed as a post-Vietnam approach to regional security consonant with the implications of pluralism (e.g. the fostering of incipient regional middle powers), it thereafter became more explicitly addressed to that task which

Kissinger characterized in 1975 as the 'problem of our age' – the containment of Soviet power.

From this perspective, the Nixon Doctrine appears less the radical departure in American postwar strategic doctrine which it ostensibly heralded than yet another point along that very same continuum. Indeed, that it was later more overtly identified with Administration attempts to contain Soviet power on the periphery suggests that the Nixon Doctrine is best viewed as a transitional strategy, more a legacy of the Truman Doctrine than a 'fresh approach' designed to meet the complexities and exigencies of a new epoch in international relations. With respect to the evolution of the means–ends relationship within American postwar foreign policy, it thus emerges as but a continuation of the process traced in chapter 1 – that is, the differentiation of means within the prevailing bipolar image of the international system. Under the new Administration, selective engagement and indirect assistance to support local efforts were to supplant the Cold War approach in which direct American intervention had remained the ultimate recourse. In these terms, the Nixon Doctrine was wholly consistent with previous attempts – from limited war to massive retaliation to flexible response – to adjust the instrumentalities of American power in the face of new domestic and international realities.

The wedding of the Nixon Doctrine to the Administration's new strategy of containment was, however, to have broad policy ramifications. As we have seen, the Nixon Doctrine's original embrace of the policy of selective engagement was motivated by the belief that if there were no longer to be 'test cases' for wars of national liberation, then the interest one would have in intervening in any particular instance could be subject to change. This was the essence of the American reaction to two decades of 'undifferentiated globalism' (as manifested in Vietnam) and the diplomacy of immobility which it had fostered. And yet, the demands of credibility – still the criterion of commitment – within the Nixon–Kissinger strategy was wholly to confound such a re-orientation of American foreign policy. Given the close interrelationship between the stability of the center and the periphery upon which the Nixon–Kissinger strategy was premised, selective engagement proved impossible. As during the preceding period, every case – whether Jordan, Bangladesh or Angola – was regarded as a test case, as part of the East–West matrix of security concerns. Such a perception of crises on the Afro-Asian periphery was the necessary complement to the notion of an indivisible détente. Paradoxically, the primacy of this belief provided the basis upon which Vietnam – that ostensible vestige of the Cold War – assumed paradigmatic importance within the Nixon–Kissinger strategy.

As discussed in chapter 1, during the Cold War period of rigid bipolarity, emphasis in American regional security policy was placed upon the elaboration of formal alliance structures which were to be bolstered by the Western great powers and envisaged to serve the ends of containment. An important complement to this regional security orientation, however, was an attitude towards (and supposed comprehension of) the dynamics of the modernization process as expressed in the slogan 'nation-building'. Here, one notable departure of the Nixon Doctrine – perhaps an honest recognition of the inefficacy of the theories of 'social engineering' so fashionable in the early 1960s – was its failure to be wedded to any specific model of Third World modernization. The Administration's relative indifference to development assistance was reflected in successive budgetary cutbacks at the Agency for International Development.[52] In light of the Nixon Doctrine's emphasis upon conventional arms transfers to developing nations, it is striking that scant, if any, consideration was devoted within the Administration to the question of the impact of these arms sales/grants – as part of the broader process entailing the wholesale transfer of Western technology – upon the domestic structure of the recipient states. This analytical failure was tacitly acknowledged by Kissinger in the aftermath of the Iranian Revolution.[53]

With the quantum increase in foreign military sales under the Nixon Doctrine, arms transfers increasingly became a major foreign policy instrument.[54] In the Kissinger diplomacy, the growing dependence of various recipients on the United States for spare parts and training was regarded as an effective means of manipulating the behavior of these allied states in much the same way as the entangling web of relations – the linkage process – was to moderate Soviet behavior. This attitude was evidenced in the Secretary of State's cryptic reference in 1974 that he was fashioning with these states 'reasons for restraint.'[55] During the post-1973 phase of the Nixon Doctrine – that is, that in which its focus was primarily, though not exclusively, on the Persian Gulf – three sets of problems emerged which confounded the Kissinger approach.

First, the Nixon Doctrine's avowed policy of selective engagement, politico-military retrenchment, and diminished involvement, paradoxically, necessitated an increased American physical presence.[56] In the case of Iran, for example, it has been reported that there were some 11,400 military related personnel and dependents operating in that country by 1975.[57] Second, contrary to Kissinger's conception of the arms relationship, the increasing reliance under the Nixon Doctrine on regional middle powers for the performance of vital functions (in Iran's case, maintaining open access through the Strait of Hormuz) had the net effect of placing Washington, in its role as the principal weapons supplier, in a dependent position.[58] Moreover, the long-term operation of such a client system was contingent upon the existence of a close correspondence (if not actual congruence) of interests between the regional actor and the United States. Given the Iranian government's rapid purchase program of over 1500 tanks and 400 advanced combat aircraft, many observers wondered aloud as to how the Administration would respond if the Shah became involved in a foreign venture which was not perceived to be in the American interest. In that situation the United States might have been confronted with the awkward choice of either supporting its client (specifically in the area of servicing high technology weapons systems) or watching its military equipment in the hands of a close ally go down to defeat. In this way, arms transfers – whatever the *pro forma* rhetorical assurances of the Nixon Doctrine – both raised the specter of unwilling involvement and established the prerequisites for a 'reverse influence' relationship between recipient and supplier. It is important that this argument be distinguished from the popularly held notion that American arms transfers to Iran, in effect, *created* the interest which the United States had in the security of that state. Indeed, the continuing American interest during the post-revolutionary period in the maintenance of a strong, territorially integral Iran is indicative of the fact that US involvement derived not from arms transfers *per se*, but rather from an antecedent interest of which those arms were only a reflection.

The third set of political problems attendant to the Nixon Doctrine's attempted utilization of arms transfers as a tool of influence stemmed from the close identification which it fostered between the United States and the various regimes of the recipient states. In the Iranian context, of course, this proved to be highly destabilizing. Yet, particularly in the Persian Gulf, arms transfers rationalized in terms of the Nixon Doctrine became the tangible symbol of American commitment and the currency in bilateral relations. Because they were the centerpiece of a process symbolizing the overall relationship, the Carter Administration subsequently found it difficult to shift away from the policy of its predecessor. As one American observer has framed the issue:

Our willingness to sell arms is seen by many, indeed most, friendly governments, as a litmus test of our bilateral relationships ... A refusal to sell invariably touches an extremely sensitive nerve, and tends to raise doubts in the minds of the affected countries about the strength of the bilateral relationship in security affairs and about the reliability of the United States as an arms supplier.[59]

As a kind of clearing-house of bilateral relations, the process of arms transfers tended to develop an inertia of its own. It became increasingly difficult for the Administration to deny Iran, for example, the AIM-54 *Phoenix* air-to-air missile system once the decision to sell F-14s was taken. The political *process* thus came to assume an importance which transcended the actual utility of the weaponry in question. In so doing, it offered an apparent confirmation of the efficacy of the US–client relationship.

The Vietnam experience exposed the dangers of an open-ended American commitment to preserve the security of a specific regime. The promulgation of the Nixon Doctrine was, in part, a response to the diplomatic immobility which invariably stemmed from such a posture. Paradoxically, however, the arms transfer policy which accompanied in particular the later phase of the Nixon Doctrine resulted in the very same kind of strong identification between the regime of the recipient state and the United States. Any attempt to differentiate somehow between the security of the 'regime' and the security of the 'nation' would have been perceived locally as having been tantamount to an act of subversion. The *amour-propre* of most Third World regimes would appear to be based upon the denial of the very possibility of such a distinction. Certainly that has been the case in the Persian Gulf over the last decade. Within the context of Iranian domestic politics, this process of identification inextricably linked American interests with the fate of the Shah. To many, the Iranian Revolution marked the end of the Nixon Doctrine era of American reliance on regional surrogates. Yet the domestic consensus behind an alternative course of action entailing a greater degree of American activism in the Third World remains elusive. The manner in which the Iranian Revolution, in tandem with the Soviet invasion of Afghanistan, has largely structured the American debate on regional security issues will be addressed in the concluding chapter of this study.

5 . THE NIXON–KISSINGER STRATEGY:
3. DÉTENTE AND THE DILEMMAS OF STRATEGIC MANAGEMENT, 1973–1976

We must never forget that the process of détente depends ultimately on habits and modes of conduct that extend beyond the letters of agreements to the spirits of relations. In cataloging the desirable, we must take care not to jeopardize what is attainable . . . We have insisted toward the Soviet Union that we cannot have the atmosphere of détente without the substance. It is equally clear that the substance of détente will disappear in an atmosphere of suspicion and hostility.

Henry Kissinger, 19 September 1974

[A] common thread runs through all [the various] definitions of détente. They all boil down to the same thing: Détente is the avoidance of nuclear war. Détente is the imposition of restraints so that the two superpowers don't blow each other up. If this is the meaning of détente, then I have a question. What is the difference between détente and cold war? Isn't cold war also an avoidance of hot war?

George Meany, President, AFL-CIO
1 October 1974[1]

The Paris agreement and beyond

The conclusion of the Paris agreement in January 1973 outwardly appeared to confirm the efficacy of the Administration's approach both to the management of adversarial relations with the Communist great powers and the disengagement of American forces from Indochina. Though later criticized as a hollow superpower peace, the Vietnam settlement marked the beginning of the end of the initial, euphoric phase of détente diplomacy under the stewardship of Nixon and Kissinger. At that time, the hope remained that the Soviet Union could become implicated in an American-inspired system of strategic co-management through the various mechanisms of linkage politics. The stabilization of superpower relations in these terms was regarded as the necessary complement to the post-Vietnam process of politico-military retrenchment

151

in Third World regions. The subtle and complex feedback process which this implied between the twin policies of superpower détente and the Nixon Doctrine was at the very heart of the Nixon–Kissinger strategy.[2]

The 'selling' of détente in the American domestic political market-place as part of the Nixon re-election campaign was, however, to generate false expectations that the 'limited adversary relationship' – properly managed – could become the cornerstone of a much-vaunted 'structure of peace'. Kissinger's characterization of the accords concluded at the May 1972 and June 1973 summit meetings as 'a code of conduct',[3] not to mention Nixon's own hyperbolic definition of détente contributed to the shaping of this public attitude. And yet, even prior to the October 1973 War – the event which triggered the dramatic public reappraisal of Soviet intentions within the United States – there was growing disquiet with both the style and substance of Administration policy. Moreover, in light of the argument advanced by Kissinger once out of office, it should be noted that the onset of this reversal *preceded* the collapse of executive authority stemming from Watergate.

The controversy surrounding the comprehensive US–Soviet trade agreement concluded in October 1972 was an early sign of the growing polarization of views within the United States on the question of détente. The anger of consumers over the adverse impact of grain sales on domestic food prices was one reflection of this public anxiety. Another, more deep-seated, source of criticism of the grain accord came from those who advocated the manipulation of trade relations – specifically, the granting of 'most favored nation' status – in order to affect internal developments within the Soviet Union. The focal point of this movement was the Jackson–Vanik Amendment which sought to link this prerequisite for the expansion of bilateral com-mercial relations with an end to restrictions on Jewish immigration.[4]

Kissinger's opposition to the Jackson–Vanik Amendment stemmed not from the belief (held by some) that trade should be kept politically neutral on the grounds that it was, like SALT, a matter of mutual interest. Rather, it followed from his assessment of the appropriate ends to which linkage politics should be addressed. Thus, the actions of Senator Jackson and his supporters (however one ascribes their motivation) created difficulties for the Adminis-tration's diplomacy insofar as they explicitly raised the awkward *value* questions which Kissinger sought to avoid. The initiation of a value dialogue with the Soviet Union, as discussed in chapter 3, was regarded as an inherently dangerous exercise given the irrefrangible nature of values and the corresponding totality of the means available to the superpowers. It was argued that the traditional dilemma of statecraft – the reconciliation of the 'just' with the 'possible' – had, in essence, been transformed under the impact of technology.[5] With the prevention of nuclear war acknowledged as the highest moral imperative, Kissinger asserted that the necessity of coexistence demanded, in turn, the adoption of an enlightened policy of the possible. While advocating the adroit use of trade relations in order to moderate the *external* behavior of the Soviet Union, he forcefully argued against its potential utilization as a diplomatic instrument to affect the evolution of that state's domestic structure. In Kissinger's terms of reference, a value-oriented strategic dialogue of the latter kind only threatened to highlight the profound incompatibility of the superpowers' domestic structures. Here, the politics of the possible – namely, the avoidance of such a clash of absolutes – was held synonymous with the prevention of the *summum malum*. As Kissinger put it in 1974:

Not by our choice, but by our capability, our primary concern in foreign policy must be to help influence the international conduct of nations in the world arena . . . We cannot gear our foreign policy to the transformation of other societies. In the nuclear age, our first responsibility must be the prevention of a war that could destroy all societies. We must never lose sight of this fundamental truth of modern international life. Peace between nations with totally different systems is also a high moral objective.[6]

Moscow's renunciation of the 1972 bilateral trade agreement came in January 1975 amidst angry charges that the Jackson–Vanik Amendment constituted an unprecedented attempt by the United States to interfere in the internal affairs of the Soviet Union. In 1973, however, the hope remained within the Administration that trade relations could be used as a diplomatic instrument to influence (and thereby moderate) Soviet *foreign* policy. From Kissinger's perspective, the manipulation of such power asymmetries through the linkage process (in this case, the Soviet Union's desire for high-level technology transfers from the West) could only occur within a political milieu in which Moscow opted for the tangible gains derived from its relationship with Washington over the uncertainties of jockeying for unilateral advantage on the periphery. Thus, in the wake of the Paris peace agreement, it was expected (or hoped) that the Kremlin's growing stake in détente would translate into a reduction in the level of its military assistance to Hanoi.[7]

Three weeks after the initialling of the Paris accord, Kissinger journeyed to the North Vietnamese capital in order to discuss the implementation of the agreement as well as the prerequisites for a normalization of relations between Washington and Hanoi. During a particularly disturbing meeting with the North Vietnamese Premier, Pham Van Dong, Kissinger was explicitly told that a majority of that country's ruling Politburo regarded the settlement as merely a cosmetic political exercise to facilitate the final withdrawal of American forces. Pham underscored that the negotiated agreement (*viz.* the ceasefire-in-place) would not be permitted to evolve into another schema for the partitioning of Vietnam.[8] Kissinger's own attitude towards the Paris agreement was reflected in answer to a press conference question shortly prior to the formal signing ceremony:

It is not easy to achieve through negotiations what has not been achieved on the battlefield, and if you look at the settlements that have been made in the postwar period, the lines of demarcation have almost always followed the lines of actual control . . . We have taken the position throughout that the agreement cannot be analyzed in terms of any one of its provisions, but it has to be seen in its totality and in terms of the evolution that it starts.[9]

Despite Kissinger's known skepticism about the efficacy of Vietnamization, it may be argued (contrary to the more cynical interpretations of the former Secretary's foreign policy) that the Paris agreement was not regarded as a political smokescreen ensuring a 'decent interval' between the withdrawal of American forces and the collapse of the Thieu government. The Administration's contention that the settlement gave the South Vietnamese 'every opportunity to demonstrate their inherent strength'[10] was premised upon the tacit assumption that the Saigon regime's long-term prospects would improve with each additional year that it was able to survive without the psychological crutch of a direct American presence.[11]

The conditions bounding this assumption, however, were hedged in two important respects. First, as suggested above, it was expected that the Soviet Union would exercise restraint *vis-à-vis* the transfer of arms to North Vietnam in order not to jeopardize the tangible benefits accruing to it through the enhancement of bilateral relations with the United States. Again, this melding of ostensibly compatible strategies – détente and devolution – was the essential aim to which the Nixon–Kissinger strategy was addressed. The second prerequisite for the successful implementation of the Paris agreement (from the Administration's perspective) was the threatened re-introduction of American tactical air power should Hanoi choose to fall back upon the military option. The position was reiterated by Nixon in personal letters sent to President Thieu on 14 November 1972 and 5 January 1973.[12] Despite these pronouncements, however, there was no political consensus within the United States to support such military contingencies. Indeed, it is significant to note that opposition to renewed bombing came from both sides of the ideological spectrum and, in fact, preceded the collapse of executive authority attendant to Watergate. Quite surprisingly, in light of their previous stance, many Congressional conservatives opposed the continuation of American air operations in Southeast Asia on the grounds that it would only lead to a new group of American POWs while not decisively affecting what was acknowledged to be a rather pessimistic political prognosis for the US clients in the region.

On 29 June 1973, Congress voted overwhelmingly to forbid the use of funds for American combat activities in Indochina after 15 August. The lopsided majority in favor of the cutoff was obtained over the heated protestations of the Administration. Kissinger claimed that the President was being denied the one policy instrument which would penalize Hanoi in the event of massive violations of the Paris agreement and which provided an ongoing incentive for the Khmer Rouge to enter into negotiations with the Lon Nol regime in Cambodia.[13] Though the vote to terminate the American air war in Southeast Asia did coincide with the dramatic first wave of revelations relating to Watergate (e.g. the testimony of John Dean before the Senate Select Committee), it would, again, be misleading to attribute the failure of Congress to sustain the Administration's position on this issue primarily to the decline in executive authority stemming from the scandal. Rather, Watergate served merely to exacerbate its political difficulties in countering a consensus against further US military activities which was already fairly well established.

The legislated termination of American involvement in Indochina provided fresh impetus to the foreign policy debate at home. If, as Raymond Aron observed, the Vietnam tragedy stemmed from the 'tendency to substitute symbol for reality in the discrimination of interests and issues,' the end of that sad episode left no self-demonstrable 'lessons' or set of criteria by which to gauge future policy.[14] Indeed, formulations such as the one encapsulated in George

McGovern's 1972 electoral slogan 'Come home America!' represented virtually the mirror image of the Cold War policy orientation which they sought to supplant. More subdued calls for 'selective engagement' were premised upon the assumption that United States' security interests might be reduced to some definable core. The inefficacy of the instrumentalities of American power called into question not only the designated ends of the nation's foreign policy, but the very morality of the intentions upon which they were rooted. Increasingly, Americans recoiled at the unsavory character of the regimes with which they found themselves in alliance. The amorphous, unmanageable nature of the Third World frustrated the clear delineation of 'pure' contingencies and thereby bolstered the atavistic impulse towards non-involvement. Within this context, as one observer has put it, diversity threatened to become an escape from commitment.

For Kissinger, the management of defeat in Southeast Asia over the long-term entailed both the preservation of US credibility and the development of a revitalized domestic consensus to sustain the imperative of America's global engagement. This latter point brings one back to the geo-strategic nature of Kissinger's foreign policy orientation and its undisputed centerpiece: the US–Soviet relationship. Though Vietnam set the emotional tenor of the American foreign policy debate, it remained bound by the broad public support which the Administration continued to enjoy on the issue of détente – the onset of Watergate notwithstanding. The political atmosphere generated by the Moscow and Washington summit meetings was reflected in the widespread perception of détente as a means of enticing Soviet acceptance of an American-inspired system of strategic management through the various mechanisms of linkage politics. This belief, as will be considered in the following section, was shattered at the time of the October 1973 Middle East War. With the nature of the Soviet–American relationship *itself* the subject of heated public controversy, the scope of the post-Vietnam debate was no longer circumscribed in the important way which it had been previously.

The October 1973 Middle East War

Despite the conclusion of the Paris agreement, American policy during the first half of 1973 (as in the latter part of 1972) remained almost exclusively preoccupied with the evolving situation in Indochina. The June 1973 summit in Washington – designed primarily to maintain the momentum of détente – provided the only major interlude. Although this concentration upon Vietnam and the development of superpower relations is clearly understandable, it was accomplished at the expense of other important issues which were, perforce, accorded secondary consideration.[15] With respect to the Middle East, this process of deferral had the net effect of transforming policy into the very kind of shallow exercise which Kissinger had scorned as an academic – that is, the projection of the future as an extrapolation of the past. In this instance, despite certain indications to the contrary, Administration policy appears to have been premised upon the assumption that the military stasis which set in following the conclusion of the August 1970 ceasefire agreement would persist.

The preoccupation of the two principal American decision-makers with other pressing foreign policy issues contributed to this diplomacy by inertia approach. As a consequence, major policy departures were rationalized in terms of previous patterns. Sadat's dramatic expulsion of Sovet military advisers from Egypt in July 1972 (to cite perhaps the principal political development in the region prior to the October 1973 War) was not vigorously followed up by the Administration. Rather than auguring a fundamental shift in the constellation of political forces in the Middle East, Kissinger reportedly regarded this move as a vindication of American support for Israel. As Nadav Safran observes:

Sadat's expulsion of the Soviets was seen in the United States as the major pay-off of a policy of close support for Israel rather than as a possible ground for changing that policy. The combination of Israeli military strength and unequivocal American backing had already proved its efficacy in deterring war and preserving a balance between friendly and hostile Arab countries; now that combination seemed also to be effective in checking and rolling back Soviet influence and diminishing the danger of a superpower confrontation. It was that policy, Washington believed, that caused the Soviets to despair of the Arabs' capacity to alter the situation by war without their own participation, maximized their fears of such participation, and impelled them to adopt the cautious course that led to the crisis between them and Egypt.[16]

In the first week of April 1972, three months prior to his announcement of the expulsion of Soviet military advisers, Sadat moved to open a secret channel to the United States.[17] The Egyptian President proposed a confidential meeting between Kissinger and his own national security adviser, Hafiz Ismail, in order to discuss mechanisms for shifting the peace process off dead center. Due to Kissinger's virtually full-time commitment to the Paris negotiations in the latter half of 1972, however, this meeting was not able to take place until February 1973. Throughout the ensuing period prior to the outbreak of hostilities on 6 October, Kissinger continued to dismiss the possibility of a combined Arab attack on Israel. This conclusion was based both upon the continuing deterrent power of Israel's military establishment and his assessment of Soviet intentions. With respect to the latter, Kissinger subsequently recorded: 'Our demonstrations of firmness on India–Pakistan and on Vietnam (not to mention the conflicts of autumn 1970) must have convinced the Kremlin that one more crisis would overload the circuit. Coupled with the firmness, our conciliatory posture in Moscow and the prospect of further moves on trade helped produce Soviet restraint.'[18]

Kissinger's sanguine assessment was not uniformly shared throughout the American foreign policy bureaucracy. Ray Cline, then director of the State Department's Intelligence and Research Bureau (INR), issued detailed reports on 31 May and 30 September 1973 which pointed to ominous developments indicating the increased likelihood of resumed hostilities. Perhaps the single most persuasive piece of evidence supporting the INR's conclusion was the interception of Egyptian war plans in late April 1972 by American defense attachés in Cairo. This specific point was, surprisingly, not raised in discussions with the Soviet leadership during the Washington summit in June.[19] While acknowledging the huge influx of Soviet arms into Egypt, the NSC staff doubted its ability to absorb them quickly so as to give Sadat an early war option. Though the quality of other intelligence reports (CIA, DIA, etc.) over the prewar period remains an open question, the known substance of the two INR reports (to which Kissinger reportedly never responded) is at variance with his subsequent assertion on 25 October that 'all the intelligence at our disposal and all the intelligence given to us by foreign countries suggested that there was no possibility of the outbreak of war.'[20]

From the onset of hostilities on 6 October 1973, Kissinger's guiding strategy (as characterized by one analyst) was 'to use the war as an extension of diplomacy.'[21] While the Arab 'confrontation states' had turned to the Soviet Union for the material wherewithal to pursue their war option, the newly confirmed Secretary of State immediately moved to seize upon what was correctly perceived as the extraordinary potential for unilateral American diplomacy during the postwar phase. Kissinger's hope of playing the role of broker within the negotiating process was premised upon the belief that the Arab states would look to Washington as the clearing house for Israeli territorial concessions (*viz.* the return to pre-1967 frontiers) once the war had succeeded in decisively shifting the political *status quo*. This line of argument was made explicit by Kissinger during his press conference of 12 October:

If the Arab objective was ... to emphasize the fact that ... permanent stability cannot be assumed in the Middle East and that there is an urgency in achieving a negotiated settlement or that it is important to achieve a negotiated settlement, then it would be our judgment that that point has been made. The United States stands ready now ... to help the parties if they want to pursue a negotiated settlement.[22]

The pre-condition of an activist diplomacy of this kind, however, was a conflict whose outcome was militarily indecisive. In operational terms, this amounted to calibrating American policy so as to deny Israel the renewed possibility for total military victory over Egypt and Syria. From this perspective emerged Kissinger's two-pronged efforts to secure a ceasefire and restrain the flow of arms to the belligerents.[23]

The use of the conflict as a political vehicle to position favorably the United States for the pursuit of postwar diplomacy was one aspect of Administration policy. Of equal importance, however, was the desire not to allow the war to disrupt the development of détente – the centerpiece of the Nixon–Kissinger foreign policy. This perhaps accounts for the relatively subdued American response to Soviet moves during the first week of fighting. These actions included, *inter alia*, the failure to consult with the Administration prior to the initiation of the conflict (according to the terms of the June 1973 agreement), the transmission of provocative messages to Arab heads of government urging their 'maximum support' for the confrontation states, and the initiation of a massive airlift to Egypt and Syria on 10 October.[24] During the press conference of 12 October, Kissinger acknowledged that these moves were not 'entirely helpful', but went on to conclude that he did not 'as yet consider that Soviet statements and actions threaten the stability of ... détente.'[25]

By the end of the first week of fighting, the increasingly dire Israeli military situation was evident. Obstacles within the American bureaucracy to the arms resupply effort prompted the Israeli Prime Minister, Golda Meir, to issue an appeal to Nixon for his personal intervention to expedite deliveries. The American President was reportedly warned in a personal note from Meir that if the airlift did not shortly begin, Israel would use every means at its disposal to ensure its national survival. Kissinger, who received a more formal version of this note from the Tel Aviv leadership on 12 October, took this last point to be an oblique reference to Israel's nuclear option. With the military balance shifting against Israel's nuclear favor (under the impact of virtually continuous Soviet An-22 cargo flights into Cairo and Damascus), the American Administration quickly moved to establish an 'air bridge' between the two countries. On Saturday, 13 October, thirty US C-130 transports laden with arms departed for Israel. By the following Tuesday, over 1,000 tons of munitions and sophisticated equipment were being airlifted into the country daily. The onset of the American resupply operation was accompanied shortly thereafter by the initiation of the awaited Israeli counteroffensive on both the Syrian and Egyptian fronts. The most dramatic aspect of this campaign was the successful crossing of Israeli forces into 'African' Egypt on 15–16 October 1973. This move coincided with the arrival of Soviet Premier Alexei Kosygin in Cairo for urgent consultations with President Sadat. Over the next two days, Kosygin apprised the Egyptian leader of the increasingly clear Israeli turnabout in the military situation and urged him to accept the Soviet ceasefire proposal. Sadat, whose faulty military intelligence had led him to believe that Egypt was still winning the conflict, only acceded to Kosygin's position when confronted with Soviet satellite photographs which revealed the extent of the Israeli counter-offensive.

The Soviet Premier departed the Egyptian capital late on 18 October, having obtained Sadat's agreement to work towards an immediate ceasefire. Soviet Ambassador Dobrynin approached Kissinger with such a proposal within hours of Kosygin's arrival in Moscow. The Soviet proposal, however, sought to link a standstill ceasefire with an Israeli commitment to withdrawal to its pre-1967 frontiers. Kissinger warned Dobrynin that these terms would be rejected out of hand by the Israeli government, but promised nevertheless to convey them to Tel Aviv. This move was followed the next morning (19 October) with an additional message from Moscow which took the Administration somewhat by surprise. Invoking the consultative mechanisms embodied in the June 1973 accords, Brezhnev invited the American Secretary of State to Moscow for urgent discussions 'on the Middle East situation.'[26] During the flight en route to the Soviet capital, Kissinger received word that Saudi Arabia had joined the other Arab members of OPEC in declaring a total oil embargo against the United States. The precipitant to this action was the President's message to Congress on the previous day requesting $2.2 billion in emergency military aid for Israel. Though the oil embargo was to play a dominant role in Kissinger's political calculations over the following weeks and months, the Saudi announcement does not appear to have had a major impact on the American negotiating strategy during the Moscow talks.[27]

Kissinger met with Brezhnev less than two hours after his arrival in the Soviet capital. The Soviet Party Chairman, cognizant of the dire Egyptian military position in the Sinai, argued for an immediate ceasefire coupled with a reassertion of UN Resolution 242. Kissinger asserted that any proposal which did not include the initiation of peace negotiations would be unacceptable to Israel. Following this initial meeting, Brezhnev was able to gain Sadat's ready acceptance of Kissinger's formulation – a telling indicator of the Egyptian President's perception of the military situation. When the two sides reconvened the following afternoon (21 October), the American delegation was surprised to learn of this decision. Attention next focused on the drafting of a UN ceasefire resolution (subsequently referred to as Security Council Resolution 338) which was adopted without dissent on 22 October. Throughout the drafting phase of this resolution, the Soviet side insisted that the strict and immediate implementation of the ceasefire arrangements was an imperative. Though Kissinger knew the inherent difficulties of such an exercise in light of his Vietnam experience, this demand was not incompatible with American interests. Indeed, the prevention of an outright Israeli victory continued to be taken as the military prerequisite for American postwar diplomacy in the region.

The Israeli leadership requested that Kissinger stop in Tel Aviv on his way back to Washington so that they might be fully briefed on the bilateral discussions in Moscow and their implications. On the basis of Kissinger's sober briefings prior to the Moscow summit, the Israelis had clearly been caught unawares by the timing of the ceasefire accord. Though closely questioned on his choice of tactics during a meeting with the Israeli cabinet, there was no suggestion that Kissinger's diplomatic activities – presented to Tel Aviv as a *fait accompli* – reflected or augured some divergence of American and Israeli interests.[28]

Upon his return to Washington on 23 October, Kissinger was confronted with angry protests from Dobrynin that the Israelis were massively violating the ceasefire agreement. Over the next 24 hours Israeli forces used sporadic Arab counter-attacks in the Sinai as the pretext for tightening their stranglehold over the Egyptian Third Army and completing their drive to the outskirts of Suez city. Increasingly concerned about the fate of the Third Army, Sadat sent urgent messages to Washington and Moscow on 24 October requesting both to despatch units of their armed forces to the Sinai to ensure implementation of the ceasefire.

Several hours after receipt of Sadat's request, Dobrynin contacted Kissinger to convey a message from Brezhnev. In a note later characterized by Nixon as having 'left very little to the imagination,' the Soviet leader denounced Israel for 'brazenly' flouting the ceasefire and repeated Sadat's request for a joint US–Soviet peace-keeping force.[29] The message went on to conclude: 'Let us together . . . urgently dispatch Soviet and American contingents to Egypt . . . I will say it straight, that if you find it impossible to act with us in this matter, we should be faced with the necessity urgently to consider the question of taking appropriate steps unilaterally. Israel cannot be allowed to get away with the violations.'[30] The credibility of this threat to undertake unilateral action was heightened by the movement of additional Soviet troop carriers into the Mediterranean and the reported alerting of seven airborne divisions in southern Russia and Hungary.[31]

In response to these developments, a meeting of what James Schlesinger subsequently referred to as the 'abbreviated' National Security Council convened in the Situation Room at the White House.[32] A consensus amongst the high-ranking officials in attendance developed in support of a DEFCON III alert of United States military forces as an unambiguous signal of American opposition to the near ultimatum contained in the Brezhnev note.[33] On the regional level, the American alert demonstrated to the Arab states the seriousness of the Administration's desire to forestall a sweeping Israeli military victory by affirming the continued American commitment to a ceasefire in the Sinai along the lines of existing force dispositions. In so doing, it bolstered Kissinger's political approach to the conflict by underscoring to the Arab states that the road to peace lay through Washington. The successful implementation of this strategy during the postwar period culminated in the great (albeit tacit) triumph of Kissinger's 'shuttle diplomacy' – the decoupling of the oil question from that of the Middle East negotiating process.

Following the inadvertently rapid public disclosure of the worldwide alert of American forces (the expectation having been that it would take at least 24 hours for news to filter out), Kissinger held a press conference to explain the Administration's position:

The United States does not favor and will not approve the sending of a joint Soviet–United States force into the Middle East . . . It is inconceivable that the forces of the great powers should be introduced in the numbers that would be necessary to overpower both of the participants. It is inconceivable that we should transplant the great-power rivalry into the Middle East or, alternatively, that we should impose a military condominium by the United States and the Soviet Union. The United States is even more opposed to the unilateral introduction by any great power, especially by any nuclear power, of military forces into the Middle East in whatever guise those forces should be introduced. And it is the ambiguity of some of the actions and communications and certain readiness measures that were observed that cause the President . . . to order certain precautionary measures to be taken by the United States.[34]

Kissinger's spirited public defense of the decision to go on alert stemmed from his privately held assessment that there existed a 'three out of four chance' of unilateral Soviet action in the absence of a firm American deterrent response.[35] Within hours of the Kissinger press conference, the sense of crisis abated when the Soviet UN ambassador ceased insisting upon the inclusion of Soviet and American contingents in the Sinai peace-keeping force. Significantly, this policy reversal coincided with the subsidence of fighting on the Egyptian front. The following day (26 October) marked the official end of the crisis when Nixon announced the return of American forces to their normal DEFCON status.[36]

In retrospect, had the ceasefire negotiated in Moscow held (and the necessity of the DEFCON III alert thereby averted), the October 1973 War's termination may well have been regarded as a prime example of strategic co-management. As it was, the war greatly reinforced the American domestic critics of détente by exposing the sharply divergent conceptions of order and stability from which each superpower was operating. Kissinger, seeking to limit the political damage to détente stemming from the alert, underscored that no 'threats' had been made by one side against the other and that the structure of relations with the Soviet Union remained essentially intact.[37] By contrast, Nixon, whose own penchant for hyperbole was in this case coupled with the desire to utilize the alert as a means of deflecting domestic political criticism over Watergate, characterized the episode as 'the most difficult crisis we have had since the Cuban confrontation of 1962.'[38]

In the public perception of the détente process, the notion of 'parity' underlying the Moscow and Washington accords had connoted more than an essential equivalence in strategic armaments. In its broader interpretation – fueled, in part, through the efforts of the Nixon Administration during the 1972 campaign to derive electoral advantage from détente – it was also taken to signify a political willingness on the part of the Soviet Union to participate in a system of strategic co-management with the United States in the Third World.[39] The Administration's approach to the Vietnam negotiations (with its emphasis upon the newly forged Moscow and Peking connections) reinforced this perception. The Nixon–Kissinger strategy's goal of melding the twin strategies of détente and politico-military retrenchment (as characterized in successive State of the World messages) was predicated upon the conception of a close interrelationship between the stability of the center and the periphery. The various modalities of linkage politics (considered above) were regarded as means of moderating Soviet behavior.

The favorable public response to détente evidenced during the period between the Moscow and Washington summits was accompanied by the generation of a certain sense of *trust* in the Soviet Union as a strategic partner. The implicit argument of the Administration – again reflecting the synthetic nature of the Nixon–Kissinger strategy – was that the moderation of Soviet policy on the periphery was evidence of its compliance to the regime of restraints governing the center. Hence, in terms of this feedback process, Vietnam (and the perceived efficacy of the Administration's strategy to implicate the Soviet Union in a settlement) became a means of politically legitimizing the SALT process. The impact of the October 1973 Middle East War was to shatter this false structure of trust. Kissinger, who in his academic writings had warned against the dangerous oscillations in American mood *vis-à-vis* the Soviet Union, sought to put the traumatic events of the month into perspective:

> There has been a misunderstanding in many respects about détente. There has been the idea that détente reflects the fact that the two sides agree with each other and that it reflects an era of good feeling or similar domestic structure. We have always believed that détente is necessary precisely because we have opposing interests in many parts of the world and totally different social systems. Détente is necessary because of the danger posed by the accumulation of nuclear weapons on both sides. That gives us the opportunity to communicate and to move rapidly if we want to. It does not eliminate the conflicting interests. It does not prevent occasional clashes – what it does make possible is a more rapid settlement and a certain amount of restraint when crises develop when both of these things occur. But there are limitations beyond which it cannot go.[40]

Despite such Administration attempts to limit its effects, the political ramifications of the war were evidenced across a range of foreign policy issues. One of the primary consequences, as suggested above, was the dramatic re-assessment of Soviet intentions which it triggered within the United States. Critical observers of the Nixon–Kissinger diplomacy pointed to the propensity of the Soviet Union towards greater involvement and risk-taking in Middle East crises (compare 1967, 1970, 1973). This development was partially attributed to the Administration's willingness to allow Moscow to attain a position of military parity. Indeed, the overall psychological impact of this Soviet power projection capability *vis-à-vis* Third World regions was heightened owing to its coincidence with the advent of American dependence on certain of these areas (particularly the Persian Gulf) for resources.

The end of the initial, euphoric phase of détente diplomacy was accompanied by the inversion of the subtle feedback process between the American perception of Soviet intentions on the periphery and the center. The perceived failure of the Soviet Union to comply fully to the spirit and letter of the Moscow–Washington accords with respect to its behavior during the October 1973 War, by implication, created a very serious crisis of confidence within the SALT forum. Though no explicit link was drawn between the two issues, the DEFCON III episode contributed to the promotion of a political atmosphere within the United States in which the questions of SALT verification and 'trust' in Soviet intentions became intertwined.[41] This shift in public attitude contributed to the often virulent domestic debate on détente (and in particular the role of Kissinger) which ensued during the two.year period preceding the 1976 presidential election.[42] That is not to say, however, that the subsequent political difficulties attendant to the SALT process may be solely attributed to the deterioration of the US–Soviet relationship following the October 1973 Middle East War. To be sure, the advent of new weapon technologies (e.g. cruise missiles) had already begun to challenge the existing SALT framework by the Autumn of 1973. The decline in the political state of the bilateral relationship operated to exacerbate the breach in the SALT II negotiations of which contending qualitative developments on the technological front served as the primary catalyst.[43]

Perhaps the most striking aspect of the American response to the October 1973 War was its reaffirmation of the centrality and primacy of the superpower relationship in international relations at a moment when new forces militated against its preponderant influence across a spectrum of issues. Clearly, the nascent multipolarity of the post-1973 period was not to be that of the 'pentagonal' system of states referred to by Nixon in 1971. However, despite the advent of multiple centers of different kinds of power, the American image of the international system remained one dominated by the notion of global engagement with the Soviet Union. This feature was largely responsible for the promulgation of a synthetic approach to détente in which favorable or adverse developments in one area (whether geographic or functional) were regarded as affecting others.

In the aftermath of the October 1973 War, Kissinger's repeated assertion of détente's 'indivisible' nature became increasingly at odds with the European perception of East–West relations.[44] While appreciative (at least in an impressionistic sense) of Western interests outside the NATO area, the European allies were loath to jeopardize the tangible benefits of détente on the continent in favor of the risks and uncertainties of the Administration's more comprehensive linkage approach. On this, as well as other divisive issues within the Alliance, Kissinger maintained that the Europeans knew that the American position was 'essentially right' – and hinted that their inability to be more supportive of the Administration stemmed from the fragilities of their own domestic structures.[45]

In dispelling the ungrounded sense of euphoria which had come to surround détente, the October 1973 War called into question the efficacy of the Nixon–Kissinger strategy. From the American perspective, the Soviet Union's continued pursuit of unilateral advantage along the Afro-Asian periphery severely challenged the notion that détente (and the pattern of restraint which it ostensibly implied) could serve to foster the conditions for regional stability so as to permit the United States to assume a less overt foreign role. The inherent dissonance between the twin aspects of the Nixon–Kissinger strategy (détente and devolution) was thus made manifest. In the wake of this development, conservative critics of the Administration's approach to relations with Moscow called for the adoption of a posture varyingly characterized as détente 'without illusion.'[46] Within the divisive political atmosphere of the period following the October 1973 War, American security policy again shifted back to reflect more explicitly the doctrine of containment.

The recasting of containment

The sharply divergent bases of superpower policy evidenced during the 1973 Arab–Israeli War served to discredit the view (largely associated with the Administration) that détente – properly managed over time – might translate into a 'stable structure' of international relations. Rather, the conflict confirmed the continuing primacy of the competitive over the consensual aspect of the bilateral relationship. Within this new context, détente emerged as less a nascent *structure* of world politics than as a contemporary *condition* of the international system. As such, détente – which sought to ease the dangers that were explicit during the Cold War – was itself shown to be inherently unstable. The sources of this instability were (and to a large part remain) essentially of a twofold nature.

On the *political* plane, a confluence of trends militated in favor of increased disorder in Third World regions, which *pari passu* provided a broadened scope for superpower competition. What one observer has characterized as the period of 'post-decolonization' has been marked by a spiralling level of violence both within and between states along the Afro-Asian *periphery*. The proliferation in the incidence of Third World conflicts (irredentism, contending nationalisms within a country challenging the existing state structure, etc.) has coincided, however, with the qualitatively new ability of the superpowers to project their power globally. The internationalization of domestic conflict in this way is what, for example, distinguishes the Congo crisis of 1961–2 from the 1975–6 Angolan Civil War.

The other source of instability in the Soviet–American relationship stemmed from *technological* advancements in strategic nuclear weaponry whose impact threatened to undermine the stability of the central balance. Since the ostensible codification of parity under the SALT I regime of restraints, the maintenance of this stability had been taken by many to be assured. This relationship between parity and stability was called into sharp question during the post-1973 period. With it, analysts both within and outside of government focused renewed attention on one of the fundamental challenges of statecraft to emerge in the postwar period – the integration of nuclear weapons and foreign policy. Given the continuingly competitive nature of the Soviet–American relationship (as dramatically demonstrated during the October 1973 War), concern was expressed that a perceived inferiority of US strategic forces – however marginal in operational terms – might permit the Soviet Union to exploit that asymmetry for political advantage.

This rationale was the motivation behind Secretary of Defense James R. Schlesinger's promulgation of a new American doctrine of flexible nuclear options in early 1974.[47] The avowed aim of this shift was 'to provide the President with a wider set of much more selective targeting options' so as to 'shore up deterrence across the entire spectrum of risk.'[48] One particular source of concern was the growing vulnerability of American land-based ICBMs to a Soviet counterforce strike. As Schlesinger argued on 10 January 1974:

Our concern is that [should the Soviet Union] marry the technologies that are now emerging in their R & D programme to the throw-weight and numbers that they have been allowed under the [SALT] Interim Agreement that they would develop a capability that was preponderant relative to that of the United States . . .

If the Soviets were able to develop these improved technologies presently available to the United States in the form of guidance, MIRVs, warhead technology, at some point around 1980 or beyond, they would be in a position in which they had a major counterforce option against the United States, and we would lack a similar option.

Consequently, in the pursuit of symmetry, meaningful symmetry, for the two forces . . . we cannot allow the Soviets unilaterally to obtain a counterforce option which we ourselves lack. We must have a symmetrical balancing of the strategic forces on both sides . . . We cannot be in a position in which a major option is open to the Soviet Union which we through a self-denying ordinance have precluded for the United States.[49]

The 'new' American doctrine of limited nuclear options was noteworthy in two respects. First, it represented less a departure than an acceleration in the direction which US nuclear strategy was already evolving.[50] Both Kissinger and Schlesinger had long argued that in an age of parity the United States would be unwilling to implement 'assured destruction' except in retaliation to an all-out Soviet attack on the American homeland. Moreover, the political consequences of the October 1973 War had underscored the inherent dissonance between the Administration's twin strategies of détente and devolution. As a result, the question of extended deterrence emerged in a wholly new context. Again, the expressed concern was that the Soviet Union might be able to exploit even marginal force asymmetries for diplomatic advantage.[51] In maintaining 'essential equivalence' through the improvement of 'deterrence across the broad spectrum', flexible nuclear options embodied (as it were) a means of re-creating the dangers that were explicit during the Cold War.[52]

This leads to a second feature of the so-called Schlesinger Doctrine, namely its fundamental difference to the counterforce doctrine promulgated by Secretary of Defense McNamara in June 1962 at Ann Arbor. The latter, as discussed in chapter 1, sought to translate American numerical superiority into a rational, credible, war-winning strategy as a means of imposing a pattern of stability on the Soviet Union. In contrast, the Schlesinger Doctrine of 'counterforce matching' was not presented as a war-winning strategy. Rather, its aim was to influence Soviet intentions and thereby reinforce deterrence at a time in which there was a 'narrowing range of credibility.' In these terms, the Schlesinger Doctrine was an important complement to the Kissinger détente.

The notion (cited as one of the prime motives behind the change in American targeting policy) that the Soviet Union might derive political utility from a marginal technical advantage was never fully elaborated by the Administration. Walter Slocombe, writing on the political implications of strategic parity, took a dissenting view:

If it is doubtful that nuclear monopoly or first-strike superiority proved effectively translatable into practical power there is even greater doubt that nuclear 'advantages' which do not reach the level of first-strike superiority affect significantly the practical ability of one nation to threaten to impose its will on another or to shape the outcome of political crises, other than those in which the continued existence of the nation (or, possibly, for a totalitarian state, the regime) is at stake. By definition, the stronger side's nuclear advantage is not enough for it to make a society-destroying retaliatory blow by the other side physically impossible. This means that there is a risk – of whatever size – that the decision to use weapons will prove suicidal.[53]

Slocombe's comment is striking and serves to highlight the paradoxical nature of the Schlesinger Doctrine – a paradox which again reflects the ongoing dilemma of integrating nuclear weapons and foreign policy. Stated in its most bald terms, one could argue that in those few areas of high-level commitment (e.g. Western Europe – where there exists a convergence of American interests and values, and is so perceived by the Soviet Union) a Schlesinger-type doctrine of limited options is of marginal utility given the fundamental inhibitions of nuclear deterrence. At best, it assists to stabilize further an existing structure of threat.[54] Conversely, in gray areas, where it is assumed that competition between the superpowers will continue, such a doctrine is of questionable relevance: there can be no direct linkage with the nuclear arena because the magnitude of interests and values at stake is of insufficient magnitude; threats lack credibility, and an attempt to utilize politically nuclear weapons under these circumstances would mark little more than a return to the arbitrary policy of massive retaliation.

Much to Kissinger's exasperation, critics of the SALT process, or at least his personal handling of it, seized upon the Schlesinger Doctrine's underlying motivation (namely, the denial of any perceived asymmetry from which the Soviet Union might derive political utility) as a means of casting doubt upon the presumed benefits of strategic arms control for the United States. This effort was held by Kissinger to constitute a direct threat both to SALT and the important process of *political legitimation* which it symbolized. Indeed, even after the October 1973 War had ostensibly discredited the Administration's notion of a stable structure, the Secretary of State continued to urge public support for SALT II on the political grounds that it would 'provide incentives for [Soviet] restraint.'[55]

At the time of the 24 November 1974 Vladivostok agreement establishing common ceilings of 2,400 strategic nuclear delivery vehicles for each side (no more than 1,320 of these being MIRV-equipped), critics condemned the accord's failure to limit the Soviet Union's pronounced throw-weight advantage. Again, the stated concern was that when wedded to the number of MIRVs permitted under the Vladivostok ceilings this disparity would give the Soviet Union a heightened counterforce capability *vis-à-vis* that available to the United States. Kissinger dismissed the question of throw-weight as a 'phony' issue and maintained that any attack on *Minuteman* would be 'plain crazy.'[56] The essential element of this argument was the technical assessment that fixed land-based missiles were 'likely to become vulnerable on both sides, regardless of the throw-weight that either side had, simply by improvement in accuracy and improvement in yield.'[57] With SALT – the centerpiece of super-power relations – under political assault on these grounds, Kissinger challenged the underlying assumptions of his critics' position: 'What in the name of God is strategic superiority? What is the significance of it politically, militarily, operationally at these levels of numbers? What do you do with it?'[58]

Domestic criticism of SALT during 1974 and 1975 was perhaps the most salient aspect of the broader political backlash against détente in the period following the October 1973 War. By an increasingly wide public margin, détente was regarded as a 'one-way street' from which the Soviet Union emerged the chief beneficiary.[59] Indeed, it was the political power of this perception which prompted President Ford (in the face of a right-wing challenge within the Republican Party from Ronald Reagan during the 1976 presidential primaries) to drop 'détente' from his political lexicon in favor of the more awkward formulation 'peace through strength.'

Conservative hostility to détente and the Kissinger diplomacy was matched by criticism of a wholly different sort from the opposite end of the political spectrum. Democratic liberals (such as Senators Kennedy, Mondale, and Church) charged that Kissinger's particular brand of *Realpolitik* had led to a fundamental betrayal of the 'core values' (rooted in the American domestic structure) which US foreign policy had traditionally sought to project. In this view, the Kissinger approach (with its concentration on the US–USSR–China strategic triangle) should be supplanted by one which emphasized the consonance of values and interests between North America, Western Europe and Japan. This contending notion of 'trilateralism' was formally embraced by candidate Jimmy Carter as one of the principal foreign policy themes of his 1976 presidential campaign against the incumbent Republican Administration. By that time, the Kissinger diplomacy was under siege by attacks from both ends of the American political spectrum. One common element of these otherwise sharply divergent critiques of Administration policy was the desire to utilize the expansion of US–Soviet relations through détente as a means of influencing domestic developments within the Soviet Union. This sentiment was reflected both in the Jackson–

Vanik amendment to the 1974 trade bill and the public controversy which later came to surround the so-called Sonnenfeldt Doctrine.[60] As discussed above, the initiation of a value dialogue with the Soviet Union was considered within Kissinger's framework of thought to be an inherently dangerous exercise. In practical terms one was left then with 'the politics of the possible.'[61] And yet, it was precisely this *style* of diplomatic conduct which contributed to the serious erosion of Kissinger's domestic base.

In the final months of 1974 (despite the competing demands of SALT and Middle East 'shuttle diplomacy') Kissinger's attention was increasingly devoted to the deteriorating situation in Southeast Asia. Within South Vietnam, the apparent breakdown of the Paris agreement was marked by geographically dispersed military action initiated by North Vietnamese regular and Viet Cong forces in order to secure greater territorial control. Since precluded by legislation from reintroducing American combat personnel into the conflict, Administration efforts centered upon securing for the Saigon government a greatly augmented military assistance package from Congress. This move suffered a severe setback in September 1974 when the House made a surprise cut, reducing the proposed authorization of military aid in fiscal year 1975 from $1.4 billion to $700 million. After the reduction of shipping costs, this was less than the total in war material supplied to Hanoi by Moscow and Peking.[62] It was within this context during the closing weeks of 1974 (according to subsequent disclosures from the North Vietnamese side) that a two-year strategic plan for 1974–6 was devised by the Hanoi leadership which called for 'widespread, large surprise attacks in 1975' in order to create conditions for a 'general offensive and uprising to completely liberate the South.'[63]

On 4 January 1975, Phuoc Binh, the provincial capital of Phuoc Long, fell to Communist forces. This was the first such governmental loss since the fall of Quang Tri city during the May 1972 offensive. Occurring at a time when the American Congress was signalling its unwillingness to underwrite the Saigon regime either militarily or economically, the capture of Phuoc Binh marked a major psychological turning point in the war. President Ford's response to the deteriorating military situation in Indochina was a request to Congress for an additional allocation of $300 million in emergency assistance for Cambodia and $722 million for South Vietnam. In a letter to Speaker of the House Carl Albert, urging swift action on the appropriation request for Cambodia, Ford emphasized the necessity of maintaining American credibility and invoked indirectly the Nixon Doctrine:

It has been a basic policy of this Government to give material support to friends and allies who are willing and able to carry the burden of their own self-defense. Cambodia is such an ally.

This is a moral question that must be faced squarely. Are we to deliberately abandon a small country in the midst of its life and death struggle? Is the United States, which so far has consistently stood by its friends through the most difficult times, now to condemn, in effect, a small Asian nation totally dependent upon us? We cannot escape this responsibility. Our national security and the integrity of our alliance depend upon our reputation as a reliable partner. Countries around the world who depend on us for support – as well as their foes – will judge our performance.[64]

Following the fall of Ban Me Thuot on 11 March, President Thieu made the surprise decision to withdraw ARVN forces from the northern and central provinces (Military Regions I and II) in favor of a new strategy concentrating upon the defense of urban centers. This precipitate announcement resulted in the unnecessary concession of large rural tracts to North Vietnamese control and greatly contributed to the disorderly nature of the ARVN retreat south. By the end of March, Quang Tri, Hue, Danang, Kontum, and Pleiku had fallen (along with most of the northern and central regions) to the NVA; a hastily organized defense perimeter was established around Saigon. At a press conference given in the wake of the collapse of his Middle East shuttle on 22 March 1975, Kissinger issued an emotional warning of 'a massive change in the international environment' if Congress decided to 'destroy' South Vietnam by denying its government essential military assistance.[65] Ignoring Administration entreaties, Congress allocated funds only to implement plans for the evacuation of American personnel and Vietnamese refugees.

The complete rout of ARVN forces in early April prompted an American embassy official in Saigon to conclude:

We should have asked ourselves long ago how an army can go on functioning when it is simply a business organization in which everything is for sale, from what you eat to a transfer or promotion. We never encouraged the Vietnamese forces to fight aggressively, to take the offensive. We fought the war for them and made them over dependent on air support. We prepared them for conventional war when the Communists were fighting unconventionally, and then, when the Communists finally adopted conventional tactics, the South Vietnamese didn't know what to do. The fact they have no leadership is largely our fault; we made them followers, so successfully that even the soldiers who were willing to fight got killed or wounded as a result of incompetence, or lost by default . . .[66]

The fall of Phnom Penh on 17 April was followed by President Ford's announcement on 23 April that, for the United States, the war was over. One week later – only hours after the departure of the last American helicopter – NVA tanks rolled unopposed into Saigon.[67]

In assessing the contributory factors to this final episode of the Vietnam debacle, Kissinger cited three conditions which had markedly changed in the 16 months following the conclusion of the Paris agreement: first, 'the total collapse, or the substantial collapse, of executive authority in the United States as a result of Watergate'; second, legislative restrictions such as the August 1973 bombing cutoff in Cambodia; and third, the sweeping reduction in military and economic assistance to the Saigon regime, by Congress.[68] From Kissinger's perspective these limitations, imposed owing to the demands of American domestic politics, had prevented the Administration from attending to one of the prime requisites of the 'stable structure': the maintenance of regional power balances.

Under these circumstances, the Soviet Union's actions *vis-à-vis* the supply of material support for the final North Vietnamese offensive, while not dismissed, were wholly comprehensible. As Kissinger put it during a nation-wide television interview on 5 May 1975:

We have to understand what détente represents. The Soviet Union is a great power that is in many parts of the world operating competitively with us. The Soviet Union is also a country that possesses an enormous nuclear arsenal and with which we have certain interests in common such as the prevention of general nuclear war, such as limiting conflict in areas where both of us could get directly involved.

In those areas détente has worked reasonably well. *What we cannot ask the Soviet Union to do is to keep itself from taking advantage of situations in which, for whatever reasons, we do not do what is required to maintain the balance.*

It is possible that Soviet arms made the conquest of South Vietnam possible. It is also true that the refusal of American arms made the conquest of Vietnam inevitable.

Therefore, while the Soviet Union does have a heavy responsibility, we cannot expect the Soviet Union to police the world for us and we have to be mature enough to recognize that we have to co-exist, even in a competitive world, and perhaps hopefully be able to moderate over a period of years the competition in peripheral areas.

Now eventually the Soviet Union must realize that it is responsible for the consequences of its actions even in peripheral areas.

But as a basic relationship détente has never meant the absence of competition [emphasis added].[69]

The sharply divergent Executive and Congressional perspectives manifested in April 1975 again confirmed the paradoxical status of the Vietnam question within the American foreign policy debate. What within the framework of the Administration constituted an important symbol of US credibility was in the view of Congress simply an anomalous, albeit tragic, vestige of the Cold War. Kissinger's fervent advocacy of policies consistent with his geopolitical image of the international system increasingly found him at odds with a post-Watergate Congress determined to reassert its traditional prerogatives in the realm of foreign policy.

To many, Kissinger's notion of national security, with its stress on the paramount importance of maintaining credibility, was considered (to borrow Bernard Brodie's language from a different context) 'an inherently expansible concept' leading to the dangerous proliferation of US security commitments. The unambiguous rebuff of this approach with respect to Vietnam was accompanied by Congressional moves to signal the continuing validity of those 'core commitments' based upon the consonance of American values and interests (e.g. Western Europe, Japan, Israel, etc.).[70] At heart, the gulf between Kissinger and his Congressional critics centered on two basic questions: first, the utility of force; and second, the centrality of the East–West competition during a period of increasing diversity and fragmentation within the international system as a whole. Within seven months of the fall of Saigon, the unfolding nature of events in Angola again led to the clash of these contending security perspectives.

The Angolan Civil War

The American policy debate over Angola which emerged to public prominence in the Autumn of 1975 must be viewed within the context of the overall evolution of executive–legislative relations during the post-Vietnam period. In rejecting Kissinger's trenchant criticism of Congressional restrictions on the Administration's conduct of foreign policy, Senator George McGovern observed that the Secretary of State's 'sadness' over insufficient 'flexibility' was 'based on the fact that history did not begin with Angola.'[71] That Congress moved to reassert its traditional role in the realm of foreign policy was, arguably, an inevitable consequence of the demise of the Cold War consensus over Vietnam. Though the 'collapse of executive authority' attendant to Watergate clearly exacerbated this trend, it was by no means the sole precipitant of it.

After 1974 the Administration and Congress clashed over a number of issues, notably including: the Jackson–Vanik Amendment linking Jewish emigration from the Soviet Union to the lifting of trade restrictions, military assistance to Vietnam and Cambodia, the cutoff of military aid to Turkey following the invasion of Cyprus, and the Congressional refusal to allow the sale of 14 batteries of *Hawk* ground-to-air missiles to Jordan. This shift toward greater Congressional activism and oversight prompted Kissinger to assert that 'the danger now is that the pendulum will swing too far . . .'[72] Owing to the unique fusion of style and substance inherent to the 'Nixon–Kissinger' approach, criticism of the former (e.g. centralization and secrecy) inevitably begged awkward questions pertaining to the latter. In these terms, the public controversy surrounding the Angolan Civil War had a broader significance which went to the very heart of the Kissinger diplomacy. As during the latter stages of the Vietnam War, domestic critics came to question both the instrumentalities and ends of American power.

Prior to the 1975 Angolan crisis, Southern Africa commanded a relatively low priority in American regional security planning. In April 1969, as part of the Nixon Administration's comprehensive foreign policy review, Kissinger ordered a survey of US policy options toward the region. Prepared by the NSC Interdepartmental Group for Africa, this study (designated NSSM-39 and presented to President Nixon in early January 1970) delineated the range of American choice in the region from overt association with the white regimes to disengagement. Of the alternative policies examined, Kissinger reportedly advocated the adoption of NSSM-39's so-called 'tar baby' option, which called for the Administration to 'maintain public opposition to racial repression but relax political isolation and economic restrictions on the white states.' This analysis was based upon the following premise:

The whites are here to stay and the only way that constructive change can come about is through them. There is no hope for the blacks to gain the political rights they seek through violence, which will only lead to chaos and increased opportunities for the communists. We can, by selective relaxation of our stance toward the white regimes, encourage some modification of their current racial and colonial policies and through more substantial economic assistance to the black states (a total of about $5 million annually in technical assistance to the black states) help to draw the two groups together and exert some influence on both for peaceful change. Our tangible interests form a basis for our contacts in the region, and these can be maintained at an acceptable political cost.[73]

Envisioned as a document to provide coherence to American policy toward Southern Africa, NSSM-39 was as striking in its omissions as in its prescriptions. The study concluded that the African liberation movements in the Portuguese colonies, Rhodesia and South Africa were ineffectual and constitute no 'realistic or supportable' alternative to the existing colonial/white minority regimes. While dismissing 'the depth and permanence of black resolve,' the NSC Interdepartmental Group for Africa did not at any point similarly question the limits of Portuguese will and commitment. Administration actions consistent with the 'tar baby' approach belied repeated State Department affirmations that the United States maintained its support for the principle of self-determination in Portuguese Africa.[74] Rather than fostering a more accommodative Portuguese attitude *vis-à-vis* political change in Southern Africa, the net effect of American actions during the 1969–73 period was to reinforce the Lisbon regime's intransigent policies toward the liberation movements operating within its colonial territories. Indeed, the Portuguese leadership went so far as to cite explicitly the Nixon Doctrine as a means of justifying its regional policy in Southern Africa.[75]

The October 1973 Middle East War served to confirm the Administration's belief in Portugal's value as a strategic ally. Having been denied access to facilities in Western Europe, the Administration was permitted by the Lisbon government to utilize the Azores base in establishing the vital American 'air-bridge' to Israel. The Caetano regime acted on the reasonable belief that Portuguese acquiescence to this direct request from the Nixon Administration in the midst of a major international crisis would translate into increased leverage during subsequent negotiations (specifically, the then pending talks over the renewal of the executive agreement governing American basing rights in the Azores). During a stop-over in Lisbon en route to the Middle East in December 1973, Kissinger publicly expressed thanks to the Portuguese leadership for its indirect assistance during the Middle East War.[76] In private discussions, the Secretary of State – much to the evident dismay of his closest aides – reportedly agreed on behalf of the Administration to supply Portugal with weapons for use in its African wars as a *quid pro quo* for continued US access to the Azores base.[77] In terms of the deleterious impact which such a policy undoubtedly would have had on Afro-American relations, one aspect of the Portuguese military coup in April 1974 was that it pre-empted the implementation of this decision.

The seizure of political power by the Armed Forces Movement on 25 April 1974 unleashed a wave of political activity within Portugal. After decades of neglect and stagnation at home, the 'Portuguese Revolution' soon took on the characteristics of a profound – if not somewhat chaotic – social revolution. This pattern of domestic instability prompted Kissinger subsequently to conclude that 'the overthrow of the Portuguese government in April 1974 and the growing strength of the Portuguese Communist party apparently convinced Moscow that a "revolutionary situation" was developing in Africa'.[78]

In contrast with Guinea-Bissau and Mozambique, the orderly transfer of authority in Angola was hampered by the existence of three contending centers of nationalist power with which the Lisbon regime had to negotiate. These rival parties were divided roughly along ethnic lines during the pre-independence period (though each made a concerted effort to expand its ethnic base). The dominant Angolan nationalist party during the 1960s was the FNLA (*Frente Nacional de Libertação*). Founded in 1962 under the leadership of Holden Roberto, the FNLA derived its major internal support from the Bakongo people of northern Angola. Significantly, the FNLA was the recipient of limited American assistance during the Kennedy Administration (as a hedge against the possible collapse of Portuguese military forces) and was, for most of the pre-independence period, the only Angolan nationalist movement officially recognized by the OAU. In 1964, the resignation of Jonas Savimbi as FNLA Foreign Minister led to the creation of UNITA (*União Nacional para Independência Total de Angola*). Savimbi's UNITA, militarily the least effective of the three contending movements, developed primarily as a movement of the southern-based Ovimbundu (the largest linguistic–ethnic grouping, constituting roughly one-third of the nation's indigenous population). The strongest challenge to FNLA predominance during the pre-independence period came from the MPLA (*Movimento Popular de Libertação de Angola*). Founded in 1956 by a small group of urban intellectuals in the Luanda area, the MPLA was dominated by the Mbundu, occupying central Angola inland from Luanda and constituting some one-fourth of the country's black population. In the early 1960s, the party began to receive small-scale Cuban and Soviet military assistance. An intra-party dispute culminated in the elevation of Dr Agostinho Neto (a medical doctor and political dissident known for his revolutionary poetry) to the presidency of the MPLA in December 1962.

During the latter half of 1974, Portuguese strategy centered upon the attempt to bring about a reconciliation of the three Angolan nationalist parties (despite the OAU's repeated failure to achieve that end). Following a preliminary round of discussions in Mombasa, Kenya, between the leaders of the MPLA, FNLA and UNITA, multilateral negotiations were convened at the Portuguese city of Alvor on 10 January 1975. The resulting agreement, signed by Neto, Roberto and Savimbi five days later, provided for the formation of a transition government to prepare for full independence on 11 November 1975. Not surprisingly, the installation of a transition government on 31 January 1975 was followed within weeks by the resumption of inter-party fighting as each movement attempted to bolster its internal position prior to the November deadline.

In late January 1975, the 40 Committee – the presidential body authorized to supervise intelligence operations and chaired by Kissinger – met to consider a CIA request of $300,000 in covert assistance for the FNLA during the pre-November transition period.[79] During the previous year the FNLA had attained a position of apparent military preponderance amongst the contending nationalist forces as a result of large-scale aid from China. On 29 May 1974, a contingent of 112 Chinese military advisers reportedly arrived in Zaire to train FNLA guerrillas. Although most aid remained covert, the FNLA publicly acknowledged the receipt of 450 tons of supplies from the PRC.[80] This military assistance complemented the already considerable material support proffered by Zaire to the FNLA. Soviet assistance to the MPLA was suspended in the first quarter of 1974 (prior to the coup in Lisbon) evidently as a result of Moscow's disenchantment with the internecine fighting between the party's contending factions. Soviet military aid to the movement was, however, resumed at a significant level in the Autumn – arguably as a response to Chinese arms transfers to the FNLA. Though also the recipient of assistance from the PRC (albeit on a more modest scale), UNITA remained the militarily least effective of the three main nationalist movements owing to shortages of both material and trained personnel. Such was the Angolan situation when the 40 Committee convened in the wake of the Alvor agreement in late January 1975.

According to one participant, Kissinger used the word 'compelling' to characterize the CIA presentation on Angola before the 40 Committee.[81] The 'routine' decision to approve large-scale funding of the FNLA was striking in that it was accompanied by the rejection of a similar request for $100,000 in assistance for UNITA. John Marcum later argued that this was motivated by 'apparently past connections and an irrepressible habit of thinking in terms of "our team" and "theirs" . . .'[82] The implications of the American decision to eschew a military relationship with UNITA during the first half of 1975 were far-reaching. It was a major factor contributing to Savimbi's eventual move toward South Africa – a decision which cost UNITA its diplomatic support within the OAU and, more importantly, legitimized large-scale Soviet/Cuban assistance to the MPLA. Several informed observers have speculated that if Western support had transformed UNITA – already a potent political force – into a coherent military organization by July 1975, the MPLA would have entered into a post-independence coalition government with them. As it was, the failure of the Administration to contemplate early assistance for UNITA represented a failure of analysis and a lost opportunity. In so doing, the success of American policy in Angola became inextricably linked to the fate of Holden Roberto's FNLA.

The relationship between the renewal of substantial American assistance to the FNLA in January 1975 and the subsequent build-up of March/April remains a matter of contention. Critics of Administration policy have maintained that Soviet policy was basically reactive. Although the $300,000 allocated by the 40 Committee in late January was designated for 'political purposes',[83] they note that (in terms of its public perception) rumors of 'heavy continuing CIA support for the FNLA' became 'very prevalent in Luanda.'[84] Nathaniel Davis, then Assistant Secretary of State for African Affairs, has cast extreme doubt, however, upon the various attempts to establish a causal relationship between the January decision and the build-up of Soviet arms which began in March:

Perhaps evidence will come to light in the future showing that the January Forty Committee decision really did trigger the step-up in Soviet aid and arms supply, but I do not believe the case is made . . . The $300,000 was for political action, not weapons, and only part of the money was expended between January and the Soviet arms build-up of March/April – probably decided upon in Moscow somewhat earlier. Considerable sums of money and quantities of arms were filtering into Angola during that period from a multiplicity of sources and to all three movements.

If one is looking for externally visible actions that might be said to have triggered the Soviet build-up, one should perhaps also consider Holden Roberto's movement of troops into northern Angola and the capital city of Luanda, and the Chinese support for Roberto in 1974–75 which no doubt had an impact on Soviet thinking. By March/April 1975, it was clear that the Alvor Accord . . . was breaking down.[85]

The strategy of the three nationalist movements during the first half of 1975 centered primarily upon the attempt to consolidate control of those areas which accorded with their respective ethnic followings. The main focal point of conflict was in the Luanda area between the MPLA and the FNLA. John Marcum notes that 'from March to July, fighting and Soviet arms shipments increased in tandem.'[86] This military assistance (estimated at over 100 tons) was considered a major escalatory move by the Administration in terms of the level of sophistication of equipment introduced into the conflict.[87] In May, Davis chaired an Interagency NSC Task Force on Angola whose report was submitted on 13 June 1975. The task force, composed of Africanists from the CIA, State and Defense Departments, recommended that the Administration eschew covert military involvement in favor of a diplomatic–political posture supportive of international mediatory efforts. In arguing against military intervention the interagency group maintained that Angola 'was basically an African problem' and that large-scale American assistance would run the risk of public exposure, have an uncertain bearing on the political outcome within the country, and seriously compromise American relations with states both within the region and beyond.[88] This study was not, however, presented to the 40 Committee in the form of a specific policy recommendation. As the House Select Committee on Intelligence subsequently reported:

The Committee has learned that a task force composed of high US experts on Africa strongly opposed military intervention; instead . . . they called for diplomatic efforts to encourage a political settlement among the three factions to avert bloodshed. Apparently at the direction of National Security Council aides, the task force recommendation was removed from the report and presented to NSC members as merely one policy option. The other two alternatives were a hands-off policy or substantial military intervention.[89]

The recommendation contained in – later excised from – the 13 June Task Force report was reiterated by Davis in lengthy memoranda submitted to Under Secretary of State Joseph Sisco prior to a meeting of the 40 Committee on 14 July.[90] The internal policy debate during this period closely paralleled that which publicly emerged between Secretary Kissinger and Congress in the final weeks of 1975. On the one side, Davis and a majority of the Africanists within the relevant federal departments and agencies advocated a policy line consistent with their 'regionalist' perspective. In sharp contrast, Kissinger and other senior Administration officials (e.g. Secretary of Defense James Schlesinger) regarded the Angolan crisis in broader 'geopolitical' terms as an important test case of American will and commitment (coming as it did within weeks of the fall of Saigon).

Though the weight of expert analysis from within the government seriously questioned the efficacy of covert assistance both in its military and political impact, the 40 Committee, meeting again on 17 July, approved the CIA Action Plan to grant an initial $14 million (of an eventual total of $31.7 million) to the FNLA and UNITA. Nathaniel Davis, who resigned as Assistant Secretary in the immediate aftermath of this decision, later commented:

Both during the final weeks of the Vietnam War and during the Angolan crisis of 1975, the Secretary and the President seem to have believed that it was better to roll the dice against the longest of odds than to abandon the competition against our great adversary. The Secretary would freely acknowledge, I believe, that he saw Angola as part of the US–Soviet relationship, and not as an African problem.[91]

The influx of large-scale foreign military assistance to the contending nationalist movements was accompanied by a marked escalation in the level of fighting. In mid-June 1975, a month before the decisive meetings of the 40 Committee, the three presidents of the liberation movements met under President Jomo Kenyatta's auspices in an ostensible attempt to salvage the Alvor agreement. *The Times* reported on 25 June that 'the ink was hardly dry on the [Nakuru] agreement between the three rival Angolan nationalist leaders to end their followers' murderous feuding when shooting broke out again in Luanda.'[92] In subsequent testimony before a Senate subcommittee, Kissinger argued that 'by mid-July the military situation radically favored the MPLA.'[93] On 9 July the MPLA launched a major military drive to expel the FNLA and UNITA from Luanda. With it, the transitional government collapsed and the country moved into all-out civil war.

During the period when the 40 Committee was considering the appropriation of large-scale covert military assistance to the FNLA and UNITA, the only Congressman closely following events in Angola was freshman Senator Dick Clark (D-Iowa), Chairman of the Senate Foreign Relations Committee's Subcommittee on African Affairs. In June and July 1975 Clark chaired a series of hearings dealing with American policy toward Southern Africa.[94] The main focus of the subcommittee proceedings was Angola, owing to the prolifer-ation of American and European newspaper reports containing charges of American aid to the FNLA conveyed via Zaire. At one point in the July hearings, Assistant Secretary Davis passed a note to Clark (who had received a CIA briefing on Angola) asking not to be pressed on certain questions because 'we both know' about American covert activities in support of the anti-MPLA factions.[95] In August, Clark journeyed to Angola and had the opportunity to meet with the leaders of three contending nationalist movements. He returned even more convinced of the mistake of American involve-ment and expressed these reservations both to William Colby (Director of the Central Intelligence Agency) and the full Senate Foreign Relations Committee.

These events occurred against the backdrop of a marked intensi-fication of the civil war within Angola. By the end of August 1975, the MPLA had secured control of 11 of the nation's 15 provincial capi-tals, as well as the oil-rich enclave of Cabinda.[96] During that same month came the first reports of significant Cuban and South African involvement in support of the MPLA and FNLA/UNITA coalition respectively. The initial military success of the MPLA during the summer of 1975 prompted President Mobutu to increase the level of the Zairean commitment to the FNLA. Between late July and mid-August, three Zairean companies and an armored-car squadron were moved across the border and into combat in northern Angola.[97]

With the Mobutu regime facing severe and chronic domestic economic difficulties, the State Department (in a move strongly endorsed by Kissinger) sought to persuade Congress to approve an immediate $160 million to Zaire in supplemental assistance.[98] This attempt to shore up the government of President Mobutu came amidst growing Congressional concern that American aid designated for Zaire was being funnelled to the anti-Soviet factions in Angola. This charge was officially denied by the Administration though reports to that effect persisted throughout the closing months of 1975.[99] In supporting the assistance measures, Kissinger is reported to have agreed that the economic crisis in Zaire threatened the Mobutu regime at a time when its help over Angola was needed most. This concern, in turn, led the State Department to give high priority to the question of aid to Zaire. Coming as it did during a period in which the general ability of the United States to support its overseas clients effectively was being widely questioned, the Administration evidently sought the aid package in order to signal firm American backing for the Mobutu regime.

The first major public disclosure of American military assistance to the FNLA and UNITA came on 25 September 1975 in an article written by Leslie Gelb of the *New York Times*. Surprisingly, this report – coming only months after the fall of Saigon – failed to generate a public debate over American involvement in Angola. Perhaps (as Nathaniel Davis has suggested) this stemmed from the article's primary emphasis being on the Administration's response to the evolving political situation in Portugal.[100] Not until early November (following Senator Clark's fact-finding mission to Southern Africa and the outbreak of large-scale fighting involving Cuban and South African regular forces) did the full Senate Foreign Relations Committee hold its first hearings on American involvement in Angola. During testimony given in closed session, CIA Director Colby and Under Secretary of State Sisco confirmed that American covert assistance was being lent to the two anti-Soviet liberation movements within the country. Both officials defended the military aid program to FNLA and UNITA on the grounds that the United States needed 'bargaining chips' in order to restore the internal military balance of power and thereby prompt the Soviet Union and its clients to seek a negotiated settlement. The publication of this testimony by the *New York Times* on the day following the Senate hearings was the first of a torrent of 'leaks' over the next two months regarding American covert activities in Angola.[101]

With the shift of the debate over Angola squarely into the public domain, Congressmen previously wary of voicing open opposition to Administration policy for fear of jeopardizing a covert operation became free to act on the legislative front (e.g. the introduction of bills to terminate American military assistance). Little more than two weeks after the public disclosure of the testimony of Colby and Sisco, Kissinger issued his first public warning to the Soviet Union on the Angolan situation. Speaking in Detroit on 24 November 1975, the Secretary of State asserted that the United States would not remain 'indifferent while an outside power embarks upon an interventionist policy – so distant from its homeland and so removed from traditional Russian interests.' The Administration, Kissinger stated, would cooperate in the pursuit of a negotiated settlement, 'but time is running out. Continuation of an interventionist policy must inevitably threaten other relationships.' Coming in the wake of the public furore created by the revelation of American covert assistance to the FNLA and UNITA, Kissinger concluded the Detroit speech with a plea to domestic critics 'to end the self-flagellation that has done so much harm to this nation's capacity to conduct foreign policy.'[102]

The acceleration of the Soviet airlift (using *Antonov*-22 transports) into Brazzaville during November brought the total of equipment transferred to the MPLA by air alone to a reported 1,000 tons.[103] Opponents of Administration policy contended that the increase in Soviet/Cuban aid constituted merely a response to prior escalatory actions by the United States, Zaire and South Africa.[104] Two days after the Detroit speech, the *Washington Post* (in a move which reflected a growing consensus of opinion) editorially called upon the Administration to terminate American covert activities in Angola. It called upon President Ford to explain publicly the political and strategic rationale underlying Administration policy and approach Congress for a 'modest open' program of support for the FNLA and UNITA. 'If the case for support cannot survive disclosure and debate,' the paper asserted, 'then let that be the end of it.'[105]

The first serious legislative challenge to the Administration's Angola policy came on 4 December 1975 when Senator Dick Clark proposed an amendment to prohibit any American involvement in the civil war without specific congressional authorization. Kissinger privately acknowledged that Clark was right 'from an African point of view' but insisted that he was wrong strategically.[106] The Secretary of State repeatedly asserted that American opposition to the MPLA stemmed not from its ideological orientation; the United States had after all, he noted, freely accepted a FRELIMO regime in Mozambique. What clearly distinguished the two cases in the view of the Administration was the degree of reliance upon Soviet/Cuban support – a theme which Kissinger returned to in his press conference of 12 December:

The United States did not become concerned until there had already taken place substantial Soviet involvement and the introduction of massive outside equipment and later the introduction of Cuban forces.

I think . . . there should not be a war by proxy of the great powers. I do not think it is a situation analogous to Vietnam, because in Vietnam the conflict had a much longer and more complicated history; but the United States cannot be indifferent to what is going on in Angola . . .

The United States favors a solution in which all of the parties in Angola can negotiate with each other free of outside interference and in which the problem of Angola is handled as an African issue. The United States will support any solution in this direction. Failing that, the United States will try to prevent one party by means of massive introduction of outside equipment from achieving dominance . . .

It cannot but affect relations between the United States and the Soviet Union . . . if the Soviet Union engages in a military operation or massively supports a military operation thousands of miles from Soviet territory in an area where there are no historic Russian interests and where it is therefore a new projection of Soviet power and Soviet interests.[107]

Kissinger argued that while the various mechanisms of linkage politics contributed to the restraint of Soviet behavior, they could not, in the final analysis, replace the maintenance of regional balances. Here, the underlying fear was that cumulative shifts along the periphery – that is, the creation of new 'precedents' such as Angola – could, by way of feedback, lead to an erosion of those understandings governing the central strategic balance.[108]

In early December, Clark was persuaded by the Democratic leadership within the Senate to yield to Senator John Tunney (D-California) on the Angolan aid cutoff question. Although Tunney lacked any expertise on Africa, he faced a difficult re-election fight and it was thought that public exposure on this issue would provide him with an important electoral boost. President Ford's veto of the Foreign Assistance Act (containing the Clark Amendment) was followed by the introduction of an amendment to the $113 billion Defense Appropriation Bill by Senator Tunney. On 18 December, the Senate rejected by a vote of 72–26 an Administration-backed amendment offered by Senator Robert Griffin (R-Michigan) which would have forbidden the deployment of US 'combat personnel' in Angola, but permitted the continuation of a military assistance program to the FNLA and UNITA. With the defeat of the Griffin Amendment, Kissinger met with some two dozen senators for almost four hours in a final effort to achieve a 'compromise' solution. Although Kissinger dismissed the analogy between Vietnam and Angola, many senators regarded the Administration's $28 million request as an open-ended commitment with clear parallels to the Gulf of Tonkin Resolution. This view reflected the broader public perception of the Angolan crisis. A public opinion poll indicated that Americans opposed by a three-to-one margin the proposal to send military supplies to the pro-Western forces in Angola because they perceived the civil war there as fitting the Vietnam model too closely.[109]

On 19 December 1975, the Senate approved the Tunney Amendment by a 43–22 vote. Two immediate factors contributed to this lopsided rejection of Administration policy. First, in terms of the military situation within Angola which had developed by the middle of December, it was evident that only a massive infusion of American military assistance with instructors and advisers could forestall a rapid Cuban/MPLA victory.[110] Second, the identification of the FNLA and UNITA with South African intervention had by the time of the Senate vote led to a dramatic enhancement of the MPLA's diplomatic standing within the OAU.[111]

President Ford strongly castigated Senate passage of the Tunney Amendment, describing it as 'a deep tragedy for all countries whose security depends on the United States.'[112] Kissinger's reaction was equally sharp. At his press conference of 23 December, he criticized Congress for imposing legislative restrictions which greatly hindered the Administration's ability to conduct a coherent policy toward the Soviet Union. 'The danger to détente that we face now,' Kissinger stated, 'is that our domestic disputes are depriving us of both the ability to provide incentives for moderation, such as the restrictions on the Trade Act [*viz.* the Jackson–Vanik Amendment], as well as the ability to resist military moves by the Soviet Union.'[113] In subsequent testimony before the Senate Foreign Relations Committee's Subcommittee on African Affairs, Kissinger contended that the congressional failure to acquiesce to the Administration's efforts to maintain an equilibrium of power within Angola had led to the collapse of prospects for a negotiated settlement:

Our diplomacy was effective so long as we maintained the leverage of a possible military balance. African determination to oppose Soviet and Cuban intervention was becoming more and more evident. On December 9, President Ford made a formal proposal to the Soviet Government through their Ambassador. Indeed, it appeared as if the Soviet Union had begun to take stock. They halted their airlift from December 9 until December 24.

By mid-December we were hopeful that the OAU would provide a framework for eliminating the interference of outside powers by calling for an end to their intervention. At that point, the impact of our domestic debate overwhelmed the possibilities of diplomacy. After the Senate vote to block any further aid to Angola, the Cubans more than doubled their forces and Soviet military aid was resumed on an even larger scale. The scope of Soviet–Cuban intervention increased drastically; the cooperativeness of Soviet diplomacy declined.[114]

While Kissinger affirmed that Soviet behavior in Angola was fundamentally 'incompatible' with détente, the future course of Administration action following the passage of the Tunney Amendment remained uncertain.[115] Informed observers pointed to the various non-military sanctions which Washington could invoke against the Soviet Union in response to the Angolan crisis. Two specific policy instruments were suggested: grain sales and the Strategic Arms Limitation Talks. Each was considered and eventually ruled out, however, by the Administration as an appropriate diplomatic counter-measure. A moratorium on grain sales was rejected on both practical and political grounds. With respect to the former, Kissinger later explained that a grain cutoff 'would not have been effective in any time frame relevant to ... the issue of Angola.'[116] Likewise, in terms of the demands of American domestic politics, there was a clear reluctance to risk the alienation of an important interest group as the nation entered a presidential election year. Addressing a predominantly agricultural audience in St Louis in early January 1976, President Ford stated: 'The linkage of grain with diplomacy would mean disruption and hardship for you, the farmer, a serious increase in tensions between the world's two superpowers and no effect in Angola.'[117]

With Kissinger scheduled to visit Moscow in mid-January to confer with the Soviet leadership over the finalization of the SALT II agreement, there was speculation that the Administration might alter its position in that negotiating forum in order to escalate pressure on the Kremlin over the Angolan situation. Citing the superpowers' profound mutuality of interest in SALT, this possibility, however, was rejected by Kissinger: 'SALT ... is in our common interest. It is not a favor we grant to the Soviet Union. It is an inherent necessity of the present period. Avoiding nuclear war is not a favor we do anybody. Avoiding nuclear war without giving up any interests is the problem that we face now.'[118]

Primary emphasis was thus placed by the Administration upon the contribution of SALT *vis-à-vis* the enhancement of the stability of the central strategic balance. An important additional factor was the continuing role of SALT with respect to the *political legitimation* of the superpower relationship. Even after the serious setbacks of the post-1973 period, SALT remained the undisputed centerpiece of détente – a negotiating process into which the leaderships of both countries had invested tremendous personal political capital. While eschewing any overt form of linkage between SALT and Angola, Kissinger did warn 'that a continuation of actions like those in Angola must threaten the entire web of Soviet–US relations'.[119] Congressional opposition to the SALT II agreement during the Carter Administration (in the wake of Soviet interventionist activities in Angola, Ethiopia and Afghanistan) demonstrated the inherent difficulties of insulating the SALT process from the broader international political environment.

Following President Ford's signing of the Defense Appropriation Bill (including the Tunney Amendment) on 10 February 1976, the CIA reportedly terminated its program of covert assistance to the FNLA and UNITA.[120] As during the aftermath of the October 1973 Middle East War, the conclusion of the Angolan episode prompted many to question the efficacy of the Administration's approach to relations with the Soviet Union. Kissinger – not without some justification – contended that Congressional restrictions had denied the Administration the ability to induce restraint in Moscow through the adroit application of incentives and penalties. As the United States entered the 1976 presidential election year, détente and the Kissinger diplomacy came under increasingly severe attack from both ends of the American political spectrum. To right-wing opponents of Administration policy, détente had long been viewed as 'a one-way street' tantamount to 'appeasement.'[121] On the orthodox left of American politics, liberals (primarily in the Democratic Party) charged that the Kissinger diplomacy was inconsistent with the core values which US foreign policy had traditionally sought to project. They advocated the eschewal of *Realpolitik* in favor of the adoption of a new foreign policy agenda embracing such concerns as human rights and the North–South dialogue.

The prevailing national mood manifested following the Angolan crisis was accurately conveyed in the summary of an influential public opinion survey published shortly prior to the 1976 presidential election:

A major US role in the world, with the activism that implies, is acceptable to – even desired by – most Americans. But our next president need understand that this desire does not translate into support for indiscriminate interventionism.

Following a number of reverses in the world arena, and perhaps prodded a bit by a measure of introspection in this bicentennial year, Americans seem infused with a certain sense of nationalism that dominated American outlook during most of our earlier history. Such nationalism is by no means logically incompatible with the aspects of unilateralism that also holds widespread appeal. *We want to be number one once more*, but we want to attain that goal with a measure of caution and without the excess of commitment that resulted in Vietnam [emphasis added].[122]

The question remained, however, as to how the contending foreign policy demands reflected in this formulation of the new 'sense of nationalism' were to be simultaneously met. In what way was the pursuit of primacy – the drive once again to be 'number one' – to be reconciled with a post-Vietnam policy of 'selective engagement'?

The Nixon–Kissinger strategy embodied one attempt (as it were) to square this circle. In seeking to distinguish itself from its predecessor, the Carter Administration offered a different answer – one ostensibly more compatible with the American national mood. Indeed, this commitment to alter the style and substance of American foreign policy was a major factor underlying the Democratic candidate's broad popular appeal in 1976. In terms strikingly similar to Nixon's inaugural address in January 1969, the Carter Administration called for the promulgation of a new foreign policy approach consonant with the new pluralism of the international system. Here, as discussed in the concluding chapter below, good regionalism – the consideration of 'local' issues outside the East/West matrix of concerns – was deemed to be the best form of geopolitics allowing the United States to maintain its preponderant international position at a sustainable cost. And yet, in excessively downgrading the importance of the East–West competition (just as Kissinger had perhaps overstated its centrality), the Carter Administration generated its own policy dilemmas and problems of coherence.

CONCLUSION

Henry Kissinger concluded his study of the Congress of Vienna system with the observation that 'men became myths, not by what they know, nor even by what they achieve, but by the tasks they set for themselves.'[1] To be sure, the momentous task which Kissinger later set for himself as a statesman was not dissimilar from that confronted by the architects of the post-Napoleonic order. Kissinger assumed stewardship over American foreign policy during a period of fundamental change in the international system. The attempt by the Nixon Administration to elaborate a coherent new approach to supplant the shattered shell of American Cold War policy was complicated by the mixed nature of that evolving system.

This complexity was reflected in the confluence of co-existent, yet contending, images of international order within whose broad bounds administration policy had to be framed. The challenge of reconciling the competitive demands of nascent multipolarity and revitalized bipolarity was – and indeed remains – perhaps the principal foreign policy dilemma to confront American decision-makers in the post-Vietnam period. While rhetorically extolling the virtues of the former ('the potential and imperative of a pluralistic world'), Nixon and Kissinger explicitly oriented Administration policy toward the latter. The emergence of the Soviet Union as a global power was described by Kissinger as 'the problem of our age.' Critics of the Nixon–Kissinger strategy asserted that the Administration's 'fresh approach' constituted little more than a continuation of the Cold War by other means.

Changes in the international system were complemented by those occurring within the American domestic realm. Two decades of 'undifferentiated globalism', culminating in the Vietnam involvement, had led to an erosion of the consensus behind containment. The year 1968 thus marked the end of the foreign policy cycle ushered in by the Truman Doctrine. The enunciation of the containment doctrine in 1947 had formalized the post-war transformation of the United States from an insular great power to a superpower with a global network of interests. The acrimonious American debate over Vietnam prompted renewed fears abroad that the United States might revert to a neo-isolationist posture. Slogans, such as 'Come home, America,' captured the mood of a considerable segment of the public. This alternative formulation of American foreign policy represented virtually the mirror image of the approach that it was intended to supplant.

Kissinger sought to steer a course between the extremes of undifferentiated involvement and disengagement. In so doing, he hoped to manage the domestic backlash stemming from Vietnam and to establish the bases of a more realistic American role in the international system. This task was complicated by the turbulent circumstances that confronted the Nixon Administration in 1969. With the major elements of the international and domestic environments in a simultaneous state of flux, Administration policy invariably assumed a transitory nature. This characteristic was acknowledged by Kissinger in his final interview before relinquishing office:

Just before I came [to Washington] I wrote an article in which I said the world is bipolar militarily, multipolar politically and fragmented economically. When you talk of world order now you have to take account of each of these realities and also the fact that probably history will record this as one of the philosophical revolutions of history. In the nature of things, this task could not have been completed . . .[2]

In reviewing the legacy of American postwar policy from the Truman Doctrine to the Nixon Doctrine, two loose stages of thought and their corresponding recipes for action have been distinguished. During the Cold War period of rigid bipolarity American strategies for regional security were notable for their architectonic nature. Emphasis was placed upon the elaboration of formal alliance structures which were to be bolstered by the Western great powers and envisaged to serve the ends of containment. An important complement to this regional security orientation was an attitude toward (and supposed comprehension of) the dynamics of the modernization process as expressed in the slogan 'nation-building'. Together, these policies – ostensibly reconciling the demands of security and modernity – were intended to successfully transform and stabilize not only the international political landscape, but the domestic structures of the developing nation-states as well. The Viet-

nam debacle called the underlying assumptions of global containment into question: it demonstrated the strength of indigenous
nationalisms, the limitations of military power, and the dangers of
putting 'local' issues into East–West matrices.[3] The net result was to
call both the *instrumentalities* and the *ends* of American policy into
question. The collapse of the domestic consensus behind global
containment as a consequence of Vietnam led to the promulgation
of a new approach to regional security under the Nixon Administration.

The Nixon–Kissinger strategy sought to harmonize the twin
imperatives of politico-military retrenchment and détente. Though
the profound disjunction between these two components of
American foreign policy later emerged, they were initially regarded
as being not only compatible, but symbiotic. To varying degrees,
each was to serve as the instrumentality of the other. Thus, the policy
of superpower détente was viewed as a means of creating and ensuring
the stable conditions along the periphery which would allow for an
orderly devolution of responsibility to incipient regional powers. In
effect, it was hoped that the rhetoric of commitment, as evidenced in
the first guideline of the Nixon Doctrine, could continue because
the reality of détente would allow the commitments to remain
unimplemented.

Within this perspective, scant attention was paid to the implications of Western policies *vis-à-vis* the dynamics of Third World
modernization (e.g. the impact of arms transfers upon domestic
structures). Rather, emphasis was placed upon the malleability of
any given national order to constitute a working part of the emerging
international system – Kissinger's 'stable structure of peace'. As for
the Nixon Doctrine, though originally depicted as a post-Vietnam
approach to regional security consonant with the implications of
pluralism, the unfolding nature of the détente process (following the
October 1973 Middle East War), prompted it to be explicitly
addressed to the task of containing the emergence of Soviet power.
Within this context, the Nixon Doctrine appeared less the radical
departure in American postwar strategic doctrine which it ostensibly
heralded than yet another point along that very same continuum. In
terms of American efforts to integrate force and diplomacy, it thus
emerged as but a continuation of the process traced in chapter 1: the
differentiation of means within the prevailing bipolar image of the
international system. In these terms, the Nixon Doctrine (as con-

cluded above) was wholly consistent with previous attempts – from limited war to massive retaliation to flexible response – to adjust the instrumentalities of American power in the face of new domestic and international realities.

The fall of the Shah in January 1979 unquestionably constituted the greatest American foreign policy setback since the collapse of South Vietnam. Many observers pointed to the Iranian Revolution as marking the end of the Nixon Doctrine era with its emphasis upon the role of preponderant local powers. And yet, the question remains as to whether a credible regional security system can be envisioned outside the context of such an indigenous power. Here, it is interesting to note that though its own foreign policy orientation was avowedly divorced from the geopolitical framework of the Nixon–Ford–Kissinger diplomacy, the initial response of the Carter Administration was strikingly similar to that of its predecessor. Zbigniew Brzezinski, President Carter's Assistant for National Security Affairs, forcefully argued that the United States should align itself with pivotal states such as Saudi Arabia, Nigeria, Brazil, Iran, India and Indonesia, which he identified as 'regional influentials.'[4]

The long-term implications of the Iranian Revolution on the evolution of American regional security policy remain uncertain. The alternatives which continue to dominate public discussion are divided along two lines. The first strand of this renewed regional security debate is that which, like the Nixon Doctrine, emphasizes the potential role of locally preponderant powers. Though ostensibly discredited by the Iranian Revolution, proponents of this view argue that reliance on regional surrogates is necessary owing to the absence of domestic support for greater American activism following Vietnam. The late President Sadat's call for a massive infusion of American arms so that Egypt might supersede Iran as the 'stabilizing' power of the region was regarded by many observers as underscoring the continuing validity of that general orientation.[5]

The alternative to a Nixon Doctrine-type approach to regional security is a renewed American commitment to overt involvement along the Afro-Asian periphery. The Carter Administration's proposal for a US Rapid Deployment Force (RDF) for possible use in the Persian Gulf region following the Soviet invasion of Afghanistan marked a move in that direction.[6] The Reagan Administration, both through its expansive rhetoric and its plans to augment significantly American conventional forces, has further accelerated this shift. And yet, the question remains as to whether the domestic support for such an activist role can be sustained over the long term without 'the appeal to moralism' (to use Aron's phrase) which led to the excesses of American Cold War policy.

In assessing these two alternative approaches to regional security, one is struck by the manner in which they have been presented as caricatured opposites within the American debate. During the Kissinger years, the Nixon Doctrine was criticized for its seeming inability to transcend its own ambiguity. In part, this stemmed from the widespread perception of it as little more than a transitional strategy. Nonetheless, the Nixon Doctrine's failure to differentiate adequately amongst the categories and levels of regional security threats – from external aggression to the domestic dislocations resulting from the modernization process – often led to a severe distortion of policy as 'localist' and 'globalist' considerations became confused. In the contemporary debate, the options of increased American involvement (*viz.* the RDF) and support of local surrogates are presented as being mutually exclusive, rather than complementary aspects of the same regional security policy.

The broad spectrum of threats manifested in a pivotal region such as the Persian Gulf clearly requires a differentiated set of responses. Threats at the high end of that spectrum (e.g. a possible Soviet move into northern Iran) can only be countered by a concerted American deterrent posture, whereas a regional response coupled with a subtle Western policy of preventive diplomacy will undoubtedly continue to be the most effective manner of meeting those (more likely contingencies) at the various lower levels of threat. What is clear is that American dependence on local and other allied (particularly British and French), assistance in the Persian Gulf region will persist so long as the Rapid Deployment Force remains, in the words of one observer, a contradiction in terms comparable to the Holy Roman Empire. Within this context, the challenge which emerges is that of melding the two strands of the regional security debate into a coherent strategy. Toward this end, it is evident that the instrumentalities of American assistance merit extensive future consideration, given the diverse nature of the threats which confront regional security systems. With the possible spectrum running from military aid to development assistance, the essential task lies in the delineation of appropriate criteria whereby policy-makers might select the requisite means, or combination of means, to meet an existing or incipient regional security threat.

The primary focus of this study has been upon the subtle and complex relationship between the Nixon Administration's twin strategies of politico-military retrenchment (as embodied in the Nixon Doctrine) and détente. The October 1973 Middle East War exposed the fundamental disjunction between these two dimensions of policy and, in so doing, underscored the central paradox of the Nixon–Kissinger strategy. Whereas détente somehow implied the mutual acceptance of a structure of international politics (Kissinger's 'legitimate order'), superpower behavior remained unswervingly committed – despite the affirmations of the May 1972 and June 1973 summit meetings – to alter favorably that very structure through the pursuit of unilateral advantage on the periphery.

Kissinger sought to moderate Soviet behavior through the adroit application of incentives and penalities. This 'linkage' approach not only severely tested Kissinger's ability to conduct a diplomacy of manipulation and maneuver, but also overstretched the tenuous American foreign policy consensus in the wake of the Vietnam War. After leaving public service Kissinger wrote that 'So strong is the pragmatic tradition of American political thought that linkage was widely debated as if it were an idiosyncracy of a particular group of policy-makers who chose this approach by an act of will.'[7] In practice, linkage worked more effectively (or, from Kissinger's perspective, more insidiously) on the American domestic plane. Thus, SALT, which was viewed by Kissinger as an instrument of international order, became hostage within the American public debate to the apparent failings of détente (e.g. Angola, Afghanistan).

By the time of the 1976 presidential election campaign, the Kissinger diplomacy was under attack from both ends of the American political spectrum. To conservative critics of Administration policy, the conferment of incentives to Moscow was tantamount to appeasement which dangerously transformed détente into what was characterized as a 'one-way street.' To their liberal counterparts, the occasional necessity of implementing penalties against the Kremlin marked not the continuation of Administration policy but its failure. In addressing these criticisms, Kissinger subsequently concluded:

Perception of linkage is . . . synonymous with an overall strategic view. We ignore it only at our peril. It is inherent in the real world. The interrelationship of American interests, across issues and boundaries, exists regardless of the accidents of time or personality; it is not a matter of decision or will, but of reality.[8]

The question of linkage and its efficacy as an approach to US–Soviet relations invariably brings the focus of discussion back to the interrelationship between regional stability and the central strategic balance. At the time of the Angolan Civil War, Secretary Kissinger forcefully argued that the provocative Soviet and Cuban military actions were part of a global signaling process to which the West by necessity must respond. With the erosion of the previous regime of precedents and restraints, Kissinger considered it vital to Western security that Soviet intervention in an area so far from its traditional sphere of activity should not become the *new* precedent. As the matter was resolved, the Congressional rebuff to the Ford Administration's request for military assistance to the FNLA and UNITA was based upon the contention that American vital interests were not at stake.

Yet the disturbing questions persist. At what point do cumulative regional shifts along the periphery begin to affect adversely the West's vital interests and perhaps even alter the central strategic balance itself? Or, phrased another way, where does a global signalling process stop and a fundamental transformation of the international system begin? This question has become all the more acute in light of the Soviet invasion of Afghanistan. Though the superpowers express the will to moderate their 'limited adversary relationship,' détente has evolved into a rigidly sectorized set of interactions whose governing 'rules of engagement' remain tacit at best. Within this context, Kissinger warned that one adverse consequence of strategic parity was that it might encourage probing by the Soviet Union at the regional level.[9] This analysis underscored the necessity of maintaining local conventional balances as a deterrent to adventurism.

Like the Nixon Administration before it, the Carter Administration came to power with the avowed commitment to change the style and substance of American foreign policy.[10] In publicly eschewing the Kissinger approach, Carter explicitly expressed his Administration's downgraded estimation both of the utility of force and the centrality of the East–West competition.[11] Kissinger's purportedly tragic philosophy of history was criticized for being out of touch with the mainstream of American civil religion. Carter's concerted attempt (in the language of one observer) to 're-Americanize' US foreign policy was predicated upon the reaffirmation of those core values which American diplomacy had traditionally aspired to project.[12] In this view, domestic support for the Administration's foreign policy would follow from the creation of a new moral consensus within the United States. At the time, Michael Howard seriously questioned whether Carter could 'succeed in creating a synthesis between the universalist liberal values which he professes and the framework of power politics which he has inherited . . .'[13]

The Carter and Reagan foreign policies represent dichotomous reactions to the Kissinger diplomacy. In sharp contrast to Kissinger's geopolitical approach to Third World security, the Carter Administration emphasized the primacy of 'local' conditions and attempted to align American policy behind the forces of 'authentic nationalism'. During the 1980 presidential election campaign, Reagan advocated a posture strikingly similar to the 'negotiation from strength' line of the 1950s and condemned the administrations of his immediate predecessors for permitting the erosion of American power. In assessing the Nixon–Kissinger, Carter, and Reagan approaches to regional security questions, it is evident that the traditional distinctions – geopolitical and local, internal and external, *inter alia* – represent less dichotomies than a broad continuum upon which interactions occur.

Balancing these competing demands remains the ultimate challenge of American statecraft. Reasoned debate cannot flow from abstract formulations (such as 'Come home, America') that reflect emotional impulses more than rational calculation. Defining a sustainable American role in international politics requires a coherent, non-universalistic conception of US national interests abroad. The delineation of a finite set of American security interests should facilitate the development of a domestic consensus in support of them. Such an exercise, while not providing any ready answers to the exigencies of the future, will at least provide a basis for choice.

NOTES

Introduction

1 George F. Kennan, 'It's History, but is it Literature?' *New York Review of Books*, 26 April 1959, p. 35.

2 Henry A. Kissinger, *A World Restored: The Politics of Conservatism in a Revolutionary Era* (London: Victor Gollancz, 1977), p. 213.

3 US President, *US Foreign Policy for the 1970s: Shaping a Durable Peace*, A Report to the Congress by Richard M. Nixon, President of the United States, 3 May 1973 (Washington, DC: GPO, 1973), p. 6.

4 Henry A. Kissinger, 'Central Issues of American Foreign Policy' in Kermit Gordon, ed., *Agenda for the Nation* (New York: Doubleday, 1969), p. 611.

5 Alastair Buchan, *The End of the Postwar Era: A New Balance of World Power* (London: Weidenfeld and Nicolson, 1974).

6 Leslie H. Gelb, 'The Kissinger Legacy,' *New York Times Magazine*, 31 October 1976, p. 85.

7 Raymond Aron, *The Imperial Republic: The United States and the World 1954–1973* (Englewood Cliffs, NJ: Prentice Hall, 1974), p. 132.

8 'Tragedy and the Common Man,' *New York Times*, 27 February 1949.

9 For an illuminating analysis of this process and its central paradox see Robert Hunter, *Security in Europe* (London: Paul Elek, 1972).

10 *International Herald Tribune*, 12 April 1965.

11 The devolutionary aspect of the Nixon–Kissinger strategy (i.e. the Nixon Doctrine) has been characterized as 'military retrenchment without political disengagement' in Robert E. Osgood *et al., Retreat from Empire? The First Nixon Administration* (Baltimore: Johns Hopkins University Press, 1973), p. 9.

12 In this regard, the following works have been particularly useful in the preparation of this study: Kenneth E. Boulding, *The Image* (Ann Arbor: University of Michigan Press, 1956); John C. Farrell and Asa P. Smith, eds., *Image and Reality in World Politics* (New York: Columbia University Press, 1968); Robert Jervis, *Perception and Misperception in International Politics* (Princeton University Press, 1976); Robert Jervis, *The Logic of Images in International Relations* (Princeton University Press, 1970).

13 Alexander George cited in Bruce Mazlish, *Kissinger: The European Mind in American Policy* (New York: Basic Books, 1976), p. 307.

14 H. H. Gerth and C. Wright Mills, *From Max Weber: Essays in Sociology* (London: Routledge and Kegan Paul, 1948), p. 280.

15 Jervis, *Perception and Misperception*, p. 9.

16 Quoted in John H. Gilbert, ed., *The New Era in American Foreign Policy* (London: St James Press, 1973), p. 1.
17 Bernard Brodie, *War and Politics* (London: Cassell, 1974), pp. 344–5.
18 Kissinger in Gordon, ed., *Agenda for the Nation*, p. 611.

1 America as the night-watchman state, 1947–1968

1 In the text of his address which was to have been delivered before the Dallas Citizens Council, President Kennedy metaphorically referred to Americans as the 'watchmen on the walls of world freedom' (see *Vital Speeches* XXX, No. 4, December 1963, p. 107).
2 Walter Lippmann, *US Foreign Policy: Shield of the Republic* (Boston: Little, Brown, 1943), p. 137.
3 See, for example: Louis J. Halle, *The Cold War as History* (London: Chatto and Windus, 1967).
4 George F. Kennan, *Memoirs, 1925–1950* (London: Hutchinson, 1968), p. 293.
5 Arthur Krock, *Memoirs* (New York: Funk and Wagnalls, 1968), p. 224. This volume includes the full text of Clifford's report in its appendix (pp. 419–82).
6 George F. Kennan ('X'), 'The Sources of Soviet Conduct,' *Foreign Affairs* 25, No. 4 (July 1947), pp. 566, 572, 575, 576, 582.
7 These columns have been collected in Walter Lippmann, *The Cold War: A Study in US Foreign Policy*, introduction by Ronald Steel (New York: Harper Torchbooks, 1972).
8 *Ibid.*, pp. 11, 14, 15, 50.
9 Arnold Wolfers, ' "National Security" as an Ambiguous Symbol,' *Political Science Quarterly* 57, No. 4 (December 1952), p. 484.
10 Lippmann, *The Cold War*, pp. 8–9.
11 Alexis de Tocqueville, *Democracy in America* Vol. I (New York: Alfred A. Knopf, 1945), p. 234.
12 Kissinger, *A World Restored*, p. 326.
13 See, for example, Stanley Hoffmann, 'Will the Balance Balance at Home?' *Foreign Policy* 7 (Summer 1972), pp. 60–84.
14 Kennan, *Memoirs*, p. 358.
15 Bernard Brodie, 'Attitudes Towards the Use of Force' (Santa Monica, CA: Rand Corporation, 12 April 1953), p. 9.
16 US Department of State, Historical Office, *Foreign Relations of the United States: 1950* Vol. I, pp. 256–8, 286–7.
17 Thomas H. Etzold and John L. Gaddis, *Containment: Documents on American Policy and Strategy, 1945–1950* (New York: Columbia University Press, 1978), p. 420.
18 Paul Y. Hammond in Warner R. Schilling, Paul Y. Hammond and Glenn H. Snyder, *Strategy, Politics and Defense Budgets* (New York: Columbia University Press), pp. 362–3.
19 Seyom Brown, *The Faces of Power: Constancy and Change in United States Foreign Policy from Truman to Johnson* (New York: Columbia University Press, 1968), p. 66.

20 Bernard Brodie, ed., *The Absolute Weapon: Atomic Power and World Order* (New York: Harcourt, Brace, 1946), p. 23.

21 Emmet J. Hughes, *The Ordeal of Power: A Political Memoir of the Eisenhower Years* (London: Macmillan, 1963), p. 13.

22 Quoted in Samuel P. Huntington, *The Common Defense: Strategic Programs in National Politics* (New York: Columbia University Press, 1961), p. 68.

23 Glenn Snyder in Schilling *et al.*, *Strategy, Politics and Defense Budgets*, pp. 407–9, 427.

24 William W. Kaufmann, 'The Requirements of Deterrence', in William W. Kaufmann, ed., *Military Policy and National Security* (Oxford University Press, 1956), p. 29.

25 Henry A. Kissinger, 'Military Policy and the Defense of the "Gray Areas" ', *Foreign Affairs* 33, No. 3 (April 1955).

26 See Henry A. Kissinger, *Nuclear Weapons and Foreign Policy* (Oxford University Press, 1957), especially chapters 6–7.

27 Robert E. Osgood, *Limited War: The Challenge to American Strategy* (University of Chicago Press, 1957), p. 279.

28 Huntington, *The Common Defense*, pp. 105–6.

29 See Albert Wohlstetter, 'The Delicate Balance of Terror,' *Foreign Affairs* 37, No. 2 (January 1959), pp. 211–34 and Bernard Brodie, *Strategy in the Missile Age* (Princeton University Press, 1959).

30 Quoted in Townsend Hoopes, *The Devil and John Foster Dulles* (Boston: Little, Brown, 1973), p. 277.

31 Henry A. Kissinger, 'Nuclear Testing and the Problem of Peace,' *Foreign Affairs* 37, No. 1 (October 1958), pp. 1–18.

32 Henry A. Kissinger, *The Necessity for Choice* (New York: Harper and Row, 1961).

33 Anthony Hartley, 'American Foreign Policy in the Nixon Era,' *Adelphi Papers*, No. 110 (London: IISS, 1975), p. 3.

34 See, for example, the seminal work by Graham T. Allison, *Essence of Decision: Explaining the Cuban Missile Crisis* (Boston: Little, Brown, 1971).

35 Philip Windsor, *Germany and the Management of Détente* (New York: Praeger, 1971), pp. 13–21.

36 This argument was advanced by Philip Windsor in an unpublished paper, 'The Future of Strategic Studies' (Spring 1978), pp. 3–5.

37 Arthur M. Schlesinger, *A Thousand Days: John F. Kennedy in the White House* (Boston: Houghton Mifflin, 1965), p. 415.

38 Doris Kearns, *Lyndon Johnson and the American Dream* (New York: Harper and Row, 1976), p. 225.

39 Philip Geyelin, *Lyndon B. Johnson and the World* (New York: Praeger, 1966), p. 15.

40 Roger Hilsman, *To Move a Nation: The Politics of Foreign Policy in the Administration of John F. Kennedy* (Garden City, NY: Doubleday, 1967), pp. 411, 421.

41 Leslie H. Gelb with Richard K. Betts, *The Irony of Vietnam: The System Worked* (Washington, DC: Brookings Institution, 1979), pp. 2, 240.

42 Stanley Hoffmann, 'Vietnam: Misconceptions in Action' in Richard M.

Pfeffer, ed., *No More Vietnams? The War and the Future of American Foreign Policy* (New York: Harper and Row, 1968), p. 115.

43 Quoted in Townsend Hoopes, *The Limits of Intervention* (New York: David McKay, 1973), p. 30.

44 US Congress, Senate, Committee on Foreign Relations, *The Vietnam Hearings* (New York: Random House, 1966), p. 288.

45 Franz Schurmann, *The Logic of World Power* (New York: Pantheon, 1974), p. 521.

46 Allen S. Whiting, *The Chinese Calculus of Deterrence* (Ann Arbor: University of Michigan Press, 1975), pp. 193–5.

47 Cited in Schurmann, *The Logic of World Power*, p. 515.

48 Herbert Y. Schandler, *The Unmaking of a President: Lyndon Johnson and Vietnam* (Princeton University Press, 1977), pp. 80–1.

49 Hoopes, *The Limits of Intervention*, p. 145.

50 Henry Brandon, *Anatomy of Error: The Inside Story of the Asian War on the Potomac, 1954–1969* (Boston: Gambit, 1969), p. 134.

51 Ernest Lee Tuveson, *Redeemer Nation: The Idea of America's Millennial Role* (University of Chicago Press, 1968), p. 213.

52 Daniel Bell, 'The End of American Exceptionalism,' *The Public Interest* 41 (Fall 1975), p. 199.

53 Robert N. Bellah, 'Civil Religion in America,' *Daedalus* 96, No. 1 (Winter 1967), p. 7.

54 Tuveson, *Redeemer Nation*, p. 213.

55 Robert E. Osgood in John H. Gilbert, ed., *The New Era in American Foreign Policy* (London: St James Press, 1973), p. 75.

56 Raymond Aron, *War and Industrial Society* (Oxford University Press, 1958), p. 56.

57 Joseph Jones, *The Fifteen Weeks* (New York: Viking Press, 1955), p. 143.

58 PPS 23 (24 February 1948) in Etzold and Gaddis, *Containment: Documents on American Policy and Strategy, 1945–1950*, p. 98.

59 Quoted in George W. Ball, *The Discipline of Power: Essentials of a Modern World Structure* (London: Bodley Head, 1968), p. 294.

60 Bellah, 'Civil Religion in America,' p. 14.

61 See Richard M. Freeland, *The Truman Doctrine and the Origins of McCarthyism: Foreign Policy, Domestic Politics and Internal Security, 1946–1948* (New York: Alfred A. Knopf, 1972).

62 Bell, 'The End of American Exceptionalism,' pp. 204–5.

2 Charting the Nixon–Kissinger strategy

1 Kissinger, *A World Restored*, p. 329; C. L. Sulzberger, 'Kissinger on Kissinger,' *International Herald Tribune*, 12 November 1977.

2 Oriana Fallaci, 'Kissinger: An Interview with Oriana Fallaci,' *The New Republic*, 16 December 1972, p. 20.

3 Hartley, 'American Foreign Policy in the Nixon Era,' p. 1.

4 Marvin Kalb and Bernard Kalb, *Kissinger* (London: Hutchinson, 1974), p. 21.

5 Roland Evans and Robert D. Novak, *Nixon in the White House: The Frustration of Power* (New York: Random House, 1971), p. 11.

6 Fallaci, 'Interview,' pp. 20–1.

7 Hartley, 'American Foreign Policy in the Nixon Era,' p. 33.

8 Richard Nixon, *RN: The Memoirs of Richard Nixon* (New York: Grosset and Dunlap, 1978), p. 234.

9 Richard M. Nixon, 'Asia after Vietnam,' *Foreign Affairs* 46, No. 1 (October 1967), pp. 114–15.

10 R. J. Vincent, 'Kissinger's System of Foreign Policy,' *The Yearbook of World Affairs: 1977* (London: Stevens, 1977), p. 19.

11 Osgood *et al.*, *Retreat from Empire?*, p. 9.

12 Nixon, 'Asia after Vietnam,' pp. 121, 123.

13 See Stanley Hoffmann, 'An American Social Science: International Relations,' *Daedalus* 106, No. 3 (Summer 1977), pp. 47–8.

14 Philip Windsor, 'Henry Kissinger's Scholarly Contribution,' *British Journal of International Studies* 1, No. 1 (April 1975), p. 27.

15 Bruce Mazlish, *Kissinger: The European Mind*, p. 181.

16 Kissinger, *A World Restored*, pp. 322, 213.

17 Henry A. Kissinger, *The Troubled Partnership* (New York: McGraw-Hill, 1965), p. 251.

18 Henry A. Kissinger, 'The White Revolutionary: Reflections on Bismarck,' *Daedalus* 97, No. 3 (Summer 1968), pp. 889–90, 919, 920.

19 James Joll, *Europe Since 1870: An International History* (London: Penguin, 1978), p. 25.

20 Sociologist Lewis S. Feuer quoted in the *New York Times*, 27 May 1976.

21 See, for example, George Liska, *Beyond Kissinger: Ways of Conservative Statecraft* (Baltimore: Johns Hopkins University Press, 1975), especially chapters 4 and 5.

22 *New York Times*, 13 October 1974.

23 Kissinger, *A World Restored*, pp. 1, 328.

24 Philip Windsor, 'Henry Kissinger's Scholarly Contribution,' pp. 27–8.

25 Kissinger addressed this theme in 'Moral Promise and Practical Needs,' *Department of State Bulletin* LXXV, 1951 (15 November 1976), pp. 597–605.

26 Kissinger, *Nuclear Weapons and Foreign Policy*, p. 360.

27 See Kissinger, *The Necessity for Choice*, especially chapter 5.

28 *New York Times*, 25 October 1968.

29 Quoted in Roger Morris, *Uncertain Greatness: Henry Kissinger and American Foreign Policy* (New York: Harper and Row, 1977), pp. 64ff.

30 Kissinger, *A World Restored*, p. 317.

31 Kissinger, *The Necessity for Choice*, p. 357.

32 Kissinger, *A World Restored*, p. 327.

33 Henry A. Kissinger, 'Bureaucracy and Policy Making: The Effects of Insiders and Outsiders on the Policy Process,' in *Bureaucracy, Politics and Strategy*, Security Studies Paper No. 17, University of California, Los Angeles, 1968, p. 5.

34 Kissinger, *The Necessity for Choice*, p. 3.

35 Fallaci, 'Interview,' p. 21.

36 Nixon, *Memoirs*, p. 110.

37 Quoted in Morris, *Uncertain Greatness*, p. 63.

38 William Safire, *Before the Fall: An Inside View of the Pre-Watergate White House* (New York: Belmont Tower, 1975), pp. 159–60.

39 Morris, *Uncertain Greatness*, p. 174.

40 Reprinted in Henry M. Jackson, ed., *The National Security Council: Jackson Subcommittee Papers on Policy-Making at the Presidential Level* (New York: Praeger, 1965), p. 39.

41 US Congress, Senate, Committee on Government Operations, Subcommittee on National Security and International Operations, *The National Security Council: Comment by Henry A. Kissinger, March 30, 1970* (91st Cong., 2nd sess., 1970), p. 2.

42 Kissinger in *Bureaucracy, Politics and Strategy*, p. 9.

43 US Congress, Senate, Committee on Government Operations, *The National Security Council*, p. 5.

44 I. M. Destler, *Presidents, Bureaucrats and Foreign Policy The Politics of Organizational Reform* (Princeton University Press 1974), pp. 118ff; see also John P. Leacacos, 'The Nixon NSC (1): Kissinger's Apparat,' *Foreign Policy* 5 (Winter 1971–2), pp. 3–27.

45 Kalb, *Kissinger,* p. 87.

46 Morris, *Uncertain Greatness,* p. 87.

47 Quoted in *The Economist*, 13 March 1971.

48 Morris, *Uncertain Greatness*, p. 71.

49 Destler, *Presidents, Bureaucrats and Foreign Policy,* p. 135.

50 Leacacos, 'The Nixon NSC,' pp. 25–7.

51 See US Congress, Senate, Committee on Foreign Relations, *Nomination of Henry A. Kissinger to be Secretary of State*, Part I (93rd Cong., 1st sess., 1973), pp. 13–19.

52 Interview in *The Observer* (London), 27 May 1979.

53 Hoopes, *The Limits of Intervention*, preface.

54 Pierre Hassner, 'Change and Security in Europe, Part I: The Background,' *Adelphi Papers*, No. 45 (London: IISS, February 1968), p. 1.

55 US President, *US Foreign Policy for the 1970s: A New Strategy for Peace*, A Report to the Congress by Richard M. Nixon, President of the United States, 18 February 1970 (Washington, DC: GPO, 1970), p. 1.

56 See, for example, Marshall D. Shulman, 'What Does Security Mean Today?,' *Foreign Affairs* 49, No. 4 (July 1971), pp. 607–18.

57 Klaus Knorr, 'The United States: Social Change and Military Power' in 'Europe and America in the 1970s, Part II: Society and Power,' *Adelphi Papers*, No. 71 (London: IISS, November 1970), pp. 2–3.

58 Joseph S. Nye, 'American Power and Foreign Policy,' *New York Times*, 7 July 1976.

59 The Nixon Administration's first explicit reference to a five-power world was made by the President in à press conference in Kansas City, Missouri on 6 July 1971; see US President, *Public Papers of the Presidents of the United States: Richard Nixon, 1971* (Washington, DC: GPO, 1972), p. 806.

60 US President, *US Foreign Policy for the 1970s: A New Strategy for Peace*, p. 2.

61 See, for example, Zbigniew Brzezinski, 'US Foreign Policy: The Search for Focus,' *Foreign Affairs* 51, No. 4 (July 1973), pp. 717–19.
62 Kissinger in Gordon, ed., *Agenda for the Nation* (New York: Doubleday, 1969), p. 602.

3 The Nixon–Kissinger strategy (1)

1 This apt characterization of the US–Soviet relationship was coined by Marshall Shulman in *Beyond the Cold War* (New Haven: Yale University Press, 1966).
2 *Weekly Compilation of Presidential Documents: 1972* 8, No. 23, p. 979.
3 Kissinger in Gordon, ed., *Agenda for the Nation*, pp. 588–9.
4 US President, *US Foreign Policy for the 1970s: Shaping a Durable Peace*, p. 6.
5 Kissinger in Gordon, ed., *Agenda for the Nation*, p. 599.
6 *International Herald Tribune*, 12 April 1976.
7 Henry A. Kissinger, 'Domestic Structure and Foreign Policy,' *Daedalus* 95, No. 2 (Spring 1966), p. 507.
8 Kissinger press conference of 6 December 1971 in *Weekly Compilation of Presidential Documents* 7, No. 49, p. 1586.
9 Mazlish, *Kissinger,* p. 258.
10 Windsor, 'Henry Kissinger's Scholarly Contribution,' pp. 34–5.
11 *Department of State Bulletin* LXVIII, No. 1762 (2 April 1973), p. 395.
12 Henry A. Kissinger, 'The Viet Nam Negotiations,' *Foreign Affairs* 47, No. 2 (January 1969), pp. 218–19.
13 US President, *US Foreign Policy for the 1970s: A New Strategy for Peace*, p. 5.
14 Hans J. Morgenthau, *Truth and Power: Essays for a Decade, 1960–1970* (London: Pall Mall, 1971), p. 428.
15 Address of 12 May 1975, *Department of State Bulletin* LXXII, No. 1875 (2 June 1975), p. 706.
16 Kissinger subsequently argued that the American defeat in Vietnam in 1975 was 'the result of domestic crisis'; *International Herald Tribune*, 6 December 1978.
17 Kissinger in Gordon, ed., *Agenda for the Nation*, p. 612.
18 *New York Times*, 9 May 1969.
19 Safire, *Before the Fall*, pp. 296–300. For Kissinger's account of the wiretaps episode, see *Years of Upheaval* (Boston: Little, Brown, 1982), pp. 115–22.
20 *New York Times*, 12 June 1974.
21 The official State Department non-verbatim summary of Sonnenfeldt's remarks appeared in the *International Herald Tribune*, 12 April 1976.
22 Kissinger, *A World Restored*, p. 286.
23 William Safire, *The New Language of Politics*, 2nd edn. (New York: Collier, 1972), p. 349.
24 *New York Times*, 28 January 1969.
25 Kalb, *Kissinger*, p. 105.
26 *New York Times*, 28 January 1969. Though Nixon directly mentioned the

Middle East within the context of his press conference remarks on linkage, it is clear that Vietnam was implied.

27 Reprinted in *International Herald Tribune*, 13 February 1969.
28 *USIS Press Release*, 8 April 1969.
29 Kalb, *Kissinger*, p. 115.
30 US President, *US Policy for the 1970s: A New Strategy for Peace*, p. 101.
31 *Ibid.*, p. 116.
32 *New York Times*, 5 March 1969.
33 Stanley Hoffmann, *Primacy or World Order: American Foreign Policy since the Cold War* (New York: McGraw-Hill, 1978), p. 46.
34 Nadav Safran, *Israel: The Embattled Ally* (Cambridge, MA: Harvard University Press, 1978), pp. 432–9.
35 *Weekly Compilation of Presidential Documents* 6, No. 12 (21 March 1970), p. 397; see also Henry A. Kissinger, *White House Years* (Boston: Little, Brown, 1979), pp. 560–4.
36 Quoted in Kalb, *Kissinger*, p. 193.
37 *Weekly Compilation of Presidential Documents* 6, No. 27 (1 July 1970), pp. 863–9.
38 Safran, *Israel: The Embattled Ally*, pp. 443–5.
39 For a full account of the Jordanian crisis see Kissinger, *White House Years*, pp. 594–631; Henry Brandon, 'Jordan: The Forgotten Crisis: Were We Masterful . . .,' *Foreign Policy* 10 (Spring 1973), pp. 158–70.
40 Publicly confirmed by *TASS* on 13 October 1970.
41 For Kissinger's account of the Cienfuegos episode see *White House Years*, pp. 632–52.
42 Recounted in Tad Szulc, *The Illusion of Peace: Foreign Policy in the Nixon Years* (New York: Viking Press, 1978), p. 366.
43 Quoted in Morris, *Uncertain Greatness*, p. 241.
44 Vladimir Kusin, *From Dubcek to Charter 77* (Edinburgh: Q Press, 1978), p. 33; cited in William Shawcross, *Sideshow: Kissinger, Nixon and the Destruction of Cambodia* (London: André Deutsch, 1979), pp. 305–6.
45 Quoted in Michael B. Yahuda, *China's Role in World Affairs* (London: Croom Helm, 1978), pp. 227–8.
46 The minutes of the WSAG meetings of 3, 4, 6 and 8 December 1971 were leaked to columnist Jack Anderson and published in the *International Herald Tribune* on 6 and 15 January 1972.
47 *Ibid.*, 6 January 1972.
48 *Ibid.*, 15 January 1972.
49 US President, *US Foreign Policy for the 1970s: The Emerging Structure of Peace*. A report to the Congress by Richard M. Nixon, President of the United States, 9 February 1972 (Washington, DC: GPO, 1973), p. 50.
50 Kalb, *Kissinger*, p. 262.
51 For Kissinger's account of the events of December 1971 see *White House Years*, pp. 886–918.
52 Safire, *Before the Fall*, p. 436.
53 *Weekly Compilation of Presidential Documents* 8, No. 19 (30 April 1972), pp. 810–11.
54 *Public Papers of the Presidents, 1972*, p. 586.

55 *Weekly Compilation of Presidential Documents* 8, No. 20 (9 May 1972), pp. 847, 848.

56 US Congress, Senate, Committee on Foreign Relations, *Détente* (93rd Cong., 2nd sess., 1974), p. 248.

57 Kissinger in Gordon, ed., *Agenda for the Nation*, p. 611.

58 Kalb, *Kissinger*, p. 130. Kissinger, *White House Years,* p. 144, reports that he approached Dobrynin on 'about ten occasions' in 1969 to enlist Soviet cooperation to help end the war in Vietnam.

59 A notable exception is Walter Slocombe, 'The Political Implications of Strategic Parity,' *Adelphi Papers*, No. 77 (London: IISS, 1971).

60 *International Herald Tribune*, 31 January 1969.

61 See US Congress, Senate, Committee on Foreign Relations, *Strategic and Foreign Policy Implications of ABM systems, Anti-Submarine Warfare, Multiple Independently Targeted Reentry Vehicles (MIRV)*, 91st Cong., 1st sess. (Washington, DC: GPO, 1969).

62 Background briefing, 3 December 1974.

63 For the text of the 'Basic Principles of Relations between the United States of America and the Union of Soviet Socialist Republics' see *Weekly Compilation of Presidential Documents* 8, No. 23 (5 June 1972), p. 943.

64 For the text of the 'Agreement on the Prevention of Nuclear War' see *Weekly Compilation of Presidential Documents* 9, No. 25 (22 June 1973), pp. 822–3.

4 The Nixon–Kissinger strategy (2)

1 US President, *US Foreign Policy for the 1970s: Building for Peace*, A Report to the Congress by Richard M. Nixon, President of the United States, 1 March 1971 (Washington, DC: GPO, 1971), p. 17; *Wall Street Journal*, 29 January 1971.

2 A Gallup poll of February 1969 indicated the steepest rise in isolationist sentiment during the postwar period. The question, 'If a situation like Vietnam were to develop in another part of the world, do you think the United States should or should not send troops?' produced the following responses: should 25%; should not 62%; no opinion 13%. Reported in *New York Times,* 23 February 1969.

3 *The Economist*, 21 December 1968.

4 Richard M. Nixon, 'Asia after Vietnam,' *Foreign Affairs* 46, No. 1 (October 1967).

5 Reported in the *Christian Science Monitor*, 20 June 1969.

6 *New York Times*, 4 February 1969.

7 *New York Times*, 13 March 1969.

8 For a statistical breakdown by region and country of the Military Assistance Program (MAP) and Foreign Military Sales (FMS) for the period under consideration within this study see: US Department of Defense, Security Assistance Agency, *Foreign Military Sales and Military Assistance Facts: 1977* (pamphlet); US Arms Control and Disarmament Agency, *World Military Expenditures and Arms Transfers 1967–1976* (Washington, DC: GPO, July 1978).

9 Quoted in Kissinger, *White House Years*, p. 223.

10 *Weekly Compilation of Presidential Documents* 5, No. 5 (10 November 1969), p. 1550. The full transcript of Nixon's informal remarks at Guam may be found in US President, *Public Papers of the Presidents of the United States: Richard Nixon, 1969* (Washington, DC: GPO, 1971), pp. 544–56.

11 US President, *US Foreign Policy for the 1970s: A New Strategy for Peace* (18 February 1970), p. 5.

12 US Department of Defense, *Statement of Secretary of Defense Laird before a Joint Session of the Senate Armed Services Committee and the Senate Subcommittee on Department of Defense Appropriations on the Fiscal Year 1971 Defense Program and Budget* (20 February 1970), pp. 10ff. By the middle of 1974, this contraction process found 'General Purpose Forces' reduced to a total of 16 active Army and Marine divisions (6 ⅓ fewer than in 1968; 3 ⅓ fewer than in 1964).

13 US Department of Defense, *Statement of Secretary of Defense Melvin R. Laird before the Senate Armed Services Committee on the FY 1973 Defense Budget and FY 1973–1977 Program* (15 February 1972), pp. 25ff.

14 US President, *US Foreign Policy for the 1970s: Building for Peace* (25 February 1971), p. 20.

15 See, for example, Zbigniew Brzezinski, 'The State of Nixon's World (1): Half Past Nixon,' *Foreign Policy* 3 (Summer 1971), pp. 3–12.

16 Testimony of Earl C. Rayenal in US Congress, Senate, Committee on Foreign Relations, *Foreign Assistance Act of 1972* (92nd Cong., 2nd sess., 1972), p. 198.

17 Earl C. Ravenal, 'The Nixon Doctrine and Our Asian Commitments,' *Foreign Affairs* 49, No. 2 (January 1971), p. 209.

18 Quoted in Evans and Novak, *Nixon in the White House*, pp. 83–4.

19 NSSM-1 was subsequently leaked to the press and placed in the *Congressional Record* on 10 May 1972. For the text of the original 28 NSSM-1 questions and an analysis of selected responses see 'NSSM-1' (based on a case by Edwin A. Deagle, Jr.) in Commission on the Organization of the Government for the Conduct of Foreign Policy (Murphy Commission), Appendices, vol. 4: *Appendix K: Adequacy of Current Organization: Defense and Arms Control* (Washington, DC: GPO, June 1975), pp. 417–36.

20 Reported in Szulc, *The Illusion of Peace*, pp. 52–4.

21 Quoted in John Osborne, 'The Nixon Watch: Doubts About Vietnamization,' *The New Republic* (3 January 1970), p. 11.

22 Kissinger, *White House Years*, p. 262.

23 For an analysis of the relationship between Vietnamization, bombing, and the negotiations see Allan E. Goodman, *The Lost Peace: America's Search for a Negotiated Settlement of the Vietnam War* (Stanford, CA: Hoover Institution Press, 1978), pp. 85–9ff.

24 Gelb with Betts, *The Irony of Vietnam*, pp. 355–7.

25 Elliot L. Richardson, 'The Altered Shape of World Power,' *Department of State Bulletin* LXI, No. 1568 (14 July 1969), pp. 28–9.

26 Quoted in Szulc, *The Illusion of Peace*, p. 150.

27 For the complete text see US President, *Public Papers of the Presidents: Richard Nixon, 1970*, pp. 405–9.

28 Safire, *Before the Fall*, p. 186.
29 US President, *Public Papers of the Presidents: Richard Nixon, 1970*, p. 409.
30 *Weekly Compilation of Presidential Documents* 7, No. 46 (12 November 1971), p. 1515.
31 Morris, *Uncertain Greatness*, pp. 176–7.
32 The North Vietnamese reaction to the Nixon Doctrine and the dramatic improvement of Sino-American relations is striking. An editorial published in the official *Nhan Dan* four days after the announcement of Kissinger's secret mission to Peking warned against the implications hidden in the new US policy moves. It characterized the Nixon Doctrine as 'the counter-revolutionary strategy of US imperialism which consists of. . . dividing the socialist countries, winning over one section and putting it against another in order to oppose the national liberation movement.' Quoted in Library of Congress, Congressional Research Service, *1971 Chronology of Events* (Washington, DC: GPO, 1972), 19 July 1971.
33 For a discussion of Japanese perceptions of Nixon Doctrine see Robert E. Osgood, *The Weary and the Wary: US and Japanese Security Policies in Transition* (Baltimore: Johns Hopkins University Press, 1972) and Katsumi Kobayashi, *The Nixon Doctrine and US–Japanese Security Relations*, California Seminar on Arms Control and Foreign Policy, Discussion Paper No. 65 (October 1975).
34 US President, *Foreign Policy for the 1970s: The Emerging Structure of Peace* (9 February 1972), p. 8.
35 For the text of Kissinger's 'Year of Europe' speech see *Department of State Bulletin* LXVIII, No. 1768 (23 April 1973), pp. 593–8.
36 *New York Times*, 27 May 1970.
37 Library of Congress, Congressional Research Service, *1971 Chronology of Events*, 7 December 1971.
38 Quoted in Shahram Chubin and Sephr Zebih, *The Foreign Relations of Iran* (Berkeley: University of California Press, 1974), p. 257.
39 *The Times*, 10 June 1969.
40 Interview with C. L. Sulzberger, *International Herald Tribune*, 9 February 1972. Sulzberger cites the incensed reaction of the Tehran newspaper, *Keyhan*, to the perceived failure of American policy during the Indo-Pakistani war: 'Pakistan, an ally of the United States through two multi-national and one bilateral treaty, has been attacked and dismembered without as much as a ripple of serious protest. There is no reason why Pakistan's plight should be treated as an isolated case that could not be repeated elsewhere in the region.'
41 Interview with Arnaud de Borchgrave, *International Herald Tribune*, 14 April 1973.
42 At the time of the termination of US economic aid to Iran, the Shah asserted: 'This means we don't need it. We have passed the stage of countries that still need it. We have "taken off" '; interview in *US News and World Report*, 27 January 1969.
43 Chubin and Zebih, *The Foreign Relations of Iran*, p. 311, put the size of the

Iranian contingent in Oman by March 1974 at three 'Special Force' ranger battalions with helicopter and air support.

44 The Iranian decision not to accept additional M-60s was reported in *The Guardian*, 6 May 1970.

45 Approval was granted during the Nixon Administration for Iran to purchase 30 F-14A fighters for $900 million; reported in *The Times*, 12 January 1974. In its first year, the Carter Administration was able to obtain Congressional approval for the sale of 7 AWACS to Iran for $1.2 billion.

46 Quoted in US Congress, Senate, Committee on Foreign Relations, *US Arms Sales Policy: Proposed Sales of Arms to Iran and Saudi Arabia* (94th Cong., 2nd sess., 1977), p. 13.

47 The designation of Saudi Arabia as the second 'pillar' was both an acknowledgment of the increasing American dependence on imported oil and an attempt to placate those Arab states which remained wary of Iranian intentions. Despite its ostensible co-equal status, the Administration hardly expected the Saudis to assume a credible regional security role. In that respect, Iran remained the center of a disguised single-pillar system in American eyes.

48 US Congress, Senate, Committee on Foreign Relations, *Multinational Corporations and United States Foreign Policy: Grumman Sale of F-14s to Iran*, Part 17 (94th Cong., 2nd sess., 1976), p. 176.

49 *Ibid.*, pp. 173ff; US Congress, House, Committee on Foreign Affairs, *New Perspectives on the Persian Gulf* (93rd Cong., 1st sess., 1973), pp. 5–6.

50 In the area of oil pricing, by way of contrast, the interests of Iran and the United States sharply diverged.

51 For an extended consideration of the US–Iranian relationship during the decade prior to the 1979 revolution see Shahram Chubin, *Security in the Persian Gulf. IV: The Role of Outside Powers* (London: Gower for IISS, 1982).

52 In 1971 alone this amounted to some 10%. In that year, total economic aid (grants and loans) was approximately $1.8 billion (of which $500 million in supporting grants was allocated for South Vietnam); *The Economist*, 6 November 1971.

53 See his interview with *The Economist*, 10 February 1979.

54 The Administration's subtle shift in military assistance policy from grant to credit purchases was affirmed in the Report to the President from the Task Force on International Development, *US Foreign Assistance in the 1970s: A New Approach* (Washington, DC: GPO, 4 March 1970), pp. 11–15. The increase in Foreign Military Sales Orders (worldwide) between 1970 and 1976 was dramatic: from a low of $952 million in FY 1970 they rose to a level of $10.8 billion by FY 1974.

55 Kissinger interview with Joseph Kraft (*Washington Post*); I am grateful to Shahram Chubin for bringing this citation to my attention.

56 For a discussion of this theme see, for example, Shahram Chubin, 'Repercussions of the Crisis in Iran,' *Survival* XXI, No. 3 (May/June 1979), pp. 98–106.

57 Department of State, Position Paper, 'The Growing US Involvement in

Iran' (1975, mimeograph). In the same report, it was estimated that the projected level of Iranian arms acquisition would necessitate a threefold increase in the number of American military related personnel by 1980 (i.e. 34,000 with a total civil/military presence of 50,000).

58 The dependency of the supplier is explored by Richard Burt in 'New Weapons Technologies: Debate and Direction,' *Adelphi Papers*, No. 126 (London: IISS, Summer 1976), pp. 26–9.

59 Lucy Wilson Benson, 'Turning the Supertanker: Arms Transfer Restraint,' *International Security* 3, No. 4 (Spring 1979), p. 17.

5 The Nixon–Kissinger strategy (3)

1 US Congress, Senate, Committee on Foreign Relations, *Détente*, pp. 247–7, 374.

2 In the case of Vietnam, a member of the Paris negotiating team, Deputy Assistant Secretary of State William H. Sullivan, emphasized the constraints which the Communist great powers were believed to have placed upon Hanoi's ability to carry on the war: The *Lao Dong* Party [of North Vietnam] will find it satisfactory . . . to keep the agreements because there are external pressures which would lead in that direction. It has discovered that the Chinese and Soviets are not willing to go to the lengths that it would like them to go to commit themselves for its ambitions . . .' *Department of State Bulletin* LXVIII, No. 1756, 19 February 1973.

3 *Department of State Bulletin* LXIX, No. 1801, 11 December 1973.

4 For Kissinger's account of the grain deal and Senator Jackson's activities see *Years of Upheaval*, pp. 246–55, 979–98.

5 See Kissinger, *A World Restored*, p. 5.

6 This speech, entitled 'Pragmatism and Moral Force in American Foreign Policy,' was delivered at the US Naval Academy on 5 June 1974; see *Department of State Bulletin* LXXI, No. 1827.

7 See, for example, US President, *US Foreign Policy for the 1970s: Shaping a Durable Peace* (3 May 1973), p. 59.

8 In *Years of Upheaval*, p. 29, Kissinger reports Pham Van Dong as asserting that the Paris accords represented 'only a temporary stabilization of the situation, only a respite.'

9 *Weekly Compilation of Presidential Documents* 9, No. 4 (24 January 1973), p. 71.

10 US President, *US Foreign Policy for the 1970s: Shaping a Durable Peace*, p. 59.

11 In *White House Years*, pp. 1375–6, Kissinger argues that the psychological dependence of the South Vietnamese on the United States was one of the major factors prompting President Thieu to delay acceptance of the draft agreement.

12 See Kissinger, *White House Years*, pp. 1412, 1462; Nixon promised 'swift and severe retaliatory action' if Hanoi failed to abide by the terms of the agreements.

13 In Laos, the *Pathet Lao* guerrillas and the government of Prince

Souvanna Phouma agreed to conditions for a ceasefire on 22 February. Thereafter, American bombing in Laos was confined to B-52 raids on the Ho Chi Minh trail. In Cambodia, Lol Nol attempted unilaterally to initiate a ceasefire, but it was not reciprocated.

14 Raymond Aron, *The Imperial Republic: The United States and the World 1945–1973* (Englewood Cliffs, NJ: Prentice Hall, 1974), p. 309.

15 While lamenting its consequences, Kissinger acknowledged the magnitude of the Administration's preoccupation with Vietnam. Following President Thieu's angry denunciation of the draft peace agreement on 22 October during a meeting with the American delegation in Saigon, Kissinger, in response, observed: 'We ... have mortgaged our whole foreign policy to the defense of one country' (*White House Years*, p. 1386).

16 Safran, *Israel: The Embattled Ally*, p. 469.

17 Kissinger, *White House Years*, pp. 1292–300.

18 *Ibid.*, p. 1297.

19 Kissinger, *Years of Upheaval*, p. 464, argues that the INR reports were more ambiguously worded than Cline suggests.

20 *Department of State Bulletin* LXIX, No. 1794 (12 November 1973), p. 585. This was merely a re-statement of the position which Kissinger had taken in his press conference of 12 October; see *Department of State Bulletin* LXIX, No. 1792 (29 October 1973), p. 534. On the question of pre-war intelligence reports, Ray Cline has argued that a major factor constraining this effort was Kissinger's refusal to apprise the appropriate agencies of the substance of his diplomatic exchanges (e.g. his private meetings with the Soviet leadership, the secret channel with Egypt, etc.); see his 'Policy without Intelligence,' *Foreign Policy* 17 (Winter 1974–5), p. 132.

21 For a more detailed consideration of Kissinger's attitude towards the October 1973 War and the ensuing negotiations see Edward R. Sheehan, 'Step by Step in the Middle East,' *Foreign Policy* 22 (Spring 1976), pp. 3–70; the author had access to the Secretary of State's written records. For Kissinger's account see *Years of Upheaval*, pp. 467–8.

22 *Department of State Bulletin* LXIX, No. 1792 (29 October 1973), p. 539.

23 Although the Administration agreed 'in principle' to replace Israeli war losses, serious bureaucratic obstacles on the American side constrained the flow of arms. The respective roles of Kissinger and Secretary of Defense James R. Schlesinger during this episode remain a matter of controversy (cf. Kalb, *Kissinger*, pp. 471–6 and Szulc, *The Illusion of Peace*, pp. 734–8). The prevailing view is that Kissinger did not decisively move to circumvent bureaucratic resistance to the 'resupply' effort until he became convinced of its immediate necessity. Kissinger rebuts this line of criticism in *Years of Upheaval*, p. 478.

24 Although the Soviet Union clearly knew of Egyptian and Syrian preparations, Mohamed Heikal reports that Moscow was apprised of the actual decision to go to war (via the Soviet ambassador in Cairo) only days before the initiation of hostilities; see *The Road to Ramadan* (London: Collins, 1975), p. 21.

25 *Department of State Bulletin* LXIX, No. 1792 (29 October 1973).

26 See Galia Golan, *Yom Kippur and After: The Soviet Union and the Middle East Crisis* (Cambridge University Press, 1977), pp. 112–15.

27 See *Years of Upheaval*, pp. 545–52.

28 *Ibid.*, p. 491. For an analysis of Israeli perceptions and policy see Matti Golan, *The Secret Conversations of Henry Kissinger: Step-by-Step Diplomacy in the Middle East* (New York: Quandrangle/New York Times, 1976), chapter 2.

29 Press conference of 26 October 1973 in *Weekly Compilation of Presidential Documents* 9, No. 43 (29 October 1973), p. 1291. Senator Henry Jackson described the note as 'brutal, rough'; quoted in *New York Times*, 26 October 1973.

30 A partial text of the message from Brezhnev was subsequently printed in *New York Times*, 10 April 1974.

31 Golan, *Yom Kippur and After*, p. 122, notes, however, that this alert had been in effect throughout the war and known by the Americans (in Schlesinger's own account of events) 'five or six' days prior to 24 October.

32 Schlesinger press conference of 26 October 1973 in *Department of State Bulletin* LXIX, No. 1795 (19 November 1973), p. 620.

33 The United States has five defense-readiness conditions or DEFCONs. With DEFCON I meaning war, several organizational components of the American nuclear arsenal, such as SAC and the *Polaris/Poseidon* fleet are routinely kept at DEFCON III. In the specific case of the 25 October alert, the declaration of DEFCON III meant that most units were elevated one grade of readiness.

34 Press conference of 25 October 1973 in *Department of State Bulletin* LXIX, No. 1794 (12 November 1973), p. 587.

35 Kissinger angrily responded to the charge that the alert was motivated by domestic political concerns (i.e. as a means of diverting public attention from the Watergate scandal); see *ibid.*, p. 589 and *Years of Upheaval*, p. 596.

36 Press conference of 26 October 1973 in *Weekly Compilation of Presidential Documents* 9, No. 43 (29 October 1973), pp. 1287–94.

37 Press conference of 26 October 1973, *Department of State Bulletin* LXIX, No. 1794 (12 November 1973), p. 592. Kissinger affirmed: 'We are not talking of a missile-crisis-type situation.'

38 Press conference of 26 October 1973, *Weekly Compilation of Presidential Documents* 9, No. 43 (29 October 1973), p. 1290.

39 Kissinger has repeatedly rejected charges that the Nixon Administration 'oversold' détente, although in *White House Years*, pp. 1255–6, he does acknowledge 'Nixon's penchant for hyperbole.'

40 Press conference of 21 November 1973 in *Department of State Bulletin* LXIX, No. 1798 (10 December 1973), pp. 715–16.

41 Charges of Soviet violations of the SALT I agreement gathered momentum during 1974–5. Kissinger himself was accused of having conducted 'sloppy' negotiations in Moscow upon which the Soviet Union was subsequently able to capitalize. Senator Jackson (*The Times*, 24 June 1974), charged that Kissinger had concluded a 'secret deal' with the Kremlin

on SALT without informing Congress. (Kissinger explained that this amounted to nothing more than a 'clarifying' agreement governing the conversion of Soviet G-class submarines; critics pointed to the 70 additional SLBMs which this clarification conceded to the Soviet side.) In testimony before the House Select Committee on Intelligence, the former Chief of Naval Operations, Elmo Zumwalt, castigated Kissinger and confirmed reports of Soviet violations of SALT; see House, Select Committee on Intelligence, *CIA: The Pike Report* (Nottingham: Spokesman Books, 1977), pp. 66–7. An *Aviation Week and Space Technology* editorial ('Pitfalls of SALT,' 24 November 1975) charged Kissinger with 'a policy of deliberate secrecy and deception that has tried desperately to conceal from the US Congress and the public the Soviet violations of SALT and the gross US policy errors that are steadily building an irreversible Soviet military advantage.' See also 'The Case Against Kissinger' in *Aviation Week and Space Technology*, 8 December 1975; Tad Szulc, 'Soviet Violations of the SALT Deal. Have We Been Had?', *The New Republic*, 7 June 1975.

42 A revealing NBC poll of March 1976 indicated that by a 69% to 22% margin, the American public 'does not trust the Russians to live up to their agreements.' Cited in Charles William Maynes, Daniel Yankelovich *et al.*, *US Foreign Policy: Principles for Defining the National Interest* (New York: Public Agenda Foundation, 1976), p. 73.

43 In his press conference of 27 December 1973, Kissinger confirmed that unexpected advances in nuclear weapons technologies were frustrating prospects for a SALT II agreement in 1974; see *The Times*, 28 December 1973.

44 See, for example, Kissinger's testimony before the Senate Foreign Relations Committee on 19 September 1974; *Détente*, p. 251.

45 See the interview with Kissinger in *Business Week*, 13 January 1975.

46 See Schlesinger's testimony in US Congress, Senate, Committee on Foreign Relations, *Foreign Policy Choices for the Seventies and Eighties*, 94th Cong. 1st and 2nd sess., 2 vols. (Washington, DC: GPO, 1976), p. 509.

47 See Lynn Etheridge Davis, 'Limited Nuclear Options: Deterence and the New American Doctrine,' *Adelphi Papers*, No. 121 (London: IISS, Winter 1975/6).

48 *Report of the Secretary of Defense James R. Schlesinger to the Congress on the FY 1975 Budget and FY 1975–1979 Defense Program* (4 March 1974), pp. 4–5.

49 *USIS Press Release*, 13 January 1974; transcript of Schlesinger's remarks to the Overseas Writers Association.

50 National Security Study Memorandum (NSSM)-3, entitled 'Military Posture,' was issued on 21 January 1969 and directed the development of criteria against which American strategic needs could be measured. The resultant study, completed in March 1969, explicitly raised the issue of limited nuclear options. For the history and current status of American targeting policy see Desmond Ball, 'Strategic Nuclear Targeting,' *Adelphi Papers* (London: IISS, forthcoming).

51 One of the major considerations in this regard was the perception of the strategic nuclear balance on third parties. For an assessment of Chinese attitudes see Michael Pillsbury, *SALT on the Dragon: Chinese Views on the Soviet–American Strategic Balance* (Santa Monica, CA: Rand Corporation, April 1975).

52 An important aspect of this was the attempt to establish the conditions for intra-war deterrence (through the creation of limited nuclear options) should deterrence fail. For a discussion of intra-war deterrence see Richard Rosecrance, 'Strategic Deterrence Reconsidered,' *Adelphi Papers*, No. 116 (London: IISS, Spring 1975), pp. 15–17.

53 Walter Slocombe, 'The Political Implications of Strategic Parity,' p. 2.

54 While the geographical context of the Schlesinger Doctrine was primarily Western Europe, the American Secretary of Defense asserted that the US would strongly consider the use of nuclear weapons if faced with aggression 'likely to result in defeat in any area of very great importance to the United States.' See Schlesinger's ABC television interview of 6 July 1975 in *USIS Press Release*, 8 July 1975.

55 Kissinger press conference of 7 December 1974 in *Department of State Bulletin* LXXI, No. 1853 (30 December 1974), p. 917.

56 Quoted in *The Sunday Times*, 1 June 1975.

57 See note 55.

58 Kissinger press conference of 3 July 1974 (in Moscow on the occasion of Nixon's final summit meeting with the Soviet leadership); see *Department of State Bulletin* LXXI, No. 831 (29 July 1974), p. 215.

59 Maynes *et al., US Foreign Policy: Principles for Defining the National Interest*, p. 73. According to an April 1976 opinion poll, 45% of the public regarded the Soviet Union as the chief beneficiary of détente as compared to a mere 3% which believed that the United States benefited most.

60 The perceived status quo orientation of Administration policy towards Eastern Europe was condemned by presidential candidate Ronald Reagan in 1976 as 'requiring slaves to accept their slavery'; quoted in Coral Bell, *The Diplomacy of Détente: The Kissinger Era* (London: Martin Robertson, 1977), p. 242.

61 This theme was addressed by Kissinger in a number of public speeches delivered across the United States during 1975 and 1976: see, for example, 'The Permanent Challenge of Peace: US Policy Toward the Soviet Union' in *Department of State Bulletin* LXXV, No. 1951 (15 November 1976), pp. 597–605.

62 Goodman, *The Lost Peace*, p. 177.

63 Van Tien Dung (North Vietnamese Chief of Staff), 'Great Spring Victory: A Summation of Senior General Van Tien Dung of the Combat Situation in the Spring of 1975,' excerpted in *New York Times*, 26 April 1976.

64 Text of letter from President Ford to Speaker Carl Albert in *Department of State Bulletin* LXXII, No. 1864 (17 March 1975), pp. 330–1.

65 *The Times*, 27 March 1975.

66 Quoted in Robert Shaplen, 'Letter from Saigon,' *The New Yorker* (21 April 1975), p. 127; cited in Goodman, *The Lost Peace*, p. 180.

67 For a more detailed chronological consideration of the events preceding and following the fall of Indochina see *Strategic Survey 1975* (London: ISS, 1976), pp. 90–100.

68 Kissinger press conference of 13 May 1975 in *Department of State Bulletin* LXXII, No. 1875 (2 June 1975), p. 733.

69 *USIS Press Release*, 7 May 1975.

70 A noteworthy example of these moves was Senator Mansfield's decision not to reintroduce his amendment for the reduction of American troop strength in Western Europe.

71 US Congress, Senate, Committee on Foreign Relations, Subcommittee on African Affairs, *Angola* (94th Cong., 2nd sess., 1976), p. 14 (hereafter cited as *Angola Hearings*).

72 *Ibid.*

73 Commissioned in April 1969, NSSM-39 was eventually leaked to the press. For what is presented as a complete and unabridged edition of this study see Barry Cohen and Mohammed A. El-Khawas, eds., *The Kissinger Study of Southern Africa* (Nottingham: Spokesman Books, 1975), pp. 66–70.

74 With respect to American compliance to the UN arms embargo against Portugal, a 1970 National Security Decision Memorandum (NSDM) produced a new set of guidelines permitting Portuguese (and South African) purchases of American dual purpose equipment (i.e. designed for civil purposes but with possible military applications). The Administration, for example, permitted Portugal and South Africa to purchase additional types of US aircraft and herbicides under the heading of agricultural/crop spraying. See US Congress, House, Committee on Foreign Affairs, *Implementation of the US Arms Embargo (Against Portugal and South Africa, and Related Issues)* (93rd Cong., 1st sess., 1973), p. 21.

75 In 1970, for example, the Portuguese Defense Minister offered NATO basing rights and associated facilities in its African territories in order to maintain Western naval predominance in the South Atlantic and Indian Oceans.

76 *Department of State Bulletin* LXX, No. 1803 (14 January 1974), pp. 25–6. After expressing American gratitude for Portuguese assistance 'during the recent difficulties,' Kissinger asserted: 'I would like to say that as far as the United States is concerned, our journey together is not finished.' Reported in *The Guardian*, 18 December 1973.

77 Reported in Gerald Bender, 'Kissinger in Angola: Anatomy of Failure' in René Lemarchand, ed., *American Policy in Southern Africa: The Stakes and the Stance* (Washington, DC: University Press of America, 1978), pp. 70–1.

78 *Angola Hearings*, pp. 16–17.

79 For an account of the January 1975 meeting of the 40 Committee see Roger Morris, 'The Proxy War in Angola: Pathology of a Blunder,' *The New Republic*, 31 January 1976.

80 John Stockwell, *In Search of Enemies: A CIA Story* (New York: W. W. Norton, 1978), p. 67.

81 Morris, 'Pathology of a Blunder,' p. 21.

82 John Marcum, 'Lessons of Angola,' *Foreign Affairs* 54, No. 3 (April 1976), p. 414.

83 See *Angola Hearings*, p. 26.

84 Kenneth L. Adelman, 'Report from Angola,' *Foreign Affairs* 53, No. 3 (April 1975), p. 563.

85 Nathaniel Davis, 'The Angola Decision of 1975: A Personal Memoir,' *Foreign Affairs* 57, No. 1 (Fall 1978), p. 120.

86 Marcum, 'Lessons of Angola,' p. 415.

87 See the testimony of William E. Shaufele, Assistant Secretary of State for African Affairs, in *Angola Hearings*, p. 175.

88 Davis, 'The Angola Decision of 1975: A Personal Memoir,' pp. 109–24.

89 House, Select Committee on Intelligence, *CIA: The Pike Report*, pp. 200, 217–18, n. 477.

90 For excerpts of the memoranda submitted to Sisco on 12, 14 and 16 July 1975 see Davis, 'The Angola Decision of 1975: A Personal Memoir,' pp. 113–16.

91 *Ibid.*, pp. 123–4. In his memorandum of 12 July, Davis questioned the two assumptions which provided the basis of Kissinger's position – first, that American credibility was at stake in Angola; and second, that American support for the FNLA/UNITA coalition would prompt the MPLA to adopt a more accommodative diplomatic posture.

92 *The Times*, 25 June 1975.

93 *Angola Hearings*, p. 9.

94 See US Congress, Senate, Committee on Foreign Relations, *US Policy Toward Southern Africa* (94th Cong., 1st sess., 1976).

95 Reported in Bender, 'Kissinger in Angola: Anatomy of Failure,' p. 97.

96 For a more detailed consideration of the fighting within Angola see *Strategic Survey 1975*, pp. 32–6. The MPLA greatly benefited from its control of the Cabinda oil fields. In September 1975, Gulf Oil paid $116 million in royalties into an MPLA bank account.

97 Davis, 'The Angola Decision of 1975: A Personal Memoir,' p. 121.

98 *International Herald Tribune*, 17 October 1975. Relations between Washington and the Mobutu regime were far from smooth during the period preceding the Angolan Civil War. In June 1975, The Zairean President ('desperately seeking a scapegoat' to divert public attention away from his regime's bleak record) had expelled the American ambassador from Kinshasha on the charge of fomenting a coup against him; see Stockwell, *In Search of Enemies: A CIA Story*, p. 44.

99 See the exchange between Senator Clark and Deputy Secretary of Defense Robert Ellsworth on 3 February 1976 in *Angola Hearings*, pp. 82–3.

100 Davis, 'The Angola Decision of 1975: A Personal Memoir,' p. 118.

101 For the text of this report by Leslie Gelb see *International Herald Tribune*, 8–9 November 1975.

102 *The Times*, 25 November 1975.

103 This estimate was offered by US intelligence sources; cited in the *Los Angeles Times*, 8 December 1975.

104 In his press conference of 9 December 1975, Kissinger dismissed this charge; see *Department of State Bulletin* LXXIV, No. 1906 (5 January 1976), p. 12.

105 'A Russian "Vietnam"?,' *Washington Post* (editorial), 26 November 1975.

106 *US News and World Report*, 23 February 1976.

107 *Department of State Bulletin* LXXIV, No. 1907 (12 January 1976), p. 54.

108 During a press conference in Phoenix on 16 April 1976, Kissinger reiterated this position: 'The tendency toward stalemate in the nuclear arms race produces new requirements for our national defense. Under the umbrella of strategic standoff, increasing attention must be given to regional defense. For it is in peripheral areas where a military imbalance can be turned into a geopolitical change that could in time affect the global balance.' See *Department of State Bulletin* LXXIV, No. 1924 (10 May 1976), p. 600.

109 *Time*/Yankelovich, January 1976.

110 The Cuban build-up accelerated between November and January. On 11 November 1975 (Independence Day) there were a reported 2,800 Cuban soldiers in Angola; by February, the Cuban air bridge ('Operation Carlotta') had brought this number to at least 12,000. See Stockwell, *In Search of Enemies: A CIA Story*, pp. 231–2.

111 With respect to the question of US–South African coordination of policy, Kissinger stated on 29 January 1976: 'Some charge that we have acted in collusion with South Africa. That is not true. We had no foreknowledge of South Africa's intentions, and in no way cooperated with it militarily.' See *Angola Hearings*, p. 13. The South African Defense Minister, P. W. Botha, directly challenged Kissinger's contention. In response to a parliamentary question, he stated that South African actions in Angola during 1975–6 had taken place with the full knowledge and encouragement of the United States, but 'they recklessly left us in the lurch.' Reported in *The Guardian*, 19 April 1978.

112 *Department of State Bulletin* LXXIV, No. 1908 (19 January 1976), p. 76. On 27 January 1976 the House of Representatives approved its own version of the Tunney Amendment by a vote of 323 to 99.

113 *Ibid.*, p. 70.

114 *Angola Hearings*, p. 18.

115 Kissinger press conference of 23 December 1975 (p. 69); see note 112.

116 Kissinger press conference of 3 February 1976; see *Department of State Bulletin* LXXIV, No. 1913 (23 February 1976), p. 215.

117 *The Financial Times*, 6 January 1976.

118 See note 112.

119 *Angola Hearings*, p. 19.

120 Stockwell, *In Search of Enemies: A CIA Story*, p. 234. With respect to the status of the anti-MPLA factions, the author notes: 'By early February the FNLA had ceased to exist as a viable fighting force and UNITA was crushed back to Huambo and Silva Porto.'

121 Theodore Draper, for example, charged that Kissinger's warning to the Soviet Union *vis-à-vis* the Angolan crisis during his 23 December 1975 press conference was 'to détente what Prime Minister Chamberlain's

reaction after 15 March 1939 had been to appeasement.' See 'Appeasement and Détente,' p. 19 in James R. Schlesinger *et al.*, *Defending America* (New York: Basic Books, 1977).
122 William Watts and Lloyd A. Free, 'A New National Survey: Nationalism, Not Isolationism' (A Report from Potomac Associates), *Foreign Policy* 24 (Fall 1976), pp. 5–6, 26.

Conclusion

1 Kissinger, *A World Restored*, p. 322.
2 *Department of State Bulletin* LXXVI, No. 1963 (7 February 1977), p. 102.
3 At this and other sections in this chapter I wish to acknowledge my debt to Dr Shahram Chubin.
4 Brzezinski discussed this theme in an interview with Elizabeth Drew in *The New Yorker*, 1 May 1978.
5 John M. Goshko, 'US Sources Report Sadat Offer to Oversee Middle East Stability,' *International Herald Tribune*, 22 February 1979.
6 In his 1980 State of the Union Address to Congress, President Carter enunciated the doctrine bearing his name; see *Department of State Bulletin* LXXX, No. 2035 (February 1980), special section, pp. A–B.
7 Henry Kissinger, 'The Morality of Power,' *The Observer*, 23 April 1978.
8 *Ibid*.
9 See Kissinger's Dallas speech of 22 March 1976, entitled 'Foreign Policy and National Security'; *Department of State Bulletin* LXXIV, No. 1920 (12 April 1976), p. 463.
10 During the 1976 presidential election campaign, Carter had criticized Kissinger's 'lone ranger diplomacy' – a teasing reference to his notorious interview in December 1972 with the controversial Italian journalist, Oriana Fallaci.
11 See President Carter's address at the University of Notre Dame on 22 May 1977 in *Department of State Bulletin* LXXVI, No. 1981 (13 June 1977), pp. 421–5.
12 This theme is explored by D. C. Watt in 'A Return to Americanism? Carter's Foreign Policy,' *Political Quarterly* 48, No. 4 (October–December 1977), pp. 429–39.
13 Michael Howard, *War and the Liberal Conscience* (London: Temple Smith, 1978), p. 130.

SELECT BIBLIOGRAPHY

Documents

Council on Foreign Relations. *American Foreign Relations, 1971–1976: A Documentary Record.* New York University Press, 1973–8.

Documents on American Foreign Relations: 1953–1969. 16 vols. New York: Simon and Schuster, 1954–70.

Jackson, Henry M., ed. *The National Security Council: Jackson Subcommittee Papers on Policy-Making at the Presidential Level.* New York: Praeger, 1965.

The Pentagon Papers. New York Times Edition. London: Routledge and Kegan Paul, 1971.

US Congress, Congressional Budget Office. 'Counterforce Issues for the US Strategic Nuclear Forces: Background Paper.' Washington DC: GPO, 1978.

US Congress, House, Committee on Foreign Affairs. *Foreign Assistance Act of 1972.* 92nd Cong., 2nd sess., 1972.

Implementation of the US Arms Embargo (Against Portugal and South Africa, and Related Issues). 93rd Cong., 1st sess., 1973.

Mutual Development and Cooperation Act of 1973. 93rd Cong., 1st sess., 1973.

New Perspectives on the Persian Gulf. 93rd Cong., 1st sess., 1973.

Subcommittee on Africa. *The Complex of United States–Portuguese Relations: Before and After the Coup.* 93rd Cong., 2nd sess., 1974.

US Congress, House, Committee on International Relations. *The Persian Gulf 1975: The Continuing Debate on Arms Sales.* 94th Cong., 1st sess., 1975.

US Congress, House, Select Committee on Intelligence. *CIA: The Pike Report.* Nottingham: Spokesman Books, 1977.

US Congress, Joint Economic Committee. *Economic Issues in Military Assistance.* 92nd Cong., 1st sess., 1971.

US Congress, Senate, Committee on Foreign Relations. *Angola: US Involvement in Civil War in Angola.* 94th Cong., 2nd sess., 1976.

US Policy towards Southern Africa. 94th Cong., 1st sess., 1976.

Subcommittee on Arms Control, International Law and Organization. *Briefing on Counterforce Attacks.* 93rd Cong., 2nd sess., 1975.

Briefing on Vietnam. 91st Cong., 1st sess., 1969.

Détente. 93rd Cong., 2nd sess., 1974.

Foreign Assistance Act of 1972. 92nd Cong., 2nd sess., 1972.

Foreign Military Sales and Assistance Act. 93rd Cong., 1st sess., 1973.

Foreign Policy Choices for the Seventies and Eighties. 2 vols. 94th Cong., 1st and 2nd sess., 1976.

Multinational Corporations and United States Foreign Policy: Grumman Sale of F-14s to Iran. Part 17. 94th Cong., 2nd sess., 1976.

Nomination of Henry A. Kissinger to be Secretary of State. 2 parts. 93rd Cong., 1st sess., 1973.

Strategic and Foreign Policy Implications of ABM Systems, Anti-Submarine Warfare, Multiple Independently Targeted Reentry Vehicles (MIRV). Part 3. 91st Cong., 1st sess., 1969.

US Arms Sales Policy: Proposed Sales of Arms to Iran and Saudi Arabia. 94th Cong., 2nd sess., 1977.

United States Security Agreements and Commitments Abroad. 91st Cong., 2nd sess., 1971.

US–USSR Strategic Policy. 93rd Cong., 2nd sess., 1974.

The Vietnam Hearings. New York: Random House, 1966.

US Department of Defense, Secretary Melvin R. Laird. *Annual Defense Department Report, FY 1971.* Washington, DC: GPO, 20 February 1970.

Secretary Melvin R. Laird. *Annual Defense Department Report, FY 1972.* Washington, DC: GPO, 9 March 1971.

Secretary Melvin R. Laird. *Annual Defense Department Report, FY 1973.* Washington DC: GPO, 15 February 1972.

Secretary Melvin R. Laird. *Final Report to the Congress.* Washington, DC: GPO, 8 January 1973.

Secretary Elliot L. Richardson. *Annual Defense Department Report, FY 1974.* Washington, DC: GPO, 10 April 1973.

Secretary James R. Schlesinger. *Annual Defense Department Report, FY 1975.* Washington, DC: GPO, 4 March 1974.

Secretary James R. Schlesinger. *Annual Defense Department Report, FY 1976.* Washington, DC: GPO, 5 February 1975.

US Department of State. *Department of State Bulletin,* 1969–76.

US Department of State, Historical Office. *Foreign Relations of the United States, 1946–1950.* Washington, DC: GPO, 1969–76.

US Foreign Assistance in the 1970s: A New Approach. Report to the President from the Task Force on International Development. Washington, DC: GPO, 4 March 1970.

US President. *Public Papers of the Presidents of the United States: Gerald R. Ford, 1974.* Washington, DC: GPO, 1975.

Public Papers of the Presidents of the United States: Richard Nixon, 1969. Washington, DC: GPO, 1971.

Public Papers of the Presidents of the United States: Richard Nixon, 1970. Washington, DC: GPO, 1971.

Public Papers of the Presidents of the United States: Richard Nixon, 1971. Washington, DC: GPO. 1972.

Public Papers of the Presidents of the United States: Richard Nixon, 1972. Washington, DC: GPO, 1974.

US President. *US Foreign Policy for the 1970s: A New Strategy for Peace.* A Report to the Congress by Richard M. Nixon, President of the United States, 18

222   *Détente and the Nixon Doctrine*

February 1970. Washington, DC: GPO, 1970.

US Foreign Policy for the 1970s: Building for Peace. A Report to the Congress by Richard M. Nixon, President of the United States, 25 February 1971. Washington, DC: GPO, 1971.

US Foreign Policy for the 1970s: The Emerging Structure of Peace. A Report to the Congress by Richard M. Nixon, President of the United States, 9 February 1972. Washington, DC: GPO, 1973.

US Foreign Policy for the 1970s: Shaping a Durable Peace. A Report to the Congress by Richard M. Nixon, President of the United States, 3 May 1973. Washington, DC: GPO, 1973.

US President. *Weekly Compilation of Presidential Documents*, 1969–76.

Books

Alroy, Gil Carl. *The Kissinger Experience: American Policy in the Middle East.* New York: Horizon Press, 1975.

Ambrose, Stephen E. *Rise to Globalism: American Foreign Policy since 1938.* London: Penguin, 1971.

Art, Robert J. and Waltz, Kenneth N., eds. *The Use of Force.* Boston: Little, Brown, 1971.

Ball, George W. *Diplomacy for a Crowded World: An American Foreign Policy.* London: Bodley Head, 1976.

Barnet, Richard J. *The Giants: Russia and America.* New York: Simon and Schuster, 1977.

Barnett, A. Doak. *China and the Major Powers in East Asia.* Washington, DC: Brookings Institution, 1977.

Bell, Coral. *The Diplomacy of Détente: The Kissinger Era.* London: Martin Robertson, 1977.

Blaufarb, Douglas S. *The Counter-Insurgency Era: US Doctrine and Performance.* London: Collier Macmillan, 1977.

Blechman, Barry M., Kaplan, Stephen S. *et al. Force without War: US Armed Forces as a Political Instrument.* Washington, DC: Brookings Institution, 1978.

Blumenfeld, Ralph. *Henry Kissinger: The Private and Public Story.* New York: Signet, 1974.

Brandon, Henry. *The Retreat of American Power.* Garden City, NY: Doubleday, 1973.

Brodie, Bernard. *War and Politics.* London: Cassell, 1974.

Brown, Seyom. *The Faces of Power: Constancy and Change in United States Foreign Policy from Truman to Johnson.* New York: Columbia University Press, 1968.

Brzezinski, Zbigniew. *Between Two Ages: America's Role in the Technetronic Era.* New York: Penguin, 1976.

Buchan, Alastair. *Change Without War: The Shifting Structures of World Power.* London: Chatto and Windus, 1974.

The End of the Postwar Era: A New Balance of World Power. London: Weidenfeld and Nicolson, 1974.

Bull, Hedley. *The Anarchical Society: A Study of Order in World Politics.* London: Macmillan, 1977.

Camps, Miriam. *The Management of Interdependence: A Preliminary View.* New York: Council on Foreign Relations, 1974.

Chace, James. *A World Elsewhere: The New American Foreign Policy.* New York: Charles Scribner, 1973.

Chubin, Shahram and Zebih, Sephr. *The Foreign Relations of Iran.* Berkeley: University of California Press, 1974.

Colby, William and Forbath, Peter. *Honourable Men: My Life in the CIA.* London: Hutchinson, 1978.

Collins, John M. *American and Soviet Military Trends since the Cuban Missile Crisis.* Washington, DC: Center for Strategic and International Studies, Georgetown University, 1978.

Destler, I. M. *Presidents, Bureaucrats and Foreign Policy: The Politics of Organizational Reform.* Princeton University Press, 1978.

Dickson, Peter. *Kissinger and the Meaning of History.* Cambridge University Press, 1978.

Dismukes, Bradford and McConnell, James, eds. *Soviet Naval Diplomacy.* New York: Pergamon, 1979.

Edmonds, Robin. *Soviet Foreign Policy, 1962–1973: The Paradox of Super Power.* Oxford University Press, 1975.

Evans, Roland, and Novak, Robert D. *Nixon in the White House: The Frustration of Power.* New York: Random House, 1971.

Freedman, Lawrence. *US Intelligence and the Soviet Strategic Threat.* London: Macmillan, 1977.

Gaddis, John Lewis. *Strategies of Containment: A Critical Appraisal of Postwar American National Security Policy.* Oxford University Press, 1982.

Gallucci, Robert L. *Neither Peace nor Honor: The Politics of American Military Policy in Vietnam.* Baltimore: Johns Hopkins University Press, 1975.

Gelb, Leslie H. with Betts, Richard K. *The Irony of Vietnam: The System Worked.* Washington, DC: Brookings Institution, 1979.

George, Alexander L. and Smoke, Richard. *Deterrence in American Foreign Policy: Theory and Practice.* New York: Columbia University Press, 1974.

Golan, Galia. *Yom Kippur and After: The Soviet Union and the Middle East Crisis.* Cambridge University Press, 1977.

Golan, Matti. *The Secret Conversations of Henry Kissinger: Step-by-Step Diplomacy in the Middle East.* New York: Quadrangle/New York Times, 1976.

Goodman, Allan E. *The Lost Peace: America's Search for a Negotiated Settlement of the Vietnam War.* Stanford, CA: Hoover Institute Press, 1978.

Gordon, Kermit, ed. *Agenda for the Nation.* New York: Doubleday, 1969.

Graubard, Stephen R. *Kissinger: Portrait of a Mind.* New York: W. W. Norton, 1973.

Haldeman, H. R. *The Ends of Power.* London: Sidgwick and Jackson, 1978.

Hoffmann, Stanley. *Gulliver's Troubles, or the Setting of American Foreign Policy.* New York: McGraw-Hill, 1968.

  Primacy or World Order: American Foreign Policy since the Cold War. New York: McGraw-Hill, 1978.

Howard, Michael. *War and the Liberal Conscience.* London: Temple Smith, 1978.

Jackson, Robert. *South Asian Crisis: India-Pakistan-Bangla Desh.* Published for the International Institute for Strategic Studies. London: Chatto and Windus, 1975.

Jones, Alan M., ed. *US Foreign Policy in a Changing World: The Nixon Administration, 1969–73.* New York: David McKay, 1973.

Kahan, Jerome H. *Security in the Nuclear Age: US Strategic Arms Policy.* Washington DC: Brookings Institution, 1975.

Kalb, Marvin and Kalb, Bernard. *Kissinger.* London: Hutchinson, 1974.

Kennan, George F. *The Cloud of Danger.* Boston: Little, Brown, 1977.

Kissinger, Henry A. *A World Restored: The Politics of Conservatism in a Revolutionary Era.* London: Victor Gollancz, 1977.

   American Foreign Policy. Expanded edition. New York: W. W. Norton, 1974.

   The Necessity for Choice. New York: Harper and Row, 1961.

   Nuclear Weapons and Foreign Policy. Published for the Council on Foreign Relations. Oxford University Press, 1957.

   The Troubled Partnership. New York: McGraw-Hill, 1965.

   White House Years. Boston: Little, Brown, 1979.

   Years of Upheaval. Boston: Little, Brown, 1982.

The Kissinger Study of Southern Africa. Nottingham: Spokesman Books, 1975.

Lake, Anthony, ed. *The Legacy of Vietnam.* New York University Press, 1976.

Landau, David. *Kissinger: The Uses of Power.* Boston: Houghton Mifflin, 1972.

Laquer, Walter. *Confrontation: The Middle East War and World Politics.* London: Wildwood House, 1974.

Liska, George. *Beyond Kissinger: Ways of Conservative Statecraft.* Baltimore: Johns Hopkins University Press, 1975.

Littauer, Raphael and Uphoff, Norman, eds. *The Air War in Indochina.* Revised edn. Boston: Beacon Press, 1972.

MacFarquhar, Roderick, ed. *Sino-American Relations, 1949–71.* Published for the Royal Institute of International Affairs. Newton Abbot: David and Charles, 1972.

Marcum, John A. *The Angolan Revolution, Volume 2: Exile Politics and Guerrilla Warfare (1962–1976).* London: MIT Press, 1978.

May, Ernest R. *Lessons of the Past: The Use and Misuse of History in American Policy.* Oxford University Press, 1975.

Mazlish, Bruce. *Kissinger: The European Mind in American Policy.* New York: Basic Books, 1976.

Morris, Roger. *Uncertain Greatness: Henry Kissinger and American Foreign Policy.* New York: Harper and Row, 1977.

Newhouse, John. *Cold Dawn: The Story of SALT.* New York: Holt, Rinehart and Winston, 1973.

Nixon, Richard. *RN: The Memoirs of Richard Nixon.* New York: Grosset and Dunlap, 1978.

Nutter, G. Warren. *Kissinger's Grand Design.* Washington: American Enterprise Institute, 1975.

Osgood, Robert E. *The Weary and the Wary: US and Japanese Security Policies in*

Transition. Baltimore: Johns Hopkins University Press, 1972.

Osgood, Robert E. *et al. Retreat from Empire?: The First Nixon Administration*. Baltimore: Johns Hopkins University Press, 1973.

Ravenal, Earl C. *Never Again: Learning from America's Foreign Policy Failures*. Philadelphia: Temple University Press, 1976.

Rosecrance, Richard, ed. *America as an Ordinary Country: US Foreign Policy and the Future*. London: Cornell University Press, 1976.

Rubinstein, Alvin Z. *Red Star on the Nile: The Soviet–Egyptian Influence Relationship since the June War*. Princeton University Press, 1977.

Safire, William. *Before the Fall: An Inside View of the Pre-Watergate White House*. New York: Belmont Tower, 1975.

Safran, Nadav. *Israel: The Embattled Ally*. Cambridge, MA: Belknap Press of Harvard University Press, 1978.

Schlesinger, James R. *et al. Defending America*. New York: Basic Books, 1977.

Schurmann, Franz. *The Logic of World Power*. New York: Pantheon, 1974.

Shawcross, William. *Sideshow: Kissinger, Nixon and the Destruction of Cambodia*. London: André Deutsch, 1979.

Shulman, Marshall D. *Beyond the Cold War*. New Haven: Yale University Press, 1966.

Snepp, Frank. *Decent Interval: An Insider's Account of Saigon's Indecent End Told by the CIA's Chief Strategy Analyst in Vietnam*. New York: Random House, 1977.

Steel, Ronald. *Pax Americana*. Revised edn. New York: Viking Press, 1970.

Stern, Ellen P., ed. *The Limits of Military Intervention*. London: Sage, 1977.

Stockwell, John. *In Search of Enemies: A CIA Story*. New York: W. W. Norton, 1978.

Stoessinger, John G. *Henry Kissinger: The Anguish of Power*. New York: W. W. Norton, 1976.

Sutter, Robert G. *China-Watch: Toward Sino-American Reconciliation*. Baltimore: Johns Hopkins University Press, 1978.

Szulc, Tad. *The Illusion of Peace: Foreign Policy in the Nixon Years*. New York: Viking Press, 1978.

Tucker, Robert W. *Nation or Empire? The Debate over American Foreign Policy*. Baltimore: Johns Hopkins University Press, 1968.

Ulam, Adam B. *The Rivals: America and Russia since World War II*. London: Allen Lane, 1973.

Urban, G. R., ed. *Détente*. London: Temple Smith, 1976.

Whiting, Allen S. *The Chinese Calculus of Deterrence*. Ann Arbor: University of Michigan Press, 1975.

Willrich, Mason and Rhinelander, John B., eds. *SALT: The Moscow Agreements and Beyond*. London: Collier Macmillan, 1974.

Windsor, Philip. *Germany and the Management of Détente*. Published for the International Institute for Strategic Studies. New York: Praeger, 1971.

Wu, Yuan-Li. *US Policy and Strategic Interests in the Western Pacific*. New York: Crane, Russak, 1975.

Yahuda, Michael B. *China's Role in World Affairs*. London: Croom Helm, 1978.

Articles and Pamphlets

Allison, Graham, May, Ernest and Yarmolinsky, Adam. 'US Military Policy: Limits to Intervention.' *Foreign Affairs* 48, No. 2 (January 1970), pp. 245–61.

Ball, Desmond. *'Déja Vu:* The Return to Counterforce in the Nixon Administration.' *California Seminar on Arms Control and Foreign Policy, No. 45.*

Bell, Daniel. 'The End of American Exceptionalism.' *The Public Interest* 41 (Fall 1975), pp. 193–224.

Brandon, Henry. 'Jordan: The Forgotten Crisis: Were We Masterful . . .' *Foreign Policy* 10 (Spring 1973), pp. 158–70.

Brodie, Bernard. 'The Development of Nuclear Strategy.' *International Security* 2, No. 4 (Spring 1978), pp. 65–83.

Brzezinski, Zbigniew. 'How the Cold War was Played.' *Foreign Affairs.* 51, No. 1 (October 1972), pp. 181–209.

'The State of Nixon's World (1): Half Past Nixon.' *Foreign Policy* 3 (Summer 1971), pp. 3–21.

'US Foreign Policy: The Search for Focus.' *Foreign Affairs* 51, No. 4 (July 1973), pp. 708–27.

Buchan, Alastair. 'An Expedition to the Poles.' *The Year Book of World Affairs 1975.* New York: Praeger, 1975.

'The Irony of Kissinger.' *International Affairs* 50, No. 3 (July 1974), pp. 367–79.

Bundy, William P. 'International Security Today.' *Foreign Affairs* 53, No. 1 (October 1974), pp. 22–44.

Campbell, John Franklin. 'What is to be Done – Gigantism in Washington.' *Foreign Affairs* 49, No. 1 (October 1970), pp. 51–69.

Chace, James. 'Bismarck and Kissinger.' *Encounter* 42, No. 6 (June 1974), pp. 44–7.

Davis, Lynn Etheridge. 'Limited Nuclear Options: Deterrence and the New American Doctrine.' *Adelphi Papers* No. 126. London: IISS, 1976.

Davis, Nathaniel. 'The Angola Decision of 1975: A Personal Memoir.' *Foreign Affairs* 57, No. 1 (Fall 1978), pp. 109–24.

Destler, I. M. 'The Nixon NSC (2): Can One Man Do?' *Foreign Policy* 5 (Winter 1971–2) pp. 28–40.

Fallaci, Oriana. 'Kissinger: An Interview with Oriana Fallaci.' *The New Republic*, 16 December 1972.

Garthoff, Raymond L. 'Mutual Deterrence and Strategic Arms Limitation in Soviet Policy.' *International Security* 3, No. 1 (Spring 1978), pp. 148–61.

'Negotiations with the Russians: Some Lessons from SALT.' *International Security* 1, No. 4 (Spring 1977), pp. 3–24.

'On Estimating and Imputing Intentions.' *International Security* 2, No. 3 (Winter 1978), pp. 22–32.

Gati, Charles. 'Another Grand Debate? The Limitationist Critique of American Foreign Policy.' *World Politics* 21, No. 1 (October 1968), pp. 133–51.

Gilbert, Stephen P. 'Implications of the Nixon Doctrine for Military Aid Policy.' *Orbis* 16 (Fall 1972), pp. 660–81.

Girling, J. L. S. ' "Kissingerism": The Enduring Problems.' *International Affairs* 51, No. 3 (July 1975), pp. 323–43.

'Pentagon Papers: The Dialectics of Intervention.' *The World Today* 28, No. 2 (February 1976), pp. 61–8.

Gray, Colin S. 'The Future of Land-Based Missile Forces.' *Adelphi Papers*, No. 140. London: IISS, 1977.

Griffith, William E. *Peking, Moscow, and Beyond: The Sino-Soviet-American Triangle.* The Washington Papers, No. 6, Center for Strategic and International Studies, Georgetown University, 1973.

Hahn, Walter F. 'The Nixon Doctrine: Design and Dilemmas.' *Orbis* 16 (Summer 1972), pp. 361–76.

Hartley, Anthony. 'American Foreign Policy in the Nixon Era.' *Adelphi Papers*, No. 110. London: IISS, 1975.

Hassner, Pierre. 'The State of Nixon's World (3): Pragmatic Conservatism in the White House.' *Foreign Policy* 3 (Summer 1971), pp. 41–61.

Hoffmann, Stanley. 'Will the Balance Balance at Home?' *Foreign Policy* 7 (Summer 1972), pp. 60–84.

Jarvenpää, Pauli. 'Flexible Nuclear Options: New Myths and Old Realities.' Cornell Peace Studies Program, Occasional Paper, No. 7, September 1976.

Kissinger, Henry A. 'Bureaucracy and Policy Making: The Effects of Insiders and Outsiders on the Policy Process in *Bureaucracy, Politics and Strategy.* Security Studies Paper No. 17, University of California, Los Angeles, 1968.

'Domestic Structure and Foreign Policy.' *Daedalus* 95, No. 2 (Spring 1966), pp. 503–29.

'Force and Diplomacy in the Nuclear Age.' *Foreign Affairs* 34, No. 3 (April 1956), pp. 349–66.

'Military Policy and the Defense of the "Gray Areas".' *Foreign Affairs* 33, No. 3 (April 1955), pp. 416–28.

'The Viet Nam Negotiations.' *Foreign Affairs* 47, No. 2 (January 1969), pp. 211–34.

'The White Revolutionary: Reflections on Bismarck.' *Daedalus* 97, No. 3 (Summer 1968), pp. 888–924.

Kobayashi, Katsumi. *The Nixon Doctrine and US–Japanese Security Relations.* California Seminar on Arms Control and Foreign Policy, Discussion Paper No. 65 (October 1975).

Kosaka, Masataka. *Détente and East Asia.* California Seminar on Arms Control and Foreign Policy, Discussion Paper No. 60 (September 1975).

Lambeth, Benjamin S. 'Deterrence in the MIRV Era.' *World Politics* 24, No. 2 (January 1972), pp. 221–42.

Laqueur, Walter. *Neo-Isolationism and the World of the Seventies.* The Washington Papers, No. 5, Center for Strategic and International Studies, Georgetown University, 1972.

Leacacos, John P. 'The Nixon NSC (1): Kissinger's Apparat.' *Foreign Policy* 5 (Winter 1971–2), pp. 3–27.

Morgenthau, Hans J. 'Henry Kissinger, Secretary of State: An Evaluation.' *Encounter* 43, No. 5 (November 1974), pp. 57–61.

Moynihan, Daniel P. 'Presenting the American Case.' *The American Scholar* 44,

No. 4 (Autumn 1975), pp. 564–83.

Nitze, Paul H. 'Assuring Strategic Stability in an Era of Détente.' *Foreign Affairs* 54, No. 2 (January 1976), pp. 207–32.

Nixon, Richard M. 'Asia After Vietnam.' *Foreign Affairs* 46, No. 1 (October 1967), pp. 111–25.

Pauker, Guy J. *US Military Options in the Third World: An Overview.* Santa Monica, CA: Rand Corporation, WN-7400-ARPA, April 1971.

Pauker, Guy, Canby, Steven, Johnson, A. Ross, and Quandt, William B. *In Search of Self-Reliance: US Security Assistance to the Third World Under the Nixon Doctrine.* Santa Monica, CA: Rand Corporation, R-1092-APRA, June 1973.

Pillsbury, Michael. *SALT on the Dragon: Chinese Views on the Soviet-American Strategic Balance.* Santa Monica, CA: Rand Corporation, April 1975.

Quandt, William B. 'Soviet Policy in the October 1973 War.' Santa Monica, CA: Rand Corporation, May 1976.

Ravenal, Earl C. 'The Case for Strategic Disengagement.' *Foreign Affairs* 51, No. 3 (April 1973), pp. 505–21.

'The Nixon Doctrine and Our Asian Commitments.' *Foreign Affairs* 49, No. 2 (January 1971), pp. 201–17.

'Nixon's Challenge to Carter.' *Foreign Policy* 29 (Winter 1977–8), pp. 27–42.

'The State of Nixon's World (2): The Political Military Gap.' *Foreign Policy* 3 (Summer 1971), pp. 22–40.

Ronfeldt, David and Einaudi, Luigi. *Internal Security and Military Assistance to Latin America in the 1970s: A First Statement.* Santa Monica, CA: Rand Corporation, R-924-ISA, December 1971.

Rosecrance, Richard. 'Strategic Deterrence Reconsidered.' *Adelphi Papers*, No. 116. London: IISS, 1975.

Salisbury, Harrison E. 'Image and Reality in Indochina.' *Foreign Affairs* 49, No. 3 (April 1971), pp. 381–94.

Shulman, Marshall D. 'What Does Security Mean Today?' *Foreign Affairs* 49, No. 4 (July 1971), pp. 607–18.

Slocombe, Walter. 'The Political Implications of Strategic Parity.' *Adelphi Papers*, No. 77. London: IISS, 1971.

Sonnenfeldt, Helmut and Hyland, William G. 'Soviet Perspectives on Security.' *Adelphi Papers*, No. 150. London: IISS, 1979.

Taylor, Trevor. 'President Nixon's Arms Supply Policies.' *The Year Book of World Affairs 1972.* London: Stevens, 1972, pp. 65–80

Vincent, R. J. 'Kissinger's System of Foreign Policy.' *The Yearbook of World Affairs: 1977.* London: Stevens, 1977.

Windsor, Philip. 'America's Moral Confusion: Separating the Should From the Good.' *Foreign Policy* 13 (Winter 1973–4), pp. 139–53.

'Henry Kissinger's Scholarly Contribution.' *British Journal of International Studies* 1, No. 1 (April 1975), pp. 27–37.

Wood, Robert Jefferson. 'Military Assistance and the Nixon Doctrine.' *Orbis* 15, No. 1 (Spring 1971), pp. 247–74.

INDEX

ABM, 113, 114
Acheson, Dean, 18, 20, 36, 42, 44, 66
Allende, Salvador, 101
Anderson, Jack, 87
Angola, 82, 84, 86, 111, 124, 179–90, 216 n.74, 218 n.120
  Alvor Agreement, 181, 182, 184
  China, 179–80
  CIA involvement, 179, 181, 183, 184, 189
  Clark, Dick, 183–6 passim
  Cuba, 179, 180, 187, 188, 218 n.110
  Davis, Nathaniel, 180–4 passim, 217 n.91
  40 Committee, 179–83 passim
  FNLA (Frente Nacional de Libertação de Angola), 178, 179, 180, 183, 184, 187, 185
  House Select Committee on Intelligence report, 181–2
  Marcum, John, 180, 181
  MPLA (Movimento Popular de Libertação de Angola), 179, 183, 185, 187, 217 n.96
  Neto, Agostinho, 179
  NSC, 181, 182
  NSSM-39, 176–7, 216 n. 73
  Roberto, Holden, 178, 179, 180
  Savimbi, Jonas, 178, 179
  Sisco, Joseph, 182, 184–5
  South Africa, 183, 184, 187, 218 n. 111
  Soviet Union, 179, 183, 185, 186, 188
  Tunney Amendment, 186–8 passim, 218 n. 112
  UNITA (União Nacional para Independência Total de Angola), 178–9, 180, 182, 183, 184, 185, 187, 195

Zaire, 179, 183–4, 217 n.98
Argentina, 139
Aron, Raymond, 3, 44, 46, 47, 155, 195

Ball, George, 42
bipolarity, 2, 3, 8, 19, 24, 37, 42, 78, 80–3 passim, 192–3
Bell, Daniel, 43, 46
Betts, Richard, 37, 129
Berlin blockade, 18, 33
Brazil, 138–9, 184
Brezhnev, Leonid, 111, 161, 162, 107
Brodie, Bernard, 6, 18, 23, 28, 29, 175
Buckley, William F., 49
Bundy, McGeorge, 36, 38, 72

Cambodia, 72, 105, 107, 128–9, 131, 132, 155; see Vietnam
Carter, Jimmy (Administration), 66, 171, 190, 194, 197–8, 219 n.10
Chile, 101
China, 18, 70, 77, 90, 103; Chou En-lai, 40, 103; US–Sino relations, 38–40 passim, 83, 84, 102, 103, 105, 133–4, 209 n.32
CIA (Central Intelligence Agency), 100, 101, 128, 182, 189; Angola, 179, 181, 183, 184, 189; Vietnam, 128, 131
Clausewitz, Karl von, 7, 27, 28, 31
Clifford, Clark, 12, 42
Cline, Ray, 158
Cold War, 8, 11–13, 23, 24, 84, 86, 109
Congress, US, 87, 155, 172–5, 176, 184–7, 189
containment, 11, 13, 14, 15, 18, 21, 25, 31, 38, 40, 147, 167, 191
Connally, John, 77, 106–7

229